global food futures

global food futures

feeding the world in 2050

brian gardner

BLOOMSBURY

LONDON • NEW DELHI • NEW YORK • SYDNEY

Bloomsbury Academic

An imprint of Bloomsbury Publishing Plc

50 Bedford Square
London
WC1B 3DP
UK

1385 Broadway
New York
NY 10018
USA

www.bloomsbury.com

First published 2013

British Library Cataloguing-in-Publication Data
A catalogue record for this book is available from the British Library.

ISBN: HB: 978-0-8578-5154-3
PB: 978-0-8578-5155-0
ePub: 978-0-8578-5157-4

Library of Congress Cataloging-in-Publication Data
Gardner, Brian, 1938–
Global food futures : feeding the world in 2050 / Brian Gardner.
pages cm
Includes bibliographical references and index.
ISBN 978-0-85785-154-3 — ISBN 978-0-85785-155-0 — ISBN 978-0-85785-157-4 (ebk.)
1. Food security. 2. Food supply. 3. Famines—Prevention. I. Title.
HD9000.5.G274 2013
338.1'90112—dc23   2013005984

Typeset by Apex CoVantage, LLC, Madison, WI, USA.
Printed and bound in India

contents

illustrations

tables

chapter 1

introduction: does the world face a continuous "food crisis"?

In the opening years of the twenty-first century there was a series of food supply and price crises. At least three times between 2005 and 2013 food was seen to be in shorter supply than it was in previous decades and prices rose to historically high levels. A combination of bad harvests, depressed stocks, and government interference led to shortages that forced up prices. The Cereal Price Index issued by the United Nations Food and Agriculture Organization (FAO) rose to 260 points in July 2012, an increase of 38 points and 17 percent from June 2012, and only 14 points below the April 2008 all-time high of 274 points. The 2012 U.S. maize crop, a major source of animal feed, dropped by an estimate of more than 50 percent due to a drought, escalating maize prices by almost 23 percent in July. As a result, the world price of wheat increased by 19 percent, which was also influenced by reduced production prospects in the Russian Federation. There had been similar price hikes in 2008 and 2011 for similar reasons.

These apparent and more frequently occurring crises have raised important questions about the security of the world's food supply. Are we reaching a point where the world's agriculture cannot be relied upon to produce enough food for the 7 billion world population? Are changing dietary demands of emerging and developing countries putting unsustainable strain on the world's basic agricultural resources? What part is the increasing use of grain for fuel playing in reducing quantities available for human food? What is the role of financial speculation in jacking up prices when supplies are short? Longer term questions include whether an increasingly stressed energy supply will raise permanently the price of food, and, probably most important, is global agriculture capable of producing enough food to feed a population expected to reach more than 9 billion by the middle of the twenty-first century?

These are the questions that this book seeks to answer.

main points

The main points to be addressed in the chapters of this book include the following issues:

- Food production needs to be increased by at least 70 percent by 2050 to feed the increased population.
- Dietary change in emerging economies and developing countries toward greater animal product consumption will put additional strain on world food production capacity.

- There are two current views of the future world food supply and demand situation—the pessimistic and the optimistic. The pessimistic view that the world's agricultural resources are overstretched and incapable of meeting rising demand for an increasing population is currently the accepted opinion, but there is gathering evidence to support a more optimistic conclusion. The optimistic view is that science and improved husbandry can maintain increased output at a level needed to feed a 30 percent increase in global population.
- Clear evidence shows that the world "food problem" remains distributional and developmental rather than because of a long-term inability to increase output.
- Climate change is a major challenge to maintaining future food supplies, particularly in those countries where increased output is most needed.
- Traditional exporters and emerging agricultural powers have considerable potential to increase output, thus maintaining and boosting global food security.
- The price of oil and probably of other energy sources will continue to increase over the long term, which is likely to be a major handicap for increased global food production.
- More scientific research, more applied science, and more money are needed to raise output in most of the hungry regions of the world.
- Impoverished nations face barriers to increasing their food supply through production and, where necessary, imports.
- The price of food will inevitably rise in the long term.

Global food production needs to increase by at least 50 percent if it is to feed the expected 9.5 billion people who will inhabit the world by 2050. While production is adequate to feed the current 7 billion population, increasing output on this scale could be seriously inhibited by oil shortages, environmental pollution, shrinking farmland areas, water shortages, and inadequate crop yield increases. According to the most pessimistic view of the future world food equation, rapidly increasing population and the demand for improved diets from expanding Asian economies is likely to lead to greater competition for a food supply that could become increasingly inadequate. In addition, production in many parts of the world will be handicapped by concern for environmental protection and sustainability.

What is not in dispute is the reality that the world's supply of food will have to be substantially increased to meet the needs of an increasing population and the changing eating habits of a large proportion of the world's inhabitants. What is in doubt is the ability of the world's food production systems to meet these needs and how the expansion of supply can be achieved without conflict with other objectives. Prime among these concerns are minimizing climate change factors, sustaining biodiversity, and avoiding conflict with the social structure of less-developed countries.

It has been estimated[1] that the world's farms need to produce 70–100 percent more food by the second half of the current century, despite climate change, energy scarcity, and regional dietary shifts. The agricultural sector's long-term objective is no longer simply to maximize productivity and production but to do so within a complex matrix of production, rural development, environmental, and food consumption objectives.[2]

The FAO stresses that while it will be possible to increase output sufficiently to meet the population challenge, this will not happen without considerable help from governments and increased investment in agricultural science. According to an FAO report, "The projected increases in yields, land and irrigation expansion will not entirely come about spontaneously (i.e., driven by market forces) but require huge public interventions and investments, particularly in agricultural research and in preventing and mitigating environmental damage. In the problem countries, public intervention will continue to be required on the one hand to develop agriculture and to adapt agriculture to local circumstances and on the other hand to establish social safety nets."[3]

the geopolitics of food

With the rise in purchasing power of oil-rich and new industrial nations, food security has become the major issue in the geopolitics of food.[4] This preoccupation has been combined with growing uncertainty about the ability of the world's agriculture industries to meet the rising demand for improved diets and the increasing number of people to be fed. This uncertainty has been heightened by the onset of climate change, which is seen as a serious factor limiting future food production increases.

The uncertainty will undoubtedly change the geopolitics of food. Climate change is most likely to affect tropical agriculture. The growing period of crops is already changing in countries like India, Ethiopia, and those of Latin America. Cultivation of crops sensitive to temperature is likely to shift toward the temperate zones or to higher altitudes. Experimental evidence suggests, for example, that global warming could lead to a 10 percent drop in the production of maize, a major food and feed crop, in the most vulnerable developing countries over the next fifty years. As a consequence of these factors, economically rich but land-poor countries are increasingly seeking ways of securing their food supplies, either by bilateral trade arrangement or by acquiring land and other food-producing resources in other countries.

In this situation of incipient shortage, there has inevitably been a tendency for parallels to be drawn with the oil industry. Those who have not studied closely enough the considerable differences between production and trade in the two commodities suggest that an organization of food producers like OPEC (Organization of the Petroleum Exporting Countries) could develop, with the supply and prices of food being controlled by a few large producers. This view was reflected in the establishment of the Organization of Rice Exporting Countries (OREC), consisting of a small group of Southeast Asia countries including Cambodia, Laos, Myanmar, Thailand, and Vietnam, in the wake of the 2007–2008 food supply crisis.

Such initiatives generally fail, simply because such groups do not generally control a large enough proportion of the supply of a given food commodity in order to exert effective pressure on prices. While the world's finite supply of oil is controlled by a relatively few producers, food is produced, in albeit varying quantities, in almost every country of the world. For various reasons, the supply of food, unlike that of oil, is not finite, and while trade in food is dominated by a few large operators, competition between these exporters is fierce. Until the end of the twentieth century world food trade was dominated by the United States, Europe, and Australasia. In the beginning of the twenty-first century, new and more powerful forces have entered the arena—most notably Brazil. The exploitation of new land and the application of modern technology means that Brazil now vies with the United States for domination of the world trade in feed grains, oilseeds, poultry meat, and orange juice. Brazil is now the major force in the world's beef trade.

On the other side of the food supply and demand equation, countries that once lived predominantly on simple rice and vegetable diets, now want to consume a more varied diet that includes meat and dairy products that once were consumed on a serious scale only in Western developed countries. This increased demand for animal-based foods has also increased the demand for animal feed grain. This phenomenon is the major reason why the margin between world grain production and consumption has steadily decreased since the mid-1990s. During the same period this relative tightness of supply has been exacerbated by the rationalization of agricultural policies by those countries with heavily managed and oversubsidized markets, most notably the United States and the European Union. At the same time, both have established new policies encouraging the production of biofuels, which has introduced further pressures on the supply of food crops.

Concern to maintain food security by land-poor nations has stimulated what has been characterized as a large-scale land grab, with oil-rich and wealthy emerging economies buying up or leasing large areas of land principally in Africa and the former communist countries in Eastern Europe. Libya for example, dependent on imports for almost 90 percent of its grain, has leased 250,000 acres of land in Ukraine to grow wheat. Egypt is seeking land acquisition in Ukraine in exchange for access to its natural gas. China is currently signing long-term leases for land in Australia, Russia, and Brazil. Qatar is leasing 40,000 hectares (98,800 acres) of Kenya's fertile coastal region to grow fruits and vegetables, in return for building a £2.4 billion port. While these developments raise serious social and economic questions, they could be a major contribution to increasing food production, general economic development, and overall world food security.

While ensuring adequate supplies of food is not a critical problem for rich countries, the obverse view is that the approximate 20 percent of the world's population living in sub-Saharan Africa and south Asia are either starving or subsisting on substandard diets. African countries currently represent thirty-six of the fifty nations whose food supplies are considered to be most at risk. Extreme droughts and high poverty rates, as well as a poor infrastructure for transporting and marketing agricultural products, makes sub-Saharan Africa particularly vulnerable. These people have no power in food geopolitics. Increasing food production and access to food for these people is dependent largely on increased indigenous production and increased economic development—both in turn dependent on political factors within the needy countries and the overseas development policies of the rich nations.

two views of the future

Of the two main views of the future ability of the world to match food supply with demand, the pessimistic view tends to gain the most publicity. In this view of the future, the world's food supply and demand system is now in a state of permanent crisis that can only be made worse by global warming. According to this school of thought,[5] deep-rooted environmental trends are contributing to the global loss of the necessary production impetus to meet rising food demand.

Among these trends are the cumulative effects of soil erosion on land productivity, desertification of cropland, and, increasingly, the conversion of cropland to non-farm uses. More recently, falling water tables and rising temperatures are reducing the world's food production capacity. In addition, farmers have diminishing reserves of unexploited technology. In support of this assessment, it is pointed out that there have been no new advances on the high-yielding varieties of wheat, rice, and maize that were developed in the so-called Green Revolution in the 1970s.

To a great extent, this pessimistic scenario is now the accepted view of opinion formers and policy-makers. The alternative optimistic view is that the world has adequate reserves of underused farmland, that plant breeding will increase yields, and that new techniques will be developed to cope with the undoubted challenges of increasing energy costs and climate change.

This more optimistic view, while accepting that increasing agricultural production will be made more difficult by global warming, energy shortages, and urban pressures, believes that production can be boosted by improved plant varieties, other technical advances, and more sophisticated land management. This would involve using more precise and less wasteful irrigation and applying fertilization to crop varieties that have been further improved by new plant breeding techniques.

No one questions the fact that all regions of the world have underused food production capacity. This is particularly true of those countries classified by official agencies as underdeveloped—the low-income food-deficit countries (LIFDCs). Similarly, all regions suffer, to differing extents, from crop-damaging weather phenomena. Most important, production can be increased in almost all areas where hunger and malnutrition are most serious. Thanks to the application of new technology, better organization, and the injection of money, production in some of these countries has dramatically increased.

To take one example, India was once regarded as locked into a cycle of low yields and permanent hunger. In the past thirty years it has more than doubled production of wheat and other food crops. Significantly, these increased levels of production have come from a largely unchanged area of land; the total crop area of the country has remained static at 141 million hectares (350 million acres) since the late 1990s. India has gone from being a major wheat importer to being a regular exporter. The fact that hunger and malnutrition still persist in India is due not to shortage but to maldistribution.

But what may be regarded as the neo-Malthusian view of the world population–food supply conflict holds that even rich, developed countries are at risk from an expected long-term food crisis. This dismal prognosis is not supported by the facts. To take the specific case of the United Kingdom, it currently produces three-quarters of its temperate food supplies and is more than two-thirds self-sufficient in all foods. Most of the remainder is imported from three main sources. Close to 70 percent comes from other European countries with similar climatic and production conditions (principally meat and dairy products), from North America (grain), and from Australasia (grain, meat, and dairy products). With the exception of Australia—which has always been the victim of wild climatic variations—none of these

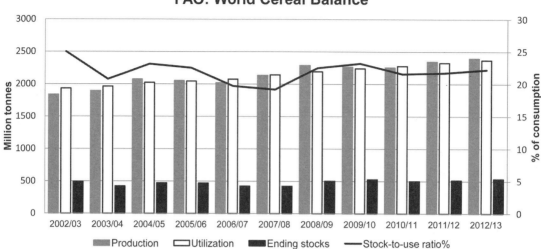

FAO: World Cereal Balance

Figure 1.1 FAO World Cereal Balance: Stocks maintain food supply when the production-consumption gap closes. In the past ten years stocks have never fallen below the critical 15–18 percent of annual consumption level.
Source of Data: FAO Food Outlook Global Market Analysis (2005–12).

exporting countries and regions is likely to suffer production reduction as a result of climatic change. Australia supplies only a minimal proportion of the UK food supply, all of which could be made up by increased domestic production.

Closer examination of the evidence suggests that recent reductions in the rate of increase in world food supply have not been caused by any innate failure of the world's agricultural system, but have been due to depressed demand and government policies. Although undoubtedly triggered by exceptional weather conditions and the depletion of world food stocks, spiraling prices were fundamentally a product of deliberate government policies such as export bans and price controls. Such policy measures depressed prices, which discouraged producers from maximizing output. The optimistic view[6] is that world agricultural production is capable of increasing with demand, provided that the right national and international policies are established.

This is especially true, for example, of Russia and the former Soviet-dominated countries (grouped for easy reference as the newly independent states). Currently, price controls and export limitations hold down farmers' prices, with the result that annual production capacity equivalent to at least 30 million metric tonnes is not being realized. The desire to contain expensive domestic surpluses has also constrained production in Europe and North America and other developed countries. Some 40 million hectares of land have been taken out of agricultural production in the United States, western Europe, and Oceania over the past three decades. This land represents production potential of a conservative 200 million tonnes—equal to about 10 percent of current global grain production.

Even in sub-Saharan Africa, the major food shortage area, there is tremendous potential for increased production, given the right social and economic conditions, but too often these conditions are not right. Of the seventeen African countries currently listed by the FAO as having the most serious hunger and malnutrition problems, only two are not suffering from war, civil unrest, revolution, or incompetent dictatorial governments.[7]

A 2012 FAO report effectively challenges the pessimistic view that world food production is now so constrained by technological limitations, water shortages, salination, and climate change that future food shortages and high prices are inevitable.[8] It supports the view that the apparent failure of the world food system to maintain market balance in the middle of the first decade of the new millennium was caused more by a failure of demand than of supply.

The recent slowdown in the rate of production increase, FAO emphasizes, "has occurred not because of shortages of land or water but rather because demand for agricultural products has also slowed. This is mainly because world population growth rates have been declining since the late 1960s, and fairly high levels of food consumption per person are now being reached in many countries, beyond which further rises will be limited."[9] But population is still increasing and production will have to rise to meet the increased demand.

access to food

The current "world food problem" therefore remains what it always was—distributional and developmental rather than due to any long-run failure of production. Two or three decades hence however, the situation could be very different as the process of increasing output will undoubtedly become more difficult.

What is more important, despite the apparent plenty, is that a large proportion of the world's population remains in absolute poverty and lacks the necessary income to translate its need for food into effective demand. While the growth in world demand for agricultural products is expected to fall from the average 2.2 percent a year of the past thirty years to 1.5 percent a year for the next thirty, the absolute demand will increase substantially. While in developing countries the slowdown in growth of demand will be significant, the problems of access to food both in economic and production terms are unlikely to decline. The reduction in the rate of increase in food demand will be concentrated in the emerging economies with plenty of money available for food imports. FAO points out that while the demand growth rate is estimated to decrease from 3.7 percent to 2 percent, this is mainly the result of China and other Asian countries having passed the phase of rapid growth in demand for food.

While the world's agriculture is probably capable of coping with increases in consumption—with or without application of new biotechnological advances—it is argued that expansion will have to be achieved without environmental stress or endangering the social structure of potential exporting countries. There is little doubt, however, that the application of biotechnology would be a positive boon to solving some of the production problems of developing countries where food production is most in need of stimulation.

climate change and future food production

Climate change is undoubtedly a challenge to maintaining an adequate world food supply. Unfortunately, the indications are that it will disadvantage most of those regions where increased production is most needed. A recent study by the International Food Policy Research Institute (IFPRI) showed that rice and wheat yields in developing countries could decrease by as much as 19 percent and 34 percent, respectively, by 2050 because of global warming.[10] The same report indicates that calorie availability in 2050 will not only be lower than in any no climate-change scenario but will actually decline relative to 2000 levels throughout the developing world. The IFPRI says that by 2050, the decline in calorie availability will increase child malnutrition by 20 percent relative to a world with no climate change. This assumes, of course, that no action is taken to counter the effects of climate change.

For Europe and North America it is probable that global warming would, overall, increase production potential, but the balance between different areas would be radically changed. The change in Europe's climate as a result of an expected rise in global temperature over the next seventy-plus years will provide advantage to some of Europe's farmers, have a significant damaging effect on others, and increase the variability of the factors governing crop and livestock production for everybody. Overall, European production is more likely to increase rather than decrease as a result of climate change.[11]

Agriculture in developing countries is the most likely to be most seriously hit by climate change. The effects—higher temperatures, changes in rainfall, rising sea levels, and weather disasters—threaten agriculture, food, and water supplies. In Africa rain-fed agriculture contributes some 30 percent of gross domestic product (GDP) and employs about 70 percent of the population. In south Asia, already suffering from a stressed and largely degraded natural resource base, this is combined with high levels of poverty and population density. Water resources are likely to be most affected by climate change, both through its effect on monsoons, which provides 70 percent of annual precipitation in a four-month period, and on the melting of Himalayan glaciers.

increasing food security?

There is little doubt that climate change will make it harder to produce enough food for the world's growing population and will alter the seasonal timing, availability, and quality of water resources. To avoid extending agriculture into already environmentally threatened areas, the current rate of agricultural productivity growth will have to be doubled, according to the World Bank, while minimizing the associated environmental damage.[12] In the extreme event of a 5°C warming, agricultural productivity would be likely to decline throughout the world, particularly in the tropics, even with changes in farming practices. This could mean that more than 3 million additional people could die from malnutrition each year. Even the more likely 2°C warming would produce new weather patterns challenging conventional agricultural practices. Between 100 million and 400 million more people could be at risk of hunger.

In these more uncertain conditions it will become even more important to spread the risk of food insecurity. A major oversimplifying assumption of those taking the pessimistic view is that there is something intrinsically good about increasing national self-sufficiency as a protection against uncertain global conditions. If world food security is to be improved however, the best use needs to made of all global food production resources. This can only be achieved by trade. Trade makes up food deficits for countries that are not self-sufficient by moving food from surplus to deficit areas—to mutual economic and probably social and environmental advantage. There is a problem only if the deficit is greater than the global surplus, but there is no evidence that this is so. In this connection, it is worth bearing in mind that so-called food miles objections to international food trade are often largely minimized when the whole energy cost of production and delivery of a food are balanced out (e.g., New Zealand lamb delivered to Europe at a lower total economic and environmental cost than European lamb).

The traditional food exporters, Australia, North America, Argentina, and Uruguay, and relatively new operators such as Brazil have the potential to continue to increase deliveries to the international market. What should not be ignored is that about half the total increase in exports in the last three decades of the twentieth century came from the European Union—then a relatively new operator on world markets. From being a net importer of 21 million tonnes of grain a year in the mid-1970s, the EU-15 became a net exporter of 24 million tonnes a year in 1997–1999. With land currently still to be removed from set-aside and further increases in productivity, it has substantial scope for increased production and exports—if the world market price rises enough. Much the same can be said for the United States, which in 2012 still had more than 10 percent of its arable land in some form of set-aside.

limitations on increasing production

Underutilized cultivable land is also plentiful in the transition economies of eastern Europe and Russia, and the scope for increasing productivity by reducing losses and raising yields is high. FAO's projections suggest that these so-called transition countries could be net exporters of 10 million tonnes of cereals a year by 2015 and 25 million tonnes by 2030.

The overall conclusion to be drawn from the facts of world agricultural resources and likely developments is that despite the obvious difficulties, food production can be increased and will continue to increase in line with increases in demand. The caveat has to be added, however, that if the problem of hunger in the poorer nations is to be diminished, production has to be stimulated in the underfarmed areas and import demand has to be aided by general economic and specific agricultural development funds from the world's richer countries.

Undoubtedly, agricultural production in important parts of the world will be constrained by irrigation water shortage, soil erosion, and water pollution. According to the pessimistic view, not only are large areas of croplands seriously eroded or polluted, but grazing rangelands are overgrazed and fisheries are depleted. However, productivity losses due to soil erosion, nutrient depletion, and salination are small on a global scale (on the order of 0.1–0.2 percent per year) compared with historic gains in productivity (on the order of 2 percent per year) due to improvements in technology and input use. But these are global figures. Fertility inadequacies and environmental constraints are much more significant in areas where the food need is greatest, particularly in parts of sub-Saharan Africa and south Asia.

the problem of rising energy cost

The energy question is paramount in any assessment of future food production potential. There is no doubt that the bulk of world agriculture is energy-intensive and vulnerable to rises in oil and gas prices. The fact that agriculture is estimated to use only 2–3 percent of current world energy output is largely beside the point; oil and other energy inputs represent 50 percent or more of agriculture's total inputs. What matters is that an inevitable long-run increase in the price of oil is likely to be the major cost-raising factor for world food production because of the large part that oil and gas play in the provision of motive power, fertilizers and crop protection chemicals.

Productivity increases, however, have reduced and are continuing to reduce the agriculture industry's energy dependency. UK agriculture for example, typical of European countries in its farming practices, is becoming more efficient in its use of energy. Total energy use by UK agriculture has fallen by more than 30 percent since 1985,[13] while output has remained constant. A similar pattern of increased efficiency is found in North America (a 40 percent reduction in the same period) and other developed countries.

The proposition that a stronger link between energy and non-energy commodity prices is likely to be the dominant influence on future developments in commodity and food markets is unquestionable. It is now generally accepted that the new equilibrium price of oil will be at least five to six times higher than the US$20/barrel of the two decades up to 2004, with proportional changes taking place in all other types of energy, at least in the long term. This must mean that food markets will be heavily influenced by the level of energy prices.

The importance of this trend in oil prices in the future cost of food is emphasized in a recently published UK Royal Society series of papers on the future of the global food system. The group of researchers on the food and energy relationship point out that "As yields and the inputs needed to support yield increase, agriculture is becoming more dependent on fossil fuels, either directly for tillage and crop management or through the application of energy-intensive inputs such as nitrogen fertiliser and pesticides."[14] While at present the world agriculture industry absorbs no more than 3 percent of total world energy supplies, this share will grow as agriculture intensifies in developing countries. The embodied energy in tractors, buildings, and other infrastructure necessary to support agriculture and food supplies will grow as developing country agricultural producers invest in the infrastructure needed to increase yields and output.

consumer concerns

It is certain that the traditional, simplistic input-output approach to maintaining or increasing agricultural production will not meet the political, environmental, and consumer challenges of the future. In developed countries, well-informed consumers will increasingly seek food that has been produced free of perceived chemical contamination, with consideration for the welfare of animals and with minimum emission of greenhouse gases (GHGs). For these three reasons in particular, consumers will force a new production and trade pattern that will result in greater national self-sufficiency in food production. While this development is undoubtedly regarded as the new protectionism by some critics, it is a reality that all sections of the food production and supply chain will have to respect.

new science and new methods

To meet these challenges, it is likely that farmers and scientists will increasingly seek to overcome the problem of the currently lower output resulting from the adoption of husbandry methods that are more economical in the use of energy and chemicals. Increasing consciousness of the environmental implications of importing food from both developed and developing countries will also affect the future pattern of trade and consumption. The impact of increased imports of, for example, beef from Brazil or palm oil from Malaysia on the land-use patterns and the environment of those countries will be of increasing concern to consumers and politicians in developed countries. The implications of production of food for export from the less-developed countries for the local social and economic structures are also likely to be of increasing concern.

trade policies and food supply

If there is to be greater global food security there has to be more fluidity in international trade in the major food commodities. An important factor in the 2006–2008 food price crisis was that rising prices of agricultural commodities produced pressure for more protectionism. Russia, for example, now operates a state grain trading company aimed at controlling up to half of its cereal exports. While it is true that Russia, and the Soviet Union and Imperial Russia before it, have always operated a state grain trading authority, such protectionism cannot be sustained in the modern global economy. It is unlikely that the modern Russian Republic will be able to maintain such an organization because the restriction of exports will lead to falling prices for farmers and falling production and increasing rural discontent.

In addition, Russia's membership in the World Trade Organization and other international economic organizations will militate against its maintaining such protectionist policies. Much the same applies to Ukraine and other former command economies; as they become more integrated into the world economy, they will find it increasingly difficult to restrict trade in this way.

As Robert Paarlberg argues in his challenging book *Food Politics* (2010): "From inside the food and farming sector, the single biggest source of this dramatic price spike [the 2006–2009 rise in global food prices] had been changes in trade policy. Once commodity prices began moving upward a number of countries decided to place restriction on food exports so as to protect their consumers from price inflation. These national trade restrictions imposed all at the same time, created a sudden shortage of food available for export on the world market, driving international prices much higher and deepening the panic buying."[15] As Paarlberg, and most other analysts, stress, the crisis did not result principally from diminished food production. "The panic in world markets was driven more by Russian and Argentinian export restrictions on wheat than by any global shortage overall."

In the short term, these activities undoubtedly lead to market distortions—both domestically and internationally—particularly when practiced by such major players as Russia and Ukraine.

the role of financial markets

Another school of thought is that a relatively new factor has emerged in world food markets that exacerbates the price-raising effect of fundamental failures in the production system—the undoubtedly massive intrusion of financial markets into food commodity trading. According to this view, one of the main causes of recent food price rises is a speculative bubble created by the massive growth in financial instruments linked to food commodities.

Undoubtedly, pension and hedge funds, sovereign wealth funds, and large banks that speculate on commodity markets have been progressively switching to commodities since the turn of the millennium. Olivier De Schutter, the UN's right to food rapporteur, argues in a 2010 working paper that the reason for this was that as other outlets for speculative capital disappeared, they were forced to switch into commodities.[16] These other outlets "dried up one by one: the dotcoms vanished at the end of 2001, the stock market soon after, and the US housing market in August 2007. As each bubble burst, these large institutional investors moved into other markets, each traditionally considered more stable than the last. Strong similarities can be seen between the price behaviour of food commodities and other refuge values, such as gold."

A study conducted by Lehman Brothers revealed that the volume of all index fund speculation in food commodities increased by 1,900 percent between 2003 and March 2008. Morgan Stanley estimated that the number of outstanding contracts in maize futures increased from 500,000 in 2003 to almost 2.5 million in 2008. Holdings in commodity index funds ballooned from US$13 billion in 2003 to US$317 billion between 2002 and 2008. The value of outstanding over the counter (OTC) commodity derivatives grew from 0.44 trillion in 1998 to 0.77 trillion in 2002 to a value of more than US$7.5 trillion in June 2007.

The De Schutter argument is that changes in supply and demand were mere catalysts to setting off a price escalation caused primarily by "excessive and insufficiently regulated speculation in commodity derivatives."

the price of failure

The most worrying factor of all for the future of the world's food supply is the extreme possibility of a long-term fall in yields, with a diminishing return to increased inputs of fertilizer, energy, and mechanization. What is more likely, however, is a fall in the rate of increase in yields, or, in other words, the failure of science to keep up with the demands of population increase—as it undoubtedly did in the last decades of the twentieth century.

The problem is likely to be concentrated in the hungry less-developed countries. Most typical of such counties are those in sub-Saharan Africa, where cereal yields average less than 1.3 tonnes per hectare, compared with yields in Asia of 2.9 to 3.4 tonnes. Cereal yields in other developing regions rose by between 1.2 and 2.3 percent a year between 1980 and 2000, while those in Africa increased by only 0.7 percent a year, according to the World Bank. This is due in part to inherent problems and to inadequate husbandry. The soil in some African countries often lacks the key nutrients nitrogen and potassium, as well as such trace elements as zinc. These problems are often compounded by poor agricultural practices.

What is most probable is that production in the developing countries will not keep pace with rising demand, unless there is a new input of scientific effort and the injection of new money into agricultural development. Although production in and exports from the major cereal-producing countries will be able to fill the shortfall, the means do have to be provided for this necessary redistribution. The net cereal deficits of the less-developed countries, which amounted to 103 million tonnes or 9 percent of consumption in 1997–1999, the FAO estimates, could rise to 265 million tonnes by 2030, representing 14 percent of global consumption.[17] But "this gap can be bridged by increased surpluses from traditional grain exporters, and by new exports from the transition countries, which are expected to shift from being net importers to being net exporters."

main factors affecting food supply and demand

There are four main factors in the food supply and demand equation; an optimistic or pessimistic result can be obtained, depending on which of these variables are fed into the calculation and how they are applied. Probably most important are assumptions on crop yield increases. Leaving aside possible environmental and social constraints, the leading economic modelers (IFPRI and the Food and Agricultural Policy Research Institute) are still expecting production to increase by 1.5–1.7 percent per year into the middle of the century. While less than the increases of the past two decades, this is still likely to be adequate to meet rising demand and to stabilize food markets—particularly since population growth rates are projected to fall even more rapidly.[18] Those with the most pessimistic view of the future global food situation tend not to regard application of the new biotechnology as likely to have a significant effect on production.

The second area of debate is the amount of land that will continue to be available for food production. Optimists expect an increase in the farmed area as new land is brought into production in developing countries and land is brought out of retirement in Europe and North America. It should not be forgotten that in the late 1990s some 40 million hectares of prime agricultural land worldwide was deliberately being held out of production by governments to reduce the taxpayer-funded cost of surplus disposal; if only half this land was producing cereals, world cereal stocks would rebuild to 1980s levels (i.e., well above the FAO's minimum safe level of 18 percent of current consumption). Analysts concerned about ecological impacts, on the other hand, believe that the available food production area, rather than increasing, will be reduced by land lost to urban and industrial use, combined with degradation of existing land.

There are also varied assumptions about how much further intensification of production can be taken. Intensification has had a major impact on food output in the period since the end of World War II, as the irrigated area in developing countries doubled and cropping intensity increased in both developed and developing countries. While the optimists expect further increases in intensification—at lower levels—the ecologists expect there to be no more new irrigation as agriculture competes for water with urban and industrial uses and that there will be significant land degradation. It should not be forgotten, however, that the scope for expansion of production on nonirrigated land is still substantial.

improving supplies to the hungry

Given that the developed countries will be able to maintain future food supplies—either by increasing production or importing more—the major issue in the world food debate is the ability or otherwise of impoverished nations to improve their supplies of food. The inability of the impoverished nations adequately to feed their people can arise from a number of factors: paucity of natural resources, lack of money to invest in agricultural development and improvement, and political obstruction. Those countries suffering from the first of these handicaps will not be able to provide adequate food supplies from their own farms; adequate nutrition will therefore depend on imports. With the right economic conditions or aid, they will have to draw on the total world food supply to improve or maintain nutrition levels. These are the most vulnerable nations.

The majority of food-poor nations, however, fall into the second category, those lacking adequate development of their agricultural resources. Agricultural advice and other extension services in these countries will need to be improved and developed if there is to be the necessary improvement in technical ability and husbandry. Better marketing networks and transport infrastructure are also vital to this process. Too many of the less-developed countries are in the third category—agricultural development, markets, and distribution disrupted and obstructed by war, revolution, and other political problems. Many of these are countries that could provide most if not all their food from their own resources. People dying of hunger or suffering from malnutrition are most usually products of inadequate supply, not an inherent lack of productive capacity.

There is little doubt that the likely rapid rise in world population will continue to push up demand, but there is also little doubt that the higher prices resulting from this increased demand will stimulate increased production. The rate at which production will have to increase in the next three or four decades is likely to be less than in the past. The annual growth rate of world demand for cereals has, according to FAO, declined from 2.5 percent a year in the 1970s and 1.9 percent a year in the 1980s to only 1 percent a year in the 1990s. The reason for this is that the annual cereal use per person (including animal feeds) peaked in the mid-1980s at 334 kg and has since fallen to 317 kg. This is the natural result of slower population growth, and more important, changes in human diets and animal feed use. This trend was accentuated in the 1990s by abnormal factors, such as serious recessions in the so-called transition countries and some east Asia and Southeast Asia countries. The FAO does expect the growth rate of demand for cereals to accelerate again to 1.4 percent a year to 2015, slowing to 1.2 percent per year thereafter.

By 2030, per capita consumption of livestock products could rise by a further 44 percent compared with 2012. As in the past, poultry consumption will grow fastest. Productivity improvements are likely to be a major source of growth. Milk yields are expected to improve, while breeding and improved management will increase average carcass weights and off-take rates. This will allow increased meat and dairy production with lower growth in animal numbers. While the obvious obstacles may prevent the agricultural potential of developing countries from being fully exploited, there is little doubt that current and new exporting countries will increase their output in response to rising effective demand.

a long-term rise in prices?

Increasing prosperity in developing and emerging economies such as China and India will stimulate dietary changes, leading to a shift to more meat and dairy product consumption. This will also lead to greater pressure on food and feed prices and exacerbate environmental and health challenges. International agriculture is capable of responding to this change in demand.

As presidents, prime ministers, and pundits are increasingly bothered about rising food prices, a multipart question inevitably arises: How serious will the rise in prices be, what are its real causes, and how long is it likely to last? More precisely, will prices fall in response to increased production or are we facing a longer period of permanently high prices?

After thirty years of falling real prices, world food prices rose to probably unprecedented levels during 2005–2008. In the subsequent four years, prices averaged out at close to the post-2008 level.

According to *The Economist*'s index, while during the three decades between 1974 and 2005 real food prices declined by 75 percent, in the three years after 2005 they rose by 75 percent. Prices of wheat, butter, and milk tripled between 2000 and 2008, and prices of maize, rice, and poultry meat nearly doubled. The prices of other basic foodstuffs such as meat, palm oil, and cassava also increased substantially. Overall, the FAO Food Price Index (FPI) rose by nearly 40 percent in 2007, following a 9 percent increase in 2006. Prices in 2008 were higher than they had been in decades; in 2010 there were further increases to new record levels. Prior to the price spike created by the harvest alarms of 2010, they settled at a new higher-than-trend level. But in August 2011 the FPI reached an average of 231 points, nearly unchanged from July 2011 but 26 percent higher than in August 2010, the index having hit its all-time high of 238 points in February 2011.[19]

The important question is whether the factors that have kept down food prices during the past thirty years are still relevant and whether they will continue to be relevant in the future. Real prices of food fell in the period 1975 to 2005 because the increase in world food output was greater than the increase in population and the increase in demand for food. The increase in production as a proportion of per capita consumption of the world's three major cereal crops since the 1970s has been 37 percent for maize, 20 percent for rice, and 15 percent for wheat. Consequently, real prices for these commodities in the period to 2007 dropped by 43 percent for maize, 33 percent for rice, and 38 percent for wheat over the same period.

The main reasons for these rises in production are likely to have been:

- continuous development of new technology such as improved seeds, better management practices, and improved pest and disease control;
- commercialization of agriculture in developing countries, which has increased the availability and quality of production inputs and created more efficient means of marketing outputs;
- the expansion of international trade, which has minimized price differences between different regions and seasons and favored production patterns based on comparative advantage.[20]

All of these are encouraging developments contributing to improved world food security. Can they be sustained into the middle of the twenty-first century?

What is probable is that prices are likely to settle at a higher real level than before 2005. This is because costs of producing the extra output needed to meet the increasing Asian demand for so-called Western style foods and for biofuel production will have increased—principally because of the rise in the price of oil. Only in the unlikely event of a reduction in oil prices, agricultural input costs, and reduced demand for biofuels would there be any return to pre-2007 food price levels. Climate change will further complicate the food supply and demand matrix.

In the real world of the immediate future there is little doubt that production is responding to the rise in prices. Following the 2007–2008 price hike there was a record cereal world harvest in 2008–2009 and record winter wheat plantings for the 2009–2010 harvest. There were further increases in plantings and production in 2011–2012. Whether production increases substantially or not, there are important

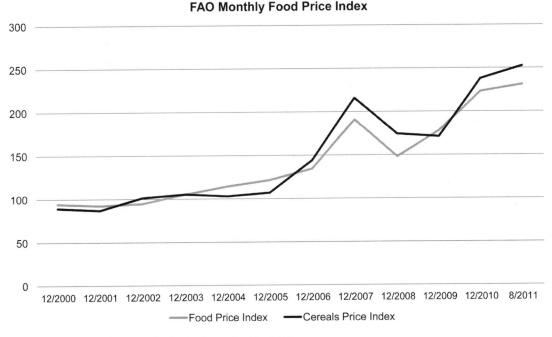

FAO Monthly Food Price Index

Figure 1.2 Breaking the trend—the food price crisis of the 2000s.
Source of Data: FAO Food Outlook Global Market Analysis (2005–12).

factors likely to raise both production costs and output prices. Oil prices continue to increase, which not only increases farmers' costs but also encourages more hectares to be allocated to maize and wheat for biofuels. A further current factor—which may not persist—is that governments are meddling with markets, as they see it, to secure scarce food supplies. It is estimated by UN World Food Programme officials that one-third of the world's population lives in countries with food price controls or export bans.

The worldwide spread of protection of agriculture markets, as currently being recommended by, for example, defenders of the EU's common agricultural policy and government advisers and politicians in other parts of the world, is unlikely to improve global food security. The alternative view that real and long-term food security is likely to come from spreading the risk of production fluctuation over as wide a geographical area as possible is difficult to promote when prices spiral and hungry people riot in the streets. In these immediate political situations, it is hard to argue that only open markets will both raise output and deliver food at stable prices in the longer term.

questions to be answered

None of the questions raised in this introductory chapter has an easy answer. The world's food supply and demand equation is a complex weave of difficult and sometimes contradictory facts, figures, and suppositions. The following chapters seek to clarify and hopefully simplify (though not oversimplify) all the factors that need to be considered in assessment of the future development of food demand and supply.

This book seeks to address the following issues:

1. Does the world face a future pattern of recurring and worsening food shortages in too many places—famine, or of increasingly plentiful food supplies?
2. How will trade in food and agricultural products develop; will it make a positive contribution to food security; and how will it foster the improvement of food supply to the most needy?
3. What role will food traders play in the delivery of food to consumers in developed and developing countries; how will international traders in food commodities influence this process; and what will be the effect of the expanding control of multinational retailing corporations?
4. What is the influence of speculation on supply and price of food? What is the impact of new financial trading instruments on the price of food?
5. How do the channels through which food supply flows affect prices, availability, and access to food?
6. How does the wider economy of developed, emerging and developing countries affect the demand for and the supply of food?
7. How will the challenges of a rising population concentrated in developing countries and the change in the world population balance affect the demand for food? How will these challenges be met?
8. What are the obstacles to access to food for the poorest nations and people?
9. What will be the response of production to increasing demand for food: land availability, production resources, productivity?
10. What will be the role of governments in facilitating or obstructing production and delivery of food? Are new policies needed?
11. How will the major challenges to increased food production—rising energy prices and climate change—be met?
12. Will liberalization improve food security and stabilize food prices?
13. Will an increase in output and trade needed to sustain a 9 billion-plus population put unsustainable pressure on the environment?

notes

1.   N. Alexandratos, ed., *World Agriculture: Towards 2030/2050—Interim Report. Prospects for Food, Nutrition, Agriculture, and Major Commodity Groups* (Rome: FAO, Global Perspective Studies Unit, 2006) and Food and Agriculture Organization (FAO) of the United Nations, "How to Feed the World in 2050: High-Level Expert Forum," (Rome: FAO, June 24–26, 2009, revised July 25, 2009).

2.   J. Pretty et al., "The Top 100 Questions of Importance to the Future of Global Agriculture," *International Journal of Agricultural Sustainability* 8, no. 4 (2010): 219–236.

3.   FAO, "How to Feed the World in 2050."

4.   According to the World Health Organization, food security exists "when all people at all times have access to sufficient, safe, nutritious food to maintain a healthy and active life."

5.   Lester R. Brown, *Outgrowing the Earth: The Food Security Challenge in an Age of Falling Water Tables and Rising Temperatures* (New York: Norton, 2004).

6.   Jelle Bruinsma, *World Agriculture: Towards 2015/2030* (Rome: FAO, 2003).

7.   FAO, "Food Supply Situation and Crop Prospects in sub-Saharan Africa," no.2, August (Rome: FAO, Global Information and Early Warning System, 1999).

8.   Nikos Alexandratos and Jelle Bruinsma, *World Agriculture: Towards 2030/2050: The 2012 Revision* (Rome: FAO Agricultural Development Economics Division, 2012).

9.   Ibid.

10.   Gerald C. Nelson et al., *Climate Change: Impact on Agriculture and Costs of Adaptation* (Washington, DC: International Food Policy Research Institute, 2009).

11.   American Economic Association: Energy & Environment and Universidad de Politécnica de Madrid, *Adaptation to Climate Change in the Agricultural Sector*, AGRI-2006-G4–05. Report to European Commission Directorate-General for Agriculture and Rural Development (ED05334), no. 1 (December 2007).

12.   World Bank, *World Development Report 2010: Development and Climate Change* (Washington, DC: World Bank, 2010).

13.   Department for Environment, Food, and Rural Affairs (DEFRA), *Ensuring the UK's Food Security in a Changing World: A DEFRA Discussion Paper* (London: DEFRA, July 2008).

14.   Jeremy Woods et al., "Energy and the Food System," *Philosophical Transactions of the Royal Society* 365B (2010): 2991–3006.

15.   Robert Paarlberg, *Food Politics—What Everyone Needs to Know* (New York: Oxford University Press, 2010).

16.   Olivier De Schutter, "Food Commodities Speculation and Food Price Crises," Briefing Note 2 by the UN special rapporteur on the right to food (September 23, 2010). Available at: http://www.srfood.org/index.php/en/component/content/article/894-food-commodities-speculation-and-food-price-crises.

17.   Ibid., iii.

18.   Joachim von Braun, *The World Food Situation: New Driving Force and Required Actions* (Washington, DC: International Food Policy Research Institute, 2007).

19.   FAO, *Food Price Index* (Rome: FAO, September 2011).

20.   UK Government, Cabinet Office, The Strategy Unit, *Food: An Analysis of the Issues. Report to Government* (London: Cabinet Office, January 2008; updated and re-issued August 2008).

chapter 2

famine or plenty?

Writers and thinkers on the vitally important issue of the future of the world's food system are broadly divided between those who believe that it is impossible for the demand for food for a population of more than seven billion to be met without unsustainable strain on the ecosystem and those who believe that human ingenuity will ensure that production will rise to meet the increased demand. In between these two extremes are those who believe that the problem can only be solved through extreme measures on population control and, possibly, prescriptive allocation of resources to agriculture.

main points

- The two main approaches to the food supply challenge are: neo-Malthusians and optimists.
- Conventional approaches to increasing agricultural production are undoubtedly under threat from urbanization, climate change, environmental constraints, contamination, and rising energy prices.
- The alternative view is that production can be increased to meet needs of rising population.
- Sources of increased productivity include new plant and animal breeding techniques.
- There is underutilized land in most regions of the world.

the neo-malthusian argument

To a great extent the pessimists, generally characterized as neo-Malthusians, currently have the run of the headlines. This is principally because their version of the future makes the better story. By invoking the ghost of the economist Thomas Malthus,[1] whose views had a truly dreadful effect on the actions of nineteenth-century politicians, this dismal thesis draws on deep fears in the human psyche. Malthus believed that population would increase exponentially, while the food supply would only increase arithmetically; the result would be starvation and shrinkage of the population to match the food supply.

There is evidence to support the pessimists' argument. The most obvious is the apparent recent increase in the volatility of prices of major food commodities. More people needing more food, more agriculturally demanding food in particular, has in recent years brought annual world food demand closer to annual production. During the first decade of the twenty-first century, the two lines on the world food graph have almost crossed over, with demand close to exceeding supply. This has meant a worrying rundown of food stocks—hence, the rocketing price increases of 2008 and 2011.

While the world is not yet in a situation where there is not enough food available to feed everyone, it soon will be, say the neo-Malthusians. Crop yields are not increasing fast enough, they maintain, and the world's cropland is stretched to the limit of sustainability and suffering the effects of contamination by the overuse of fertilizers and pesticides, the declining amount of water to nourish crops, and climate changes that will handicap food production in those countries that most need to increase output. To add further to the difficulty of increasing or even sustaining food production, oil, the basic element of the world's commercial agricultural production, is in increasingly short supply and will therefore become progressively more expensive.

a broken world food system?

Followers of this pessimistic school of thought tend to argue that the world food system is broken or generally deteriorating under the weight of technical unsustainability and the domination of monopolistic food buyers, processors, shippers, retailers, and commodity speculators. According to this argument, this structural flaw is responsible for putting smaller food producers out of business in both the developed and underdeveloped world and thus diminishing food security because of increasing dependence on industrialized agriculture. In the case of the most food insecure countries, they are increasingly being made dependent on expensive food imports.

The acknowledged leader of the pessimistic school is Lester Brown of the Earth Policy Institute in Washington, DC. He believes that high food prices are here to stay and that shortages will increase as a result of climate change, increasing population, water scarcity, and soil erosion. While prepared to admit that some (actually, most) of his earlier warnings of disaster were not fulfilled,[2] Brown argues that the difference between past food crises and now is what many believe is a very different phenomenon:

> Whereas in years past, it's been weather that has caused a spike in commodities prices, now it's trends on both sides of the food supply/demand equation that are driving up prices. On the demand side, the culprits are population growth, rising affluence, and the use of grain to fuel cars. On the supply side: soil erosion, aquifer depletion, the loss of cropland to non-farm uses, the diversion of irrigation water to cities, the plateauing of crop yields in agriculturally advanced countries, and—due to climate change—crop-withering heat waves and melting mountain glaciers and ice sheets.[3]

These climate-related trends seem destined to take a far greater toll in the future.

Examples, albeit some extreme, of those stresses on the global food system are cited by Brown and others. On the supply side, Saudi Arabia once relied on its own aquifer, or an underground water supply, which is now dried up. From 2007 to 2010, Saudi wheat production fell by two-thirds, and "by 2012, wheat production will likely end entirely," according to Brown. (The classical economist's answer to this would be Saudi Arabia should not be growing wheat, a product for which it has nil comparative advantage, but should be, more efficiently, importing wheat in exchange for its oil for which it has maximum comparative advantage.)

On the demand side, Brown admits there is some good news in terms of our increasing popula-tion: "World population growth, which peaked at 2 percent per year around 1970, dropped below 1.2 percent per year in 2010." But none would dispute his point that the challenge comes from the actual increase in population, "because the world population has nearly doubled since 1970, we are still adding 80 million people each year." In addition to these new mouths, 3 billion people are "moving up the food chain" and consuming more grain-intensive livestock and poultry, generating even more demand for grains. A new and undoubtedly important factor in the food demand picture is the development of biofuels, both bioethanol from grain and biodiesel from oilseeds. In support of his argument, Brown points out that in the United States, which harvested 416 million tonnes of grain in 2009, 119 million tonnes went to ethanol distilleries to produce motor fuel for cars—the equivalent of a year's food supply for 350 million people.

Because of these new factors in the world food equation things can never be the same again ac-cording to the Brown thesis; the easy outpacing of increasing demand by increasing production seen throughout the industrial age until the twenty-first century is a thing of the past.

water shortage a major problem

Water shortage is an increasing handicap to increasing food production in the most food-poor coun-tries, as well as in some of the most prosperous countries.[4] Current and future water availability has been identified as one of the foremost global challenges.

Nine of the ten most vulnerable countries are from the Middle East and North Africa. These countries include Saudi Arabia (4), Libya (5), Yemen (7) and Jordan (10). The insecurity created by water shortage and other fundamental obstacles to increased production is stimulating a continued high rate of land grabs by larger, wealthier countries with emerging economies, that have taken to offsetting their own water shortages by buying up land in the water-rich but economically poor countries in sub-Saharan Africa. China is one such buyer, and given recent severe droughts, it seems likely that it will continue to seek more and more opportunities to purchase arable land.

The more enthusiastic proponents of the pessimistic worldview found their position fully supported by a 2011 publication by Oxfam International: "Now, as climate chaos sends us stumbling into our sec-ond food price crisis in three years, little has changed to suggest that the global system will manage any better this time around. Power remains concentrated in the hands of a self-interested few. The paralysis imposed upon us by a powerful minority risks catastrophe. Atmospheric concentrations of greenhouse gases are already above sustainable levels and continue to rise alarmingly. Land is running out. Fresh water is drying up."[5]

climate change will make things worse

The effects of climate change have to be added into this dismal equation. Oxfam expects maize prices to increase by nearly 180 percent, with paddy rice prices rising by 140 percent and wheat prices by 120 percent within two decades. Maize is forecast to suffer the biggest climate-induced productivity losses: south and southeastern Africa would see a 35 percent loss in maize productivity by 2030 due to climate change, while west, central, and eastern Africa would also lose in more than 20 percent of maize productivity. But the basis for the claims of these massive food price rises in this new research is difficult to find.

While no one questions that climate change will affect the world's food production pattern—and probably harm most those in need of more food—the optimists argue that there are countervailing factors that challenge Oxfam's dismal predictions. Cautious assessments of the world's future food production capacity and its ability to meet increased demand by such internationally recognized organizations as the Food and Agriculture Organization (FAO) of the United Nations and the International Food Policy Research Institute (IFPRI) are optimistic about the ability of future production to meet demand.

the optimistic view

Individual researchers looking at future crop production possibilities are also optimistic. Professor Wally Huffman at Iowa State University has made a study of the long-term trend of maize and soya bean yields in Iowa, wheat in Kansas and France, rice in Japan, and potatoes in the Netherlands. The study indicates that there is no indication that the rate of increase in yields of food crops is slowing and concludes that there is no reason to fear falling crop yields.[6] Huffman predicts that the rate of increase in yields for maize and soya beans in major production areas will rise much faster than it has in the past fifty years: "From 2010 to 2019, corn yields are going to increase quite substantially, maybe at four to six bushels [65 kg to 98 kg] per acre, per year [156 kg to 235 kg/hectare/year]." (*Note:* 1 hectare = 2.47 acres.)

Much of the increase will be due to genetic improvements in hybrid maize varieties produced by genetic manipulation aimed at chemical-free insect protection and herbicide tolerance that will permit a major increase in plant populations. Also, better equipment and improved husbandry techniques, including reduced and no-till farming, will contribute to rising maize yields. Other crops will also have improved yields and continuing increases in output, according to Huffman: U.S. and French wheat, without genetic modification (GM) (increasing at 0.5 bushels/acre/year and more than 1.5 bushels/acre/year, respectively); Japanese rice yields are improving without GM at a rate of 0.5 bushels/acre/year and are now at 113 bushels/acre/year compared to around 90 bushels/acre/year in 1960; and Netherlands' potato yields are increasing by about 4.6 bushels/acre/year. European crop yields could be increased further with adoption of genetically modified varieties.

Huffman believes that production and availability of food crops will continue to increase because of the research efforts of both private companies and government. Higher yields will result from application of new techniques in breeding crops, including new research methods that allow breeding and testing techniques to be dramatically speeded up. Supply of crop products to food markets will also be increased by a reduction in pressure from biofuel production with the continuing switch from a maize base to a biomass base over the coming decades.

There is no doubt that the global climate is changing and all assessments of food supply potential in both developed and less-developed countries now have to factor in this reality. Whatever governments do or do not agree on greenhouse gas emission control, it will make little difference to the influence on world food production of a changing climate during the next forty years. More relevant to the world food problem are the methods and policies adopted to counteract climate change and ensure the rapid acceleration of production and delivery of food to where it is most needed.

No one with knowledge of the current state of world agriculture would quibble with the argument that meeting the challenge of feeding 9.5 billion people is daunting. But with or without global warming, those with a more optimistic view argue that the world's agricultural resources are adequate to feed everyone— today, tomorrow, and in forty years' time. They argue that if practical food production stimulation policies were to be applied at international, national, and regional levels, local food supply in the most vulnerable areas could be substantially increased and hunger significantly reduced. The experience of the past two decades shows that well-designed schemes, specifically targeted at agricultural production and food supply problems in once crisis-ridden areas, have yielded massive dividends. They have also prevented the world's hunger and malnutrition problems from being much greater than they would have been.

hunger reduced

Thanks to agricultural development and the application of new technology in developing countries— plus the delivery of grain and other staples from increasingly productive developed world agriculture— the incidence and risk of hunger has been massively reduced. In 1980 at least one-third of the world population of about 3.3 billion were near to starving. Today the number suffering hunger and malnutrition has been reduced to one-sixth of a twice as large population. This does not of course diminish the scale of the reality that of the current 7 billion world population, one billion or more people still remain undernourished.

In the words of a recent report from IFPRI: "Five decades of investment in agricultural development have contributed significantly to feeding billions of people."[7] The application of modern science, improvements in rural infrastructure and public policy, and international collaboration have combined to enhance yields and increase food output to feed millions.

What is important is that these advances in agricultural productivity have been combined with schemes to improve access to food. "Many later interventions sought to integrate community participation and environmental sustainability into agricultural development, "says IFPRI, "with important repercussions for the use of local knowledge resources and natural resources in combating hunger. Other interventions worked to strengthen the role of markets and agricultural incomes by encouraging the commercialisation of small-scale farmers' production, improving supply chain efficiencies, and loosening the state regulation of both input and commodity markets."

Despite earlier pessimistic prognostications, agricultural production and agricultural trade has boomed in countries and regions once high on the food crisis list. Most spectacular examples are China and India. China cut the number of hungry people from 303 million in 1979–1981 to 122 million in 2003–2005. Given that country's one-sixth share of world population, this made a single massive contribution to reducing world hunger. Despite rapid population growth, India also reduced the number of people suffering from chronic hunger from 262 million in 1979–1981 to 231 million in 2003–2005.

There are outstanding examples of the success of such focused approaches. In Argentina, the use of zero tillage, the introduction of herbicide-resistant soya bean varieties and other factors, and improved soil fertility by reversing decades of erosion created an estimated 200,000 new agricultural jobs and provided the international market with new supplies of soya beans that contributed to keeping global food prices lower. This result was achieved with lower inputs and production costs, with the added benefits of reducing land degradation, conserving soil fertility, and economizing on scarce water resources. By 2008, the area of Argentinean land under zero tillage reached nearly 22 million hectares.

In India, the backing of supportive policies ensured the dairy industry's steady growth and development. The country went from being a net importer of dairy products to being a significant exporter. Between 1970 and 2001, dairy production in India increased at 4.5 percent per year, and is currently expecting to produce 100 million tonnes of milk a year.

trade necessary for food security

Improvement and maintenance of the worlds' food security is not only dependent on the ability of the hungriest countries to grow more of their own food, it is also necessary that developed and major developing countries increase their production capacity to meet inevitable demand increases from increasingly prosperous countries that cannot adequately increase their own food production.

Economists who believe that free markets will increase global food security argue that the continuing liberalisation of trade in agricultural products, which began with the World Trade Organization's 1994 Marrakech Agreement, is essential to the maintenance of world food security. There is no doubt that the underlying causes of the recent worldwide food price inflation are still present—protectionism, food production distorted by subsidies and market manipulation, government subsidized demand for biofuels, low agricultural productivity in the poorest countries, and an emergency food aid system that often works too late and too little. The higher prices of the early twenty-first century have also stimulated increased production in the major producing and exporting countries. It is also argued by leading scientists that higher prices for food will continue to stimulate rising agricultural productivity and production.[8]

Supporters of this argument point out that, for example, western European agriculture is currently operating at probably more than 15 percent undercapacity because of political obstructions of various types, and production potential in central and eastern Europe has still not been fully realized, Russia and Ukraine are estimated to be producing less than 70 percent of their full potential, and Brazil and other South American countries have yet to reach maximum output. The longer term rising price of oil will increase worldwide agricultural production costs. The price of food will consequently rise, but food will not be in short supply.

To take the example of Brazil, now the world's second largest agricultural exporter after the United States, it could still substantially increase its output without cutting down even one more rain forest tree. In the period 1990–1991 to 2008–2009 Brazil's production of grains rose from 58 million tonnes to 144 million tonnes, despite an increase in planted area of only 26 percent, from 37.9 million hectares to

47.7 million hectares. Productivity can therefore be seen to have almost doubled. Brazil's milk production has increased from 11.2 billion to 27.1 billion liters since the early 1980s, with a productivity gain of 86 percent. In the 1994 to 2009 period, beef production rose 77 percent, pig meat by 133 percent, and poultry meat by 217 percent. Potential for further increase in output is substantial. Of the current 340 million hectares of Brazil's existing agricultural area, some 96 million hectares remain underutilized or not used.

Significantly, international organizations concerned with monitoring the world's food supply and demand tend toward the more optimistic view of the future. They point out that recent reductions in the rate of increase in world food supply have not been caused by any innate failure of the world's agricultural system, but have been due to depressed demand and government policies. These are the main factors that have discouraged producers from increasing output.

The FAO is confident that the world has the necessary agricultural resources to increase output. It lists the three main sources of growth in crop production: expanding the cultivated land area, increased cropping frequency—often with the aid of irrigation, and increased yields. The pessimistic view that we have reached the limits on these three fronts is effectively contradicted by FAO: "It has been suggested that we may be approaching the ceiling of what is possible for all three sources. A detailed examination of production potentials does not support this view at the global level. There is adequate unused potential farmland."[9]

Global Land Use

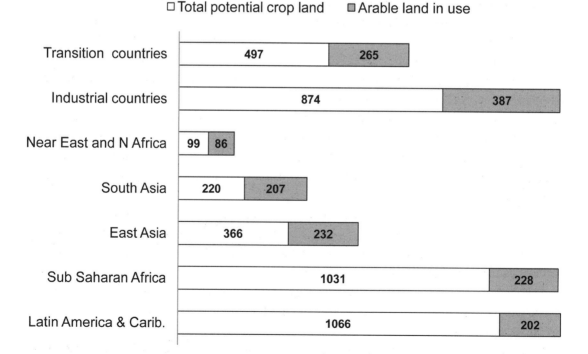

Figure 2.1 Land in use and available for crop production according to FAO (million hectares).
Source of Data: Nikos Alexandratos and Jelle Bruinsma, World Agriculture: Towards 2030/2050: The 2012 Revision *(Rome: FAO Agricultural Development Economics Division, 2012).*

Table 2.1 THE SOURCES OF INCREASED PRODUCTION ACCORDING TO THE FAO

	Arable land expansion %		Increases in cropping intensity %		Yield increases %
	1961–2005	2005/7–2050	1961–2005	2005/7–2050	1961–2005
All LDCs	23	21	8	8	70
Sub-Saharan Africa	31	25	31	6	38
Near East/N Africa	17	−7	22	17	62
Latin America & Caribbean	40	30	7	18	53
S Asia	6	5	w	8	82
E Asia	28	2	−6	12	77
World	14	9	9	14	77
LDCs less than 40% of potential arable land in use 2005		30		15	
LDCs with +80% of arable land in use 2005		2		9	

Source: Nikos Alexandratos and Jelle Bruinsma, *World Agriculture: Towards 2030/2050: The 2012 Revision* (Rome: FAO Agricultural Development Economics Division, 2012)

Comparison of soils, terrains, and climates with the needs of major crops suggests that an extra 2.8 billion hectares are suitable in varying degrees for rain-fed (nonirrigated) production of arable and permanent crops—almost twice as much as is currently farmed. It is conceded that only a fraction of this extra land is realistically available for agricultural expansion. There are also likely to be serious structural and political obstacles to further exploitation of potential arable land.

According to an FAO report, "There is little evidence to suggest that global land scarcities lie ahead. Between the early 1960s and the late 1990s, world cropland grew by only 11 per cent, while world population almost doubled. As a result, cropland per person fell by 40 per cent, from 0.43 ha to only 0.26 ha. Yet, over this same period, nutrition levels improved considerably and the real price of food declined. Fears of an imminent crunch between population growth and land availability are unwarranted."[10]

Most of the increased production needed in the future will come from increased yields in both developed and developing countries, but future yield growth does not need to be as rapid as in the past. While wheat yields, for example, in the developed countries are not likely to be sustained at the 2 percent a year increase of the past fifteen years, an annual rise of only 1.2 percent a year is needed over the next thirty years.

vital increased yields

Given the constraints on expanding the world's farmed land, it is clear that most of the increased production needed in the future will come from increased yields in both developed and developing countries. To meet production projections, future yield growth will not need to be as rapid as in the past. While wheat yields, for example, in the developed countries are not likely to be sustained at the 2 percent a year growth of the past fifteen years, an annual rise of only 1.2 percent is needed over the next thirty years.

The FAO believes that application of biotechnology, in its broadest sense, to agriculture in the developing countries offers the best way of improving food security and reducing pressures on the environment, provided that possible environmental threats from biotechnology itself are addressed. According to an FAO report, "Genetically modified crop varieties—resistant to drought, waterlogging, soil acidity, salinity and extreme temperatures—could help to sustain farming in marginal areas and to restore degraded lands to production. Pest-resistant varieties can reduce the need for pesticides."[11]

While the obvious obstacles may prevent the agricultural potential of developing countries from being fully exploited, the current and new exporting countries will increase their output in response to rising effective demand.

The traditional exporters, Australia, North America, Argentina, and Uruguay, have the potential to continue to increase deliveries to the international market. Unutilized cultivable land is plentiful in the transition economies of eastern Europe and Russia, and the scope for increasing productivity by reducing losses and raising yields is high. The FAO's projections suggest that the transition countries could be net exporters of 10 million tonnes of cereals a year by 2015 and 25 million tonnes by 2030. Thus, despite the obvious difficulties, food production can continue to increase in line with increases in demand. If the problem of hunger in the poorer nations is to be diminished however, production has to be stimulated in the underfarmed areas and import demand has to be aided by money from the world's richer countries.

better functioning markets needed

The view that better functioning markets are an important contribution to improved food security is backed by the Organisation for Economic Co-operation and Development, which argues that "agricultural trade enhances national and global food security by increasing the sources of food supply and lowering prices in importing countries, stimulating food production in countries that have a natural or structural advantage in agriculture, and increasing overall economic growth rates through a more efficient allocation of resources."[12] The long-held OECD position is that trade reform would deepen world markets and, as a result, reduce international price volatility and encourage farmers around the world to produce according to their respective comparative advantages.

The case for trade liberalization is reinforced by the prospect of climate change, the authors of a UK government report[13] maintain, "Trade helps mitigate geographic-specific risks, so that if there is a constraint on supply in one region, whether within Europe—which is not immune to animal disease outbreaks or weather affected harvests—or another part of the world, alternative suppliers can fill the gap. In short, international trade is a key underpinning of food security at all levels."

The report bucks the conventional wisdom that the shortfall in the 2007 Australian harvest and a large increase in the use of the U.S. maize crop for biofuel production were the major causes of the 2007–2008 food supply and price crisis. These can clearly be seen to be a relatively small part of the cause when it is considered that Australian wheat production and exports (about10 percent) represent a relatively small proportion of total world production and exports and, likewise, that bioethanol production from U.S. maize was a small proportion of total world production and export availability (U.S. maize exports actually increased in the 2007–2008 marketing year). The reasons for the price hike identified by the UK paper are more fundamental—and feasible.

The paper puts forward four main factors that, in varying degrees, underlay the sudden increase in prices. Most obvious was the depletion of grain stocks, with global stocks to use ratios for wheat, maize, and rice in 2007–2008 declining to around 15 percent, followed by the inevitable uncertainty about the following year's crop. The prospects for a response from agricultural producers and exporters to the high prices was made more sluggish by the rapid increase in global energy prices, which increased the cost of agricultural inputs, especially fertilizers. Commodity prices were further stoked by weakening of the U.S. dollar, increasing dollar-denominated international prices, affecting particularly importing countries whose exchange rates did not appreciate against the dollar. The situation was unnecessarily exacerbated by export restrictions in a number of countries, most notably Ukraine, which fueled the price spike for wheat and maize, and could have added pressure to the rice market price inflation.

A fundamental issue in solving the problem of hunger in the most vulnerable regions is, how can the transition from today's smallholder-based agriculture to sustainable agricultural intensification occur in ways that maintain livelihoods for smallholder farmers?

The future maintenance of an adequate food supply in the end comes down to the very basic question of whether the long-term capacity of fossil fuels and stocks of nitrogen, phosphorus, and potassium fertilizer are adequate to support intensive, or more intensive, production systems globally. Given that such resources are finite, how can food production systems that reduce dependence on externally derived nitrogen, phosphorus, and potassium resources be developed?

What is all too clear from these questions is that the quantity and price of the world's future food supply is dependent on the availability and cost of energy, principally oil. It is also clear that if there is to be any reduction in oil dependency of the industry and amelioration of agriculture's pressure on the environment, there has to be a large and consistent investment in agricultural research.

summary

Current volatility in food prices lend support to neo-Malthusian food shortage arguments. Annual food production has undoubtedly moved closer to demand—unlikely the period of comfortable surplus that lasted until the late twentieth century. The pessimistic view on current and future food supply holds that the world food system is broken under the pressure of technical inadequacy, but also because of speculative and food trade monopolists. The rising expectations of the new, third world middle class, with its demand for more protein foods, is putting additional strain on the world's food production capacity. Climate change and environmental stress will exacerbate further the obstruction of production increases needed to feed a more than 9 billion population.

The international food monitoring agencies are, on the contrary, cautiously optimistic. There is both additional and increased productivity potential sufficient to continue to meet increasing demand for both carbohydrate and protein foods. Scientists believe that, given the right financial encouragement, there can be adequate future increases in production. But better functioning markets are needed, both locally in food-needy countries and internationally to ensure long-term food security.

notes

1. Thomas Robert Malthus, *An Essay on the Principle of Population* (London: J. Johnson, 1798; reprint, London: Macmillan, 1966).

2. Lester R. Brown, "The Great Food Crisis of 2011," *Foreign Policy Magazine*, January 2011.

3. N.B.J. Koning et al., "Long-term Global Availability of Food: Continued Abundance or New Scarcity?," *NJAS: Wageningen Journal of Life Sciences* 55(3): 229–292.

4. Report on global water stress by the Report: Global water stress. From British risk assessment firm Maplecroft, 2011.

5. Robert Bailey, *Growing a Better Future: Food Justice in a Resource-constrained World* (Oxford: Oxfam International, 2011).

6. Wallace Huffman, "Technology and Innovation in World Agriculture: Prospects for 2010–2019," Iowa State University Working Paper # 09007, April 2009.

7. David J. Spielman and Rajul Pandya-Lorch, eds., *Millions Fed: Proven Successes in Agricultural Development* (Washington, DC: International Food Policy Research Institute, 2009).

8. Keith W. Jaggard, Aiming Qi, and Eric S. Ober, "Possible Changes to Arable Crop Yields by 2050," *Philosophical Transactions of the Royal Society* 365B (2010): 2835–2851.

9. Nikos Alexandratos and Jelle Bruinsma, *World Agriculture: Towards 2030/2050: The 2012 Revision* (Rome: FAO Agricultural Development Economics Division, 2012).

10. Ibid.

11. Ibid.

12. OECD, *Agricultural Policy Monitoring and Evaluation 2011: OECD Countries and Emerging Economies* (Paris: OECD Publishing, 2011).

13. Global Food Markets Group, *The 2007/08 Agricultural Price Spikes: Causes and Policy Implications* (London: UK Government, DEFRA, 2010).

chapter 3

world agricultural trade

The pattern of world trade in food is changing. For most of the second half of the twentieth century North America and Europe exported bulk temperate products, principally grains, to developing countries in the southern hemisphere and imported bulk tropical products from those countries. More recently however, developing countries have increased their production of staples such as wheat and maize. As a result, they are exporting to each other and increasingly exporting high quality fruit, vegetables, and meat to Europe and North America. The once simple pattern of two way north-south trade has now become much more complex. Food trade can be broken down into three main categories: bulk staples, semiprocessed foods, and highly processed foods. Trade in high value foods has increased rapidly. Large multinational retailers and processors are having an increasing influence on food trade. World exports of food grains and feed grains are dominated by North America, Europe, and Brazil, while Asia, North Africa, and the Middle East are the major import regions. The grain trade is also still dominated by only a few large companies. Major year-to-year uncertainty is created in the animal feed grains market by China, with China and the other BRIC countries (Brazil, Russia, India) increasingly involved in world food trade, both as importers and exporters. With the growth of emerging economies, the international grocery retailing industry is having an increasingly important influence on world food trade.

main points

- Trade in agriculture and food products is hampered by many restrictions.
- Traditional north-south food trade flow is changing, with increased Southern Hemisphere production and exports.
- Changing dietary patterns in developing and emerging economies are creating new trade flows.
- There is a changing balance of agricultural trade between developed and developing countries.
- Geographical spread of major grain exporters increases global food security.
- World food trade is increasingly dominated by a few large operators.
- Multinational retailers have the power to exploit farmers and other suppliers.
- Food processors are becoming larger to counter the market power of supermarkets.

A fluid pattern of trade in agricultural commodities and food is an essential element in maintaining future global food security. While until relatively recently the farm product trade was far from fluid, it is likely that trade in agricultural products will follow and extend the gradual liberalizing developments of the past half century. Put simply, basic food staples, including largely grains and oilseeds, have been produced in increased quantities in developed northern hemisphere countries and traded among themselves and increasingly with developing countries. Southern hemisphere developing countries have increased their production of grains, rice, and oilseeds, with which they have fed their increasing populations and exported in increasing quantities to other developing countries as well as to the more prosperous northern countries. Those developing countries with inadequate production resources have increased their import dependency.

This generalized picture, however, obscures a much more complex matrix of interlocking trading arrangements based on changing patterns of economic development and food consumption. One of the most obvious features of this is the increasing growth in both hemispheres of meat and dairy product consumption. This has had a fundamental influence on production, consumption, and trade. In the past three decades there has been increased specialized agricultural production in several major emerging economies, which has led to changed lines of trading, both south-south and south-north, as well as the traditional north-south flow.

This changing web of trade is likely to develop further in meeting global food demand over the next thirty to forty years. Because of asymmetric population changes and climatic adjustment, developed countries will probably provide an increasing share of their food needs, but will also continue to import larger quantities of agricultural products that they cannot produce themselves; most obviously, fruit, oilseeds, sugar, and tropical beverages. The trade of the developing countries is also not homogenous. While the group as a whole will increase its net exports of tropical products and import more temperate-zone food, within the group there will remain important net exporters of temperate-zone commodities such as grains, oilseeds, sugar, as well as exclusively tropical oilseeds such as palm oil.

It is important to note that while agricultural trade has expanded during the past half century, it has not grown as much as could have been possible in a more liberal trading atmosphere—and one more favorable to developing country exporters. Growth has only been equal to about the rate of global economic output. The main reason for this has been the perpetuation of trade barriers—import tariffs and taxes—in agriculture well above the rates for industrial products. The failure to include agriculture fully in the postwar multilateral trade negotiations under GATT, until the Uruguay Round of the 1980s and 1990s, was the main reason for this. Despite the 1994 Marrakech Agreement, which began the dismantling of farm trade tariffs, agricultural tariffs were still as high in 2011, on average, as industrial tariffs were in the 1950s. The effects of high border protection have been made worse by domestic farm support policies in most developed countries and in some developing countries that have aimed at greater self-sufficiency at the expense of international trade.

"If, for instance, the reform process that began under the Uruguay Round Agreement on Agriculture were to achieve a [further] fundamental reform of the sector, and if there were significant reductions in production-enhancing subsidies and protection in industrial countries, this could have an impact on predicted trading patterns," the FAO commented.[1] "And if policy reforms extended beyond the developed countries and led to the removal of the remaining bias against agriculture in the policy of several developing countries, this could mobilize resources to enhance productivity and stimulate development of the rural economy." The inference is that the overall increase in production and trade would generally enhance global food security.

There is little doubt that the structure of agricultural trade has changed markedly over the past three decades. An important feature of this change has been the balance in trade in food and agricultural products between developed and developing countries. This has been to the detriment of the less-developed countries. While developing countries as a whole had an overall agricultural trade surplus of US$6.7 billion at the beginning of the 1960s, this surplus gradually disappeared, so that by the end of the 1990s trade was broadly in balance, with periodic minor surpluses and deficits. The FAO outlook to 2030 indicates a widening agricultural trade deficit for the developing countries, possibly reaching an overall net import level of US$31 billion (at the 1999 dollar value). The forty-nine countries designated by FAO as least-developed countries (LDCs) have been most affected by this change. Even by the end of the 1990s, their imports were more than twice as high as exports. Estimates for 2030 suggest that this trend will continue. The agricultural trade deficit of the group of forty-nine LDCs is expected to widen further and quadruple by 2030.

It has to be kept in mind that increasing economic growth and prosperity in the more advanced LDCs will contribute to this changed configuration of trade. As countries develop their nonagricultural exports and their imports increase, agricultural exports remain static or decline. As a result, imports of temperate-zone commodities have grown rapidly. The net imports in this product category increased by a factor of thirteen over the forty years to the turn of the millennium, rising from a minor deficit of US$ 1.7 billion in 1961–1963 to US$24 billion in 1997–1999.

What is also significant in the development of food and agriculture trade is the shift in the change in the patchwork of products moving between countries.[2] What is most noticeable is the shift in trade from cereals to livestock products, notably to meats and dairy products. This is the result of various mutually reinforcing developments that took place coterminously in developed and developing countries. In developed countries, technological and organizational progress in livestock production and therefore overall productivity was greater than gains in cereal production. This made it more profitable to convert cereals into meat domestically and then to export higher value meats and meat products, rather than cereals. In the emerging developing economies of Asia, increasing prosperity and migration to towns has led to a shift in consumption patterns—with rapidly rising per capita consumption—from grain-based diets to livestock-based diets. The richer developing countries have also established the infrastructure facilities such as rapid transport, cold stores, and supermarkets that have stimulated demand for livestock product imports.

Competition in agricultural trade has grown between developed and developing countries, particularly in what are regarded as competing commodities, which can be produced in both north and south, but originating from different primary products. These include most notably sugar from beets or cane, and vegetable oil from several different oil crops. More recently, particularly with the development of cheap air freight, there has been increasing competition from developing countries in commodities such as fruits and vegetables at certain seasons. Too often, producer subsidies in developed OECD countries offset the comparative advantage of developing country producers. The history of the sugar industry and trade is an outstanding example.

Trade in essentially tropical commodities mainly produced in developing countries is primarily a south-north flow. Tropical products, such as palm oil, coffee, cocoa, or tropical fruits are the main items in this flow. Developing countries have been increasing output and exports of these products substantially over the past decades. Developed countries' import markets for these commodities have become increasingly saturated. Since developed countries do not produce these commodities in significant quantities, they do not support or protect these markets.

The structure of global agricultural trade can be broken down into four categories: bulk commodities, processed intermediate products, fresh horticultural products, and processed consumer goods. From 1980 to 1997 the share of bulk products steadily dropped while the shares of nonbulk categories have subsequently increased, to the extent that bulk commodities are no longer a valid indicator for measuring world agricultural trade growth. However, the share of intermediate processed commodities in total agricultural trade has not decreased, as has trade in bulk commodities. Only a few commodities account for a large share of total agricultural trade. Among major commodities, there are dramatic differences in the rates of growth in trade. Growth in many of the processed intermediate products such as soya bean oil, flour, and soya bean meal has also exceeded growth rates for total agricultural trade (3.5 percent per year)—indicative of the change in food consumption trends. Import demand for these commodities is derived from consumer's increased demand for finished processed food and livestock products.

Wheat, corn, coffee, and cocoa beans now account for most trade in bulk commodities. An important factor in the changing structure of world agricultural trade is the continuing dominant role of developed countries. Most of the growth of trade in processed consumer products is developed country imports. Developed countries import a much greater share of processed consumer goods than developing countries, while the opposite is true for bulk commodities.

The future level of imports will depend on how competitive domestic producers are and the presence or absence of tariff protection. Clearly, input costs, technology, and levels of productivity, particularly in the livestock sectors, vary by region, with soil and climatic conditions having important influences on these aspects. For these reasons some production regions are likely to be expanding beef producers (e.g., South America) and others not. Traditionally, world imports of red meats are concentrated in a few developed countries: Japan's meat imports alone account for nearly as much as all developing countries put together. Emerging Asian economies are also becoming important meat importers.

summary of global pattern of food trade

Over the long term, the trend in world agriculture and food trade is influenced mainly by declining expenditures on staples such as rice and wheat and increased spending on higher valued food items—meat, dairy, fruits, and vegetables.[3] Food trade is becoming more determined by the level of processing. Trade can be divided into four main categories:

- traditional bulk commodities such as wheat, rice, and maize
- horticultural products such as fresh fruits and vegetables

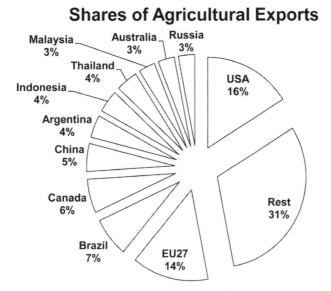

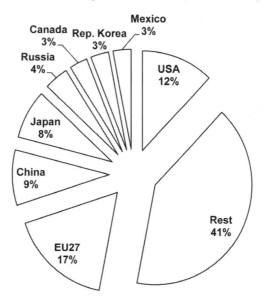

Figure 3.1 The pattern of world agricultural trade.
Source of Data: USDA Economic Research Service, "Global Food Markets" (2012).

- semiprocessed products such as flour and oils
- processed food products such as pasta and prepared meats

Horticultural, semiprocessed, and processed products are considered high-value products. Unlike bulk commodities, high-value products are often ready to eat and are generally more perishable. These characteristics make high-value products subject to greater quality and safety scrutiny compared with bulk agricultural commodities; these nontariff barriers make market access for developing country exporters more difficult. Given these characteristics, food suppliers sometimes choose to meet consumer demand through locally processed food products rather than through imported food. Sometimes domestic and trade policies can be impediments for trade in high-value products.

Trends in food demand have increased trade in high-value foods and reshaped food marketing globally:

- Food suppliers and retailers have responded to demand by importing food from around the world and modifying their products and retail formats to better meet consumer needs.
- Large multinational retailers have expanded in the developing countries, and the top fifteen companies now account for more than 30 percent of global supermarket sales.
- Multinational food manufacturers have invested in a variety of industries in many host countries.

trade in primary commodities

Approximately 8.5 percent of worldwide goods trade consists of agricultural commodities, while their share in the total trade in primary products accounts for 27.5 percent (2008).[4] The most striking feature of world agricultural and food product trade is the low share of exports and high share of imports, in terms of total goods trade and primary products trade, held by Africa, the Middle East, and former communist non-EU Commonwealth of Independent States (CIS). The most outstanding feature of the development of this trade is the increased share of Brazil as an exporter and the increased share of China as importer. Both of these countries are continuing to increase their importance in the world food market.

The pattern and direction of agricultural product trade is continuingly changing with increased south-south trade in addition to the traditional north-south trade. On the import side, the developing countries are becoming increasingly integrated into world agricultural trade and regional markets. Other, emerging economies like China, which have a well-developed trade role, are seeking to diversify their sources of supply. This is stimulating new economic interactions and trade between developing and other countries that are effectively reshaping worldwide flows of agricultural trade. In addition, developing country groupings that have become well-integrated into the world trade infrastructure, are assuming greater prominence in international trade negotiations and their agendas (see Chapter 15).[5]

While the developing countries are showing the strongest growth in agriculture and food exports, these countries are still expected to remain very large net importers for the foreseeable future. The more expansionary developing countries, however, are displacing traditional exporters and competitors through lower-cost products and rapid growth. They are also becoming dominant in regional markets that are likely to provide a springboard for further expansion of exports. According to the OECD, non-OECD countries are projected to show the strongest percentage increase in exports by 2019, relative to the 2007–2009 base, for oilseeds (59 percent), poultry (54 percent), wheat (50 percent), skim milk powder (43 percent), and cheese and vegetable oils (39 percent). Traditional exporting OECD countries that once dominated the export trade will tend to lose export shares in many commodities to non-OECD countries.[6]

trade in basic foods: grains

Wheat

Global trade in the world's major food grain, wheat, is dominated by the United States. While producing only 10 percent of the world wheat crop, the United States is consistently the world's biggest wheat exporter. The U.S. share of world wheat exports has fluctuated from a high of 50 percent in 1973–1974 to 30–40 percent in 1982/1983–1995/1996, and between 20–30 percent thereafter. Increased planting flexibility in U.S. farm legislation and low returns relative to competing crops has led to a decline in U.S. wheat area, limiting export potential.

U.S. exports played an important part in rebuilding the world wheat supply after the supply crisis of 2006–2008 Although in the 2007–2008 marketing year, total world wheat trade grew by 4 million tonnes, U.S. exports increased by almost 10 million tonnes—the largest year-on-year increase in twenty years.

It should be noted that a major reason why U.S. wheat exports grew at the expense of other exporting countries in this period is that in 2007–2008 the United States had large stocks of wheat. These declined by 4 million tonnes after 2008. U.S. exports were also highly competitive due to depreciation of the dollar against other world currencies. Between 2006 and mid-2008, the U.S. dollar depreciated by about 25 percent, thus reducing the price of U.S. wheat compared to that produced by other countries.

Usually, around 90 percent of the world's wheat exports are accounted for by the United States, Canada, Australia, the EU-27, Argentina, and the countries of the former Soviet Union exporters—Russia, Ukraine, and Kazakhstan.

Because these major exporters are spread over a diverse geographical area, their exports provide significant stability to world wheat trade and prices.[7] There is also a spread of the types of wheat grown—adding further to the risk-spreading effect of trade. Although most of the world's wheat output is grown as winter wheat in the Northern Hemisphere, there are large areas of spring wheat in Canada, Kazakhstan, Russia, and the United States. Spring wheat is planted much later and thus escapes the hazard of frost damage. If therefore Northern Hemisphere wheat is hit by winter-kill, as is often the case, there is a large element of safety in both the spring crops and the Southern Hemisphere seasonal production. In the Southern Hemisphere, the Australian and Argentinian wheat crops are planted after the Northern Hemisphere's spring wheat. Moreover, due to wheat being planted and harvested at different times, there is normally rapid response to supply fluctuations in other regions. Higher or lower prices on world markets continually influence farmers' planting conditions.

It is important to bear in mind that the amount of wheat traded between countries each year represents a relatively small percentage of total global production—no more than 6 percent. In the period up to 2005/2006, world wheat trade peaked in 1987/1988 at 111.5 million tonnes, when China and the Soviet Union were importing very large amounts. After that and up until 2005/2006, imports by China and countries that were formerly part of the Soviet Union were much lower, and world wheat trade fell away from its 1987/1988 level despite increasing imports by developing countries. In 2003, the EU established trade barriers to lower quality wheat imports, also limiting world wheat trade. In 2005/2006, world wheat trade reached 114 million metric tonnes. Import demand for wheat is highly sensitive to price, which is an important factor when considering the problem of access to food by the less prosperous developing countries. While total wheat trade increased modestly toward the end of the first decade of the twenty-first century, in 2007/2008 high prices choked off any rise in wheat trade.

The rising population in various parts of the developing world combined with strong economic growth is increasing demand for both food for people and feed grains for raising livestock. As a result, increasing quantities of wheat are needed to meet demand for staple food products in countries with low incomes and expanding populations in sub-Saharan Africa (Nigeria, Republic of South Africa, Sudan, and Kenya) and North Africa (Egypt, Algeria, and Morocco), south Asia (Afghanistan, Bangladesh, and Pakistan) and Southeast Asia (Indonesia, Philippines, and Vietnam), and Latin America (Brazil and Mexico).

While only five nations or regions dominate wheat exports, the opposite is the case on the import side. In addition to significant wheat importers, such as the EU-27, Japan, Indonesia, South Korea, and Brazil, there are many more countries heavily dependent on imports. Large quantities of wheat are imported by developing countries with limited production potential. Trade is likely to expand further with population growth in Egypt, Algeria, Iraq, Brazil, Mexico, Indonesia, Nigeria, and other developing countries.[8]

Maize

As with wheat, trade in maize (corn), the world's major animal feed and industrial use grain, is dominated by the United States—both in output and exports. However, exports account for only a relatively small portion of demand for U.S. corn—about 15 percent. Nevertheless, world price levels are largely determined by supply and demand in the U.S. market. This is because the concentration of the major export supply is much more concentrated in one country than is the case for wheat. This makes world maize trade and prices highly dependent on weather in the U.S. Corn Belt.

The U.S. share of world maize exports averaged 60 percent during the period 2003/2004 to 2007/008. U.S. corn exports soared in the 1970s from 13 million tonnes at the start of the decade to a record 62 million in 1979/1980. The growth was due to strong demand in Russia as well as in Japan, western and eastern Europe, and developing countries. Over the next few years, U.S. corn exports dropped, bottoming out at 31 million tonnes in 1985/1986, due to poor global economic growth, expansion of the European Union (EU), and U.S. government support for domestic corn prices. In the second half of the 1980s, U.S. exports rebounded, reaching 60 million tonnes in 1989/1990 because of large domestic supplies and more competitive prices as the government reduced support to grain growers. Exports in the early 1990s declined again because of external factors, notably the breakup of the Soviet Union and rising Chinese corn exports.

To some extent the U.S. influence over the maize market is moderated by Argentina, the other major exporter, which is in the Southern Hemisphere. Argentinian producers plant their maize after the state of the U.S. maize crop is known, providing a quick, market-oriented supply response to any shortfall in the U.S. crop. Other producers, including Brazil, Ukraine, Romania, and South Africa, have significant corn exports when their crops are large or international prices are attractive.

A major unknown in the world maize market is China, sometimes an exporter and at other times an importer. The country's exports are closely linked to government export subsidies and tax rebates, because maize prices in China are normally higher than those in the world market. It is likely that in the future China will be predominantly a maize importer. Government stocks are expensive to maintain, and export policy therefore fluctuates with little relationship to production levels, making China's maize trade difficult to predict.

World maize trade peaked in 1980/1981, with large imports by the Soviet Union and Europe. Since then, corn imports by European Union countries have declined steadily as the Common Agricultural Policy limited grain imports and EU membership and domestic production expanded. As significant exporting countries like Hungary joined the EU, their exports that had previously been sold to non-EU countries were diverted into the EU. The collapse of the Soviet Union and following economic restructuring of the Soviet bloc countries at the end of the 1980s, reduced livestock numbers and led to a consequent fall in maize imports into the former Soviet Union and eastern Europe. On the other hand, at the same time, Japan, South Korea, and Taiwan continued to increase maize imports to support increasing meat production and consumption.

One constant in the world maize market is the steady increase in demand from developing countries, which have continued to increase maize imports at a fairly steady pace since 1980. This growth in developing-country imports is the major factor pushing global trade above 70 million tonnes each year since 1999/2000.

Japan is by far the world's largest maize importer. While growing no feed or industrial grains itself, and being a large meat producer, Japan has to be a continuous importer of maize and other feed grains. With meat consumption leveling off, livestock feed demand has stagnated, but imports for industrial use and starch manufacture have increased. South Korea is the second largest importer of maize in the world. Mexico is a growing importer. While a large maize producer itself, Mexico processes much of its production of white corn into human food products, but has turned to imported yellow corn and sorghum for livestock feed to support increased meat production.

Import demand for maize is dependent not only on the demand of importing countries for feed ingredients, but also on importing countries' internal policy measures that adjust prices as well as the availability of competing products. The various coarse grains—maize, oats, barley, and so forth—can often be substituted for each other in feed use. Maize competes with other feed grains, as well as with wheat and non-grain feedstuffs such as cassava. Oilseed meal and other protein sources are often used as complements to grains but can also be substitutes, especially those protein meals with low-protein content. The extent to which such substitution can take place is limited by the types of animals fed, the desire to maintain stable rations, local preferences, and import tariffs and other barriers to trade.

food trade in the emerging economies

There is a small group of countries that have substantial agricultural production and export potential but have suffered past economic or social problems that have hampered the development of their full potential in the world agricultural trade. These are what are commonly called the BRIC group—Brazil, Russia, India and China. Of this group, Brazil is already a formidable force on world markets, having displaced the United States as the major exporter of soya beans, become the world's largest and most competitive beef exporter, and is a major player in global poultry meat and orange juice markets.

At the other end of the spectrum in this group is India. It is the seventh largest country in the world in terms of its geographical size. Today it has a population of nearly 1.1 billion, which makes it the second most populous nation in the world. With current population growth, by 2025 India may even have caught up with China according to the UN. India is a country with still large underutilized agricultural production potential. For good and obvious reasons, the country has pursued a policy of increasing production to increase self-sufficiency in staple food commodities like rice and wheat. Nonetheless, there are important foods that it has been unable to produce itself, while it has been able to produce an export surplus of other commodities. Both these developments have involved India increasingly in world agricultural trade.

India's agricultural imports are focused mainly on intermediate products.[9] These account for 56 percent of imports; final products are 31 percent, while the share of primary agricultural commodities is just 13 percent. The biggest recent growth has been in intermediate products, which have increased nearly fourfold in the decade to 2010. This reflects the importance of vegetable oils in Indian imports. Palm oil is by far the biggest import at 29 percent of the total. Together with soybean oils, they represent, pre than 40 percent of imports. Protein-rich peas are also within the top five. The significance of these foodstuffs imports is that they are indicative of the response to population growth. There are also trades that are indicative of the importance of first-stage food-processing industries in India. While cashew nuts and cotton are among the top exports, they also appear among the top ten imports. Cashew nuts are imported for further processing as are silk and cotton, which are used in the Indian textile industry.

Also indicative of rising prosperity is the growth in imports of vegetable oils, with an increase of more than 800 percent between 1993–1995 and 2003–2005, with soybean oil and other oils and fats taking a growing share of an expanding market. Given the importance of vegetable oil imports, it is not surprising that India depends on a few key suppliers. Palm oil is supplied essentially by two ASEAN (Association of Southeast Asian Nations) trading partners, with more than 72 percent of India's palm oil imports coming from Indonesia and 27 percent from Malaysia. This concentration is almost perfectly mirrored in the soybean oil market, with Argentina supplying 72 percent and Brazil around 24 percent.

Despite the expansion of India's wheat production, it still needs to be an intermittent importer of wheat—principally from the EU. Having been a small net exporter of wheat since 1999/2000, India became a net importer in 2006/2007. India bought €120 million worth of wheat from the EU in 2006. Dried peas accounted for 6 percent of exports in 2006 but have fluctuated over the period.

In pursuit of its food self-sufficiency policy, India has maintained a high level of import tariffs on food products. The current average applied tariff is 40.8 percent, according to the WTO, but the actual applied tariffs are subject to frequent adjustment, being diminished by the government when domestic supply needs to be supplemented by imports. For example, the wheat tariff was reduced in 2006, as India needed imports to compensate for its poor harvest. Therefore, the EU was able to export wheat to India at zero tariff that year. In contrast, EU exports of dairy products are currently very low mainly due to high Indian tariffs; the intention here is to protect the country's expanding domestic dairy industry.

Due to a combination of increasing domestic production and manipulation of its tariff system, India is a net exporter of agricultural food products, with a small surplus of just under $4 billion. Between 1993–1995 and 2003–2005, exports nearly doubled while imports grew almost threefold. The value of exports grew from $4 billion to $7.7 billion while imports rose from $1.8 billion to $5.2 billion within a decade. The balance of agricultural trade has always been in surplus, though there were sharp fluctuations during the 1990s. Since 2000 both imports and exports have grown steadily.

India is diversifying its export markets but is clearly dependent on the prosperous developed countries for its most lucrative trade. The EU remains its top market, accounting for 16 percent of the value of export sales in 2003–2005, although this is a decline from 21 percent in the mid-1990s. Other Asian countries in the ASEAN group form its other main market, with 14 percent, although its share has also fallen. This trend may be reversed as a result of India's new free trade agreements with the EU and ASEAN. Meanwhile, food trade with neighboring Bangladesh and China (currently 7.5 percent) is growing fast. The U.S. market share has remained steady at 10 percent, as has that of Saudi Arabia.

The composition of India's agrifood trade is concentrated on finished tertiary products rather than primary commodities. While basic commodities represent around one-third and intermediate products over one-quarter, final products account for the remaining 40 percent of total agrifood exports. However, the biggest recent growth has been in the export of commodities, which increased by 134 percent from 1993–1995 to 2003–2005 and have continued to grow at a similar pace through the decade. The single biggest export is milled rice, accounting for 16 percent of the value of exports.

Two other commodities, cotton and wheat, are also within the top ten exports. Soybean meal, an intermediate product, is the second most important export, with 9 percent of sales. Six out of the top ten are final products, including cashew nuts, beef, coffee, and tea, which together represent about 14 percent of the value of exports. In the 1990s the value of India's exports fluctuated widely. The principal reason for this was the wide variations both in the price and the volume of rice exports, the latter depending on the balance between production and consumption. Since the turn of the millennium, India's exports have grown steadily. In addition to rice, beef (buffalo meat), and soybean meal, exports are also expanding.

As a food importer, in 2006/2007 India became a net importer of wheat, having been a net exporter for the previous five years. It is not expected to be a big net exporter in the immediate future. India is expected to be an expanding market for exports of high quality processed milk products. Not surprisingly, given its likely population and income increase, India is projected to remain a leading vegetable oils importer, absorbing one-quarter of world soybean oil imports and 14 percent of palm oil imports. This is an expected increase in imports from 5 million tonnes to 6–8 million tonnes by 2016/2017. Indian consumption of vegetable oils has grown faster than production since the mid-1990s and the trend is expected to continue. Combined with the recent hike in prices, this could lead to a doubling of India's vegetable oil import bill in ten years.

importance of china in the world's agriculture economy

China has all the characteristics that emphasize the global need for fluid trade in agriculture and food products and the need for efficient producing countries to increase their export availability. Without increased production and deliveries from agriculturally advantaged countries, China's demand on the world food economy could have an increasing inflationary effect on world food prices. For example, China dominates the world trade in the major global source of protein for feeding livestock, soya beans, now accounting for almost half (44 percent) of total world trade in the commodity. While China' share was only 21 percent in 2002, it is expected to reach 57 percent by 2017/2018, as its net imports increase from 34 million tonnes in 2007/2008 to 52 million tonnes. China is also responsible for major shares of word imports of palm oil and soya oil—31 percent and 23 percent, respectively.

China has a massive population, a booming economy, rising average incomes, and an agricultural sector that is incapable of feeding a population of more than 1.2 billion. While the urban share of the population at 41 percent (2003) is considered by the OECD to be low when compared to countries with a similar level of development, a rapid increase is projected. By 2016 the urban population will be bigger than the rural population and the urban share should reach 60 percent by 2030, says the UN. The growth of the economy has improved living standards in China. According to the OECD, income growth lifted 400 million people out of poverty between 1979 and 2002.

Seven out of China's top ten imports are commodities.[10] China's major import is soya beans for both human consumption and livestock feeding, valued at $7.5 billion in 2006 and accounting for 28 percent of the value of the country's agricultural imports. Compared to 2002 (the year import tariffs were cut to 3 percent), this represents a tripling in the value of imports. Edible oils such as palm oil (7.2 percent) and soybean oil (4 percent) have also increased sharply, reflecting changing consumption patterns.

Dependency of agricultural exporting countries on trade with China can be seen from the picture of key suppliers for its top five imports: Soya bean imports are supplied by the United States (41.5 percent), Brazil (33.5 percent), and Argentina (24 percent), with a small amount coming from Uruguay. The United States has lost market share to Brazil since1999, when it had 58 percent of the market, compared to Brazil's 19 percent—to the benefit of Chinese consumers, because Brazil is now the world's lowest cost producer of soya. The concentration of suppliers is even more pronounced for edible oils. There are just two suppliers of palm oil, Malaysia and Indonesia, with the former accounting for 70 percent of the trade. Argentina dominates the soybean oil trade, accounting for 76 percent of China's market, leaving the rest to Brazil.

The latest projections of the Food and Agricultural Policy Research Institute (FAPRI) are for growth in China's overall agricultural trade, but, significantly, imports are expected to grow faster than exports as the domestic agriculture industry fails to keep up with economic growth.[11] However, the agricultural trade deficit will still be small relative to the size of China's overall trade surplus. Trade in food and feed between China and the rest of the world will be a busy two-way traffic, since its potential exports of fruits and vegetables will grow (possibly up to 40–50 million tonnes by 2030) alongside imports of both food and feed.

Seen from a world food production and trade perspective, China is expected to increase steadily its demand for meat and other nontraditional foods as growth in income and urbanization drive a westernization of diets, especially increased demand for meat. Given China's intention to encourage domestic livestock production, its feed imports are forecast to grow over the coming decade. FAPRI is projecting domestic use of soya beans to grow by 40 percent in the next decade.[12] Faced with burgeoning demand and the limitations of its own agriculture, China gave up its self-sufficiency policy for oilseeds over a decade ago. Self-sufficiency in soya beans (which accounts for 80 percent of oilseed consumption) has consequently fallen from 95 percent in 1997 to 30 percent in 2007. Since 2002, more than half of soybean consumption has been covered by imports. When considered as a share of the world market, China's imports are large. The growth in livestock feed demand means that China is also expected to switch from being a net exporter of maize (900,000 tonnes in 2007/2008) into a consistent net importer of 2.6 million tonnes by 2020.

Expected increases in income and urbanization will lead to a shift in Chinese diets away from food staples and toward proteins, especially meat. If China continues to import feed and encourage livestock production, then its feed imports should grow sharply over the coming decade. China's dominance of the world's soya imports will be complemented by increased importance in the trade in other animal feed grains. It is predicted to become a net importer of maize, wheat, and meats. With exports, especially of fruits and vegetables, also on the increase, China's impact on world agricultural markets can only become stronger.

the structure of world food trade

Dominant forces in the food delivery chain

The world food business is now dominated by the retail grocery trade—the retail tail wags the production dog. This sector in turn is increasingly dominated by a smaller number of large operators. With the growth in power of these groups, they have increasingly controlled the way food is produced, traded, and delivered to the consumer. In the words of a leading food market economist, "None of these changes is consistent with the tenets of traditional models of competitive agricultural markets."[13]

While the United States, the European Union, and Japan together currently account for more than 60 percent of total retail processed food sales in the world, market growth is faster among developing countries, particularly the lower-middle-income countries such as China, Morocco, the Philippines, and many eastern European countries. The new markets of the former communist economies of eastern Europe, such as Bulgaria, Romania, and Ukraine, are experiencing much more attractive double-digit growth rates in food and beverage retail sales. As retail sales growth in these markets has stabilized, their place in the growth league has been taken by Asian markets, where processed food product sales are attractively increasing.

And these new markets are easier to exploit than they once might have been. "With rising income levels and global expansion of food retailing and food service outlets, food consumption patterns, as measured by spending on different types of food products, appear to be converging across countries," according to Professor Richard Sexton.[14] Processed food products and multinational retail and food service chains from the United States and other high-income countries have become increasingly common in middle-income nations such as China and Thailand. For example, fast-food sales in China more than doubled between 1999 and 2005, while sales from Western-style supermarkets increased almost sixfold, from $16 billion to $91 billion during the same period. Changes in food preferences and food delivery mechanisms appear to be mutually enforcing, with worldwide tastes and diets evolving along with increasingly modern food retailing and food service outlets. This cyclical relationship between food demand and delivery mechanisms is increasing the similarity of food delivery and consumption around the world—a phenomenon referred to as convergence.

The scale of this international business is now truly massive. According to a recent analysis by the Economic Research Service of the U.S. Department of Agriculture, "Global food retail sales are about $4 trillion annually, with supermarkets/hypermarkets accounting for the largest share of sales. Most of the leading global retailers are U.S. and European firms, as large multinational retailers expand their presence in developing countries and small retail firms increasingly account for a smaller share of total food sales. The top 15 global supermarket companies account for more than 30 percent of world supermarket sales. With improved technologies and economies of size, these retailers enjoy operating cost advantages over smaller local retailers."[15]

The same report concludes: "Income growth and globalization of the food retail and food service industry are giving rise to increasingly similar food consumption patterns across the world. Food consumption patterns of middle and high income countries, as indicated by their food spending across different food types over time, are converging. The expansion of Western-style retail and food service outlets is modernizing the food marketing sector in developing countries. At the current rate, ERS estimates that within about 20 years form 2011, food purchases in middle-income countries through Western-style grocery stores will approach 50 percent of the level of the sales in higher income countries."

The increasing dominance of the market by a few large food processors has been startling in the United States and Europe. According to Professor John Connor of Purdue University, a long-term analyst of food supply chain concentration, the market share of the top twenty U.S. food manufacturers has doubled since 1967. Only 100 firms now account for 80 percent of all value-added arising from the movement of the primary commodity to the finished food on the plate. In Europe, Nestlé and Unilever dominate, while in the United States, Kraft and General Foods have the major share. Operating on a massive scale, Nestlé, the world's biggest food manufacturer, has a turnover approaching than $70 billion in 2010.

Major players in the world food market

The international grain trade

Grain has been an internationally traded commodity almost since the beginning of recorded time. The modern phase in the trade begins with the Industrial Revolution, when the populations of the western European countries outgrew their own domestic production capacity and had the cash to buy from countries with surpluses like Russia and Ukraine. This Black Sea trade saw hundreds of thousands of tonnes of mainly wheat shipped westward into the mills of Great Britain, the Low Countries, and Germany. The repeal of Britain's import-restricting Corn Laws in the mid-nineteenth century opened the way to this booming trade. Later, the exploitation of the plains of North America led to the growth of the trans-Atlantic grain trade, which still forms the basis of the modern international trade pattern. With the growth of the Asian economies a much greater proportion of U.S. and Canadian exports now flows eastward.

But what all three phases of the development of the international grain trade have in common is domination by a very few large—very large—companies. The world grain trade is now dominated by four huge operators: Cargill, the largest and most diversified, and its main competitors, which include Archer Daniels Midland (ADM), Bunge, and Dreyfus. These four companies are alleged to control 90 percent of the world's trade in cereals and most other major agricultural commodities.[16] Almost all the grain that moves between nations, about one-fifth of world production, passes through Cargill, ADM, or Bunge. Others operators include Gavilon, a commodities trader, which counts among its shareholders Soros Fund Management, and Mitsubishi, the Japanese trading house that took over Cook Industries, the sixth largest international grain trader, before Cargill swallowed another major competitor, Continental, in 1999.

Companies with this scale of operation and global reach are able to exploit economies of scale in transport, storage, and finance. While the profit margins from global trading in bulk commodities are generally slim, there are significant profits to be made by exploiting global market instability. Such multinational traders can utilize their unsurpassed market intelligence system to capture the profit that can be made from such instability. With widespread and diverse sources of supply, it is possible to exploit temporary and what can be often only fleeting but substantial opportunities for profit. Diversification into non-grain products, as with most notably Cargill, also gives added scope for risk spreading and increased profits.

All of these major companies have diversified into activities other than trading in the grain market and food markets in general. Most notably, they have sought greater control over their markets by horizontal and vertical integration of food production, road and rail transport, and international shipping. They have also sought to reduce competition by taking over smaller operators in international food markets. They also seek further control by joint ventures with agricultural input suppliers, in particular plant breeders and agrochemical manufacturers. Large multinational enterprises (MNEs) such as Cargill, ADM, and Bunge have developed collaborative contracts with other large enterprises that specialize in major inputs such as agrochemicals and seeds. What are regarded as these food industry clusters result in substantial control over what is produced, what is consumed, and the commercial bases on which these decision are made.

The scope and influence of these primary food supply companies may be judged by an examination of the activities of the major actor in this theatre, Cargill.

"At present Cargill is both a principal buyer and seller of commodities," wrote Richard Gilmore in 1982, "a 'fobber' (a grain handler responsible for moving the crop to port), an exporter and importer, a grain handler, a processor, and a livestock and poultry farmer; it is a broker for all modes of transportation and an owner of trucks, railroad cars and ships; it is a speculator, hedger and Futures Commission Merchant (FCM) on the commodity exchanges; and it is a borrower and lender in commercial credit. It is the world's largest miller and second largest meat packer."[17] Little has changed in the Cargill approach, but the scale and scope have grown immensely.

Cargill is now the largest private corporation in the United States. To reduce its dependence on the legendary fickleness of the grain business, the company in the 1980s and 1990s adopted a policy of radical diversification. This process gave it even greater control of important shares of both the national and international food business. It saw itself as no longer simply a commodity merchandiser, but a processor of commodities as well—effectively an extension of its activities, both up and down the food chain. By the turn of the millennium, in addition to being the world's principal grain merchant and the number three food company in the United States, Cargill also boasted ownership of the eighth largest U.S. steel producer in its North Star Steel subsidiary, the top position in European cocoa processing, and the number one ranking among pet food processors in Argentina. But the move that gave it almost complete domination of the global trade in food staples was its highly controversial takeover its largest rival, Continental Grain. Despite opposition from the farm lobby, antitrust activists and important sections of the U.S. political establishment, Cargill agreed to acquire Continental Grain's worldwide grain storage, transportation, export, and trading operations.

MONOPSONY*—DOMINANT POWER OF LARGE BUYERS OVER FOOD PRODUCERS

To reinforce its monopsonistic power in the medium to long term, companies such as Cargill foster relationship marketing with consequent vertical coordination, which can lead to serious market dysfunctions. For all practical purposes, producers—who take the risk in producing for an often volatile market—wind up with a single buyer even if there are several buyers who could theoretically compete to buy from them. The favored farmers and suppliers are under unspoken economic pressure to work with the retailer or processor without complaint. If there are problems, then the processor or retailer can simply refuse to buy. The buyers can control their costs under these conditions, and can ensure that they will have a docile group of suppliers. Through the creation of joint ventures and partnerships with farmers' cooperatives in the United States, Cargill has in effect created captive suppliers of grains and oilseeds without having to take risk or to increase its investment in production. The cooperatives are effectively absorbed into Cargill's business, rather than obtaining the countervailing market power that cooperatives were originally set up to achieve.

*Market in which goods or services are offered by several sellers but there is only one buyer.

Middlemen: The Food Processing Giants

The monopsonistic relationship between buyers and suppliers now increasingly applies to the supermarkets and their relationship with suppliers—in their case not only farmers, but also farmers' cooperatives, food processors, and wholesalers.

In the past, supermarkets have sought to thin down milk, beef, or fresh produce suppliers to only a few suppliers, or even devolve management of an entire food category to a leading supplier as leader and coordinator of supply of that food product. In doing so, they found that they had created large intermediaries with countervailing market power, which they found increasingly difficult to manipulate. As result, they have increasingly adopted a policy of divide and rule by buying from a larger number of smaller suppliers.

This has not always been successful. Some supermarkets that have not succeeded in achieving this diversity of supply now find themselves facing the market dominating power of a number of large operators in the food processing industry. For example, ABP, Dawn Meats, and Kepak handle about 25 percent of UK beef cattle slaughtering and processing, and because of their close links with most of the major retailers (Sainsbury's, ASDA, and Morrison), they are able to exert important market pressure on the retailers. The major supermarkets are now aiming to ensure greater security of supply with flexibility through what have been characterized as "virtual production networks,"[18] whereby buyers maintain a small but interchangeable pool of suppliers, switching competitively between them, depending on price. Online auctions also give the buyers further power to screw down their supplier's margins.

Dominance of the few in major commodity sectors

Markets for most of the major agricultural commodities—particularly those of particular importance to small producers in the world's least prosperous agricultural exporting countries—are increasingly controlled by a few large buyers.

Sugar

The major sugar traders are highly integrated, controlling both production and processing. The world trade in sugar is dominated by just three companies: Cargill, Louis Dreyfus, and Tate and Lyle. Cargill trades and ships over 6.5 million metric tonnes of sugar annually and is the largest shipper of raw sugar from Brazil. Cargill also compensates for the vicissitudes of the world sugar market by having a controlling interest in Cerestar, the large French sweetener and starch company. This gives it a strong position in the market for maize and wheat-based sweeteners such as high-fructose maize syrup.

Tate and Lyle's trade house (TLI) handles 4–5 million tonnes of raw and white sugar a year. It has a share in a bulk sugar terminal in Santos, Brazil, and has opened sugar distribution centers in Egypt, Israel, Algeria, and Indonesia. Dreyfus also trades both raw and white sugar and handles more than 4 million tonnes of sugar annually. The Dreyfus Group is the largest supplier of sugar to U.S. cane refiners, handling approximately 1.1 million tonnes a year, one-third of total cane refiner utilization.

Dreyfus owns two Brazilian plants that produce 250,000 tonnes of sugar and ethyl alcohol annually. Because of the regulatory protection provided by the European Union's sugar market support regime, the sugar processors in the EU enjoy a privileged position. Until recently EU exporters received so-called export refunds (subsidies to export) on sugar, based on the difference between the world market and the tariff and production quota protected EU sugar price. Until recently export refunds for sugar generally cost the European taxpayer more than €300 million a year.

Dairy processing

Dairy production and processing is globally a highly protected industry because of its political importance to both dairy farmers and consumers. Across all the OECD countries the degree of protection as measured by the percentage producer subsidy equivalent (PSE)—the premium above prevailing world market prices—for milk is generally about 30 percent. As a consequence, overproduction and disposal of surpluses at prices well below cost of production is a drug on international and local markets, such as the Dominican Republic and parts of the Caribbean where EU milk is sold at 25 to 30 percent below the cost of local production. In the EU, export refunds for milk and milk products, currently running at around €300 million a year, are paid to processors and exporters such as Nestlé and Danone, rather than to dairy farmers. The EU dairy regime is meant to put a floor in the market, but too often European dairy farmers do not necessarily get the benefit of this taxpayer largesse. Fortunately, the level of subsidization is declining as a result of EU reforms (in the 1990s EU expenditure on dairy export subsidies exceeded €1 billion a year). The relative importance of subsidized exports is declining, and nonsubsidized exporters such as New Zealand, Australia, Argentina, and Uruguay are becoming more important global players. New Zealand, which has no producer subsidies nor subsidies for exports, holds approximately one-third of world dairy export trade.

In developed country markets some large operators have moved out of processing milk into staple commodities and moved into branded higher value-added products. Such specialization is part of the trend of consolidation in dairy processing and manufacturing, largely as a counter to concentration in the retail sector.

In 2011 the leading twenty-one dairy processors handled 24 percent of world milk production—or 39 percent of all milk delivered to processors worldwide. Significantly, the world's largest milk processor is the New Zealand farmers' cooperative marketing arm Fonterra, which processes 3 percent of world milk production.[19] According to Rabobank International, the top twenty dairy processing companies globally accounted for a combined turnover of more than US$200.2 billion in 2010.[20]

The five largest companies accounted for 41 percent of this turnover. The momentum of consolidation is expected to accelerate in the future because of the need for increased expenditure on research and development, commercial product development, and quality assurance schemes from the farm to the plate—the classic quandary of being a preferred supplier in buyer-driven chains.

Downward pressure on processors' margins from increased supermarket purchasing power already apparent in the UK, exacerbated by a tradition of below-cost selling, is also becoming apparent not only in other European countries but also worldwide. The phenomenon of major supermarkets rationalizing their supplier bases to benefit from scale economies and lower costs, already explained above, is putting further pressure on the liquid milk processors. The six largest retailers in the UK, for example, are all now supplied with liquid milk from the leading three dairy companies (Arla, Express, and Wiseman). The large dairies are also raising the stakes by introducing new large-scale superdairies to enhance their production and delivery capabilities further along the supply chain.

Multinationals and dairy smallholders in the developing world

The role of multinational companies in the dairy industries in developing countries will always be controversial. On the one hand, commercial arrangements with large processors and retailers can allow technical upgrading and market growth, such as the Cafra local cooperative of dairy farmers in southern Chile. The cooperative could only sell its cheeses locally for many years until it gained access to a major supermarket chain. Its market has grown significantly and it now supplies a large number of stores nationwide. On the other hand, the impacts on domestic market structures can be predatory and extractive. An extreme example is the inordinately large market shares in poor countries of multinationals such as Nestlé's control of 80 percent of milk production in Peru.

The problem for many developing country dairy producers is that the global dairy industry is undergoing fundamental change. Restructuring in industrialized and middle-income countries is having profound impacts not only internally, but also on the production systems of neighboring low-income countries. Upgrading and intense price competition in middle-income countries, driven by the demands of powerful food processors and retailers, leads to saturation of markets with exportable high-quality, low-price, and long shelf-life milk. These types of longer-life dairy products can be transported across borders into fragile developing markets, thereby displace domestic fresh product output. Production systems once judged to be sustainable at a regional or national level, such as those developed in the high Andes of Bolivia, are uncompetitive against such imports.

Poultry and pig meat

Poultry meat is an important source of protein in developing country markets because production is easily increased and is the most attractive in terms of the efficiency of the conversion of feed to meat. The international trade in poultry meat has risen rapidly, with the rise in prosperity of the emerging Asian economies and of the post-communist transition economies. China and Russia account for more than one-third of global imports. By 2001 poultry meat represented nearly 43 percent of the world meat trade, up from 25 percent in 1990; with the boom in exports from Brazil, chicken now (2011) accounts for close to 60 percent. Food trade analysts believe that the world poultry markets are now saturated, in other words unlikely to expand much further, particularly with increased production in the LDCs.

In marked distinction to the international poultry market, trade in pig meat is relatively small. Less than 4 percent of world pork production is traded internationally. However, international competition in both commodities is increasing as a result of the retail and food service sector's increasing internationalization and trend to regional sourcing. This has changed radically the competitive conditions of the industry and tended to put even the largest national players at a disadvantage in competition with giants such as Tyson and Smithfield in the United States, Danish Crown in Europe, or the CP Group in Southeast Asia.

The easy international movement of capital is an increasingly important feature of global poultry and pig meat trade. Companies can move products and production to meet different specifications (provenance, quality, animal welfare, and so forth), thus allowing them to exploit differences in labor costs and serve different market sectors. For example, investments by European-based companies in Brazil and Thailand allows them to use domestic production for fresh meat sales, where the consumer is more sensitive to provenance, and use cheaper imports for ready meals and food service customers. A typical instance of this is UK's Grampian Country Food Group, producer of fresh and frozen meat products for not only the retail market, but also wholesale and food service sectors, which bought the business of a Thailand-based chicken products manufacturer.

The largest of the international integrators is probably the U.S. firm Tyson, which processes and markets chicken as well as red meat. The company is worth $7.1 billion and has an astonishing 25, 27, and 21 percent of the U.S. chicken, beef, and pork markets, respectively. Tyson sells to every major U.S. retailer including Walmart and is also the market leader in food service. It has more than 7,000 contract poultry growers and 55 chicken processing plants. The company has poultry processing plants in China, Mexico, and Panama. International sales are in excess of $10 billion; the company has an 18 percent share of world poultry exports. Tyson de Mexico is the number three chicken processor and top producer of value-added chicken in Mexico, serving retail and catering customers.

The retail behemoths

"Modern food systems are accelerating towards a highly concentrated structure, in which most power and leverage resides at the retail end, and in which benefits are passed to customers and shareholders rather than producers. These structures are also becoming the norm in many middle-income and some low-income countries, causing parts of domestic markets to resemble export markets." That was how the current development between the producers and the retailers of food was summarized by a report from the UK Department for International Development in 2004.[21] This process has since intensified.

The growth in size and market power of the supermarkets is a relatively recent phenomenon. Until the 1980s, small-scale grocers mostly had to accept the prices charged by wholesale suppliers. The rapid growth in the size and scope of the super grocers—the ASDAs, the Carrefours, the Tescos—through the retail revolution of the past three decades has changed all that. These giants have effectively turned the tables on their suppliers. Wholesalers have been practically eliminated from the food chain as pioneering companies like Tesco—originators of the slogan "pile it high and sell it cheap"—have largely eliminated wholesalers from their large share of the food chain and have gone direct to the growers and processors of food in order to obtain the lowest possible supply prices.

When such companies control a large share of the food selling business—the Big Four supermarkets now control close to 80 percent of all retail food sales in for example the UK market and about 60 percent in western Europe—they are able to decide the prices they are prepared to pay. They are also able to dictate the conditions, standards, and delivery conditions. The food retailer has thus changed from being a humble intermediary between the shopper and the food processing giants to being the gatekeeper of the modern agrifood system.[22]

In highly developed markets like the UK, Belgium, and Germany producers and food processors in many sectors now face a monopsony situation in which their customers—the supermarket chains and food service companies—have such gigantic market power that they, not the producers, completely control access to the final consumer. While first developed in North America and western Europe, the power and influence of the retail giants is now being extended to the former communist countries of eastern Europe, to Asia, and even to the less-developed countries of sub-Saharan Africa.[23] The world's largest four supermarkets in 2011 accounted for close to 80 percent of total global food sales. This compares with a 33 percent share of global sales in 2002 and 29 percent in 1999.

The buying power of the multinational grocers, led by ASDA-Walmart, Carrefour, Ahold, Tesco, and so-called hard discounters such as ALDI, has pushed many smaller supermarket operators out of established markets and is effectively preventing the rise of any new smaller chains in emerging economies. Walmart grew to be the top grocery retailer in the United States only fourteen years after entering the food business. Subsequently, twenty-nine smaller chains have been bankrupted, with Walmart identified as the major catalyst in the demise of twenty-five of them.

The monopsonistic power of the major retail companies arises essentially from their size, conferring "market power through acquisition, leading to logistical control, economies of scale, barriers to entry of competitors, and/or the ability to remould the social and political environment to a company's own benefit. Size also confers 'absolute cost advantage'—the ability to outbid smaller companies for resources and ideas, invest more heavily in research and development, set predatory prices, manipulate futures markets, raise external capital, or mount lavish promotional campaigns."[24]

The large retailers are able to manipulate their suppliers through bulk buying, by playing suppliers against each other, or through threatened removal from their list of guaranteed suppliers and thus to obtain substantial discounts.[25] By such means the largest supermarket operating in the UK market, Tesco, is consistently able to achieve discounts from suppliers at least 4 percent below the industry average. The UK Food Group says, "With retail margins often quite small, these differences in supplier prices have a profound impact on supermarket profitability, and are a frank demonstration of the link between size and buyer power."

The large retailer can insidiously or overtly gain control of the entire food supply chain from field to kitchen by imposing its own standards of hygiene, harvesting, packaging, and delivery or by assisting the conformity of producers with state-imposed standards. This is particularly true of the overwhelming body of health and hygiene regulations being imposed on producers in Europe and North America. The giant retailers also gain savings not only by extracting more favorable terms in the form of lower merchandise prices from bound suppliers, but also by providing (charged for) greater provision of services, such as special packaging or third-party food safety certification, often demanding payment of fees for these self-beneficial services.

Margins are maximized by paying great attention to managing and evaluating store shelf space, and to distribution logistics with just-in-time delivery provisions imposed on suppliers, whose costs and risks are increased, while the store's costs and working capital requirements are minimized. The distribution and delivery systems are the major cost-saving area. Substantial savings are achieved by eliminating the traditional wholesaler through direct supply from primary producers and manufacturers to regional distribution centers (RDCs), and then on to superstores, and subsequently by taking over key areas of the upstream distribution network from suppliers.

The drive toward market domination is spurred by the lower unit costs and higher net margins to be gained from increased market share and sales density. This imperative is what has led to the pattern of global supermarket growth during the past three decades. The result of this process, which is certainly not in the interests of food producers and probably not in those of consumers, is that absolute costs and barriers to entry for potential competitors are increased and subsequent growth in the retail market becomes dominated by only one or two organizations.[26]

multinational retailers and the developing world

If it is accepted that the monopsonistic power of the supermarket multinational enterprises (MNEs) allows them to exploit the market-aware and business-oriented farmers of the developed world, and few now question this conclusion, then it must be even easier to achieve the same objective among the myriad small peasant farmers of the developing countries.

"Supermarket dominance of agrifood is no longer an industrialised world phenomenon. Ground-breaking work in Latin America has shown that penetration of transnational retail firms is proceeding at a rapid pace even in rural areas of the 'developing' world, and this is having a marked impact on market structure," says a 2003 report by the UK Food Group.[27] What the supermarket MNEs are only too well aware of is that most of the population growth in the next three decades is likely to take place in the new and growing urban agglomerations of low- to middle-income countries. As a consequence, the global retailers are organizing their operations to follow these growing demand points. More than half of the likely growth in global food retail markets is forecast to arise in emerging markets. China and India are said to be among the five most attractive countries for expansion of modern food systems.[28] While this development may be beneficial to consumers, it is also likely to mean that primary producers and processors "face domestic markets that start to take on the characteristics of export markets."

An almost European-level of dominance of the retail food market has already been achieved by both indigenous and MNE retail chains. Supermarkets now control 50–60 percent of the food retail sector in Latin America—a phenomenal increase from 10 to 20 percent in the mid to late 1990s. Much the same has happened in Central America; in Guatemala, for example, a leading supermarket chain has concluded that only 17 percent of the population is precluded from shopping in a supermarket, due to low income or geographic isolation.

As a result of this predominance in the food-buying sphere, the power in the market of thousands of small and medium rural enterprises, which have played a fundamental role in job creation and rural income diversification, is being seriously undermined. In Brazil, as in western Europe, the buying conditions of the supermarkets in the red meat sector have eliminated large numbers of small slaughterhouses, traders, and transport operators from the food business.

supermarkets in east asia

Prior to 1990 the supermarket was an unknown concept in China. It was inevitable however that this massive and increasingly prosperous potential market, with a population of 1.25 billion, would be targeted by the grocery MNEs. The country has more consumers than Europe and the United States put together. The rising urban middle class is now estimated to be close to 600 million. In the coming ten years, China will therefore be the largest market and a magnet for international supermarket businesses.

Close to two-thirds of the country's population will still be rural, and the majority of food retail business will still handled by small, individually owned stores and large state-owned shops. But the two decades since 1992, when foreign direct investment was first allowed in China, has seen the movement of consumers—especially younger shoppers—from traditional wet market shopping into supermarkets for fresh foods.

These consumers are attracted by lower prices, more choice, and more convenience. The attraction of the Chinese market can be judged by its sheer scale. Retail sales hit $1.8 trillion in 2009, up 15.5 percent year on year. The enormous grocery retail market in China is estimated at US$285 billion in 2009. This level of sales is underpinned by the steady rise in household incomes. In 2009, the per capita disposable income in urban areas reached $2,515, nearly triple what it was at the turn of the millennium. In economically advanced cities such as Beijing and Shanghai, the average per capita disposable income is of course higher, $3,810.[29] By the end of 2010, when the retail food market was worth US$18.4 billion, the sales volume of chain supermarkets all over China amounted to more than 40 percent of the total retail food turnover of the entire country.

Since China's WTO membership accession, Tesco and other foreign traders have been able to develop in the world's most profitable market with a potential customer base of more than 1.3 billion people (*Straits Times,* 2010). In 2009 Tesco set up a series of joint ventures for the development of shopping malls in China. This has subsequently included three malls in Anshan, Fushan, and Qinhuangdao. Another eighteen new hypermarkets had opened in China by 2010.

What of the future development of food marketing? This was summed up by a leading business consultancy in 2009. The result of surveys conducted among senior food executives and policymakers in nineteen countries, its "State of the Art in Food" report concluded: "The consolidation and internationalisation of the food retail and manufacturing industry can be expected to continue. In the near future, four or five large retail organisations will operate on a worldwide scale. There will, however, also be a number of dominant regional and national retailers. A similar situation will exist among the large manufacturers. About 10 food manufacturers will operate globally, with 20 to 25 global brands, along with a number of consumer goods companies that will be dominant in particular countries or regions."[30]

summary

While the trade in agriculture and food products is hampered by many restrictions, the traditional north-south food trade flow is changing with increased Southern Hemisphere production and exports. Because of the changing dietary patterns in developing and emerging economies, new trade flows are being created. Principally this is changing the balance of agricultural trade between developed and developing countries. Due to the changing dietary demand of newly prosperous consumers, livestock products are becoming more prominent in the global trade picture. Most outstanding is the increased importance of Brazil as a food exporter and China as an importer. The increase in trade and the geographical spread of major grain exporting countries is likely to increase global food security. While the international grain trade has traditionally been in the hands of a few international companies, trade in second and third stage processed foods is increasingly coming to be dominated by a few large operators. Supermarkets are increasing their share of retail food sales worldwide with the multinational retailers using their market power to exploit farmers and other suppliers. Food processors are tending to become larger and to control a larger proportion of production in order to counter the market power of the supermarkets. The increasing power and influence of Western food processors and retailers in developing and emerging markets is symptomatic of this development.

notes

1. FAO, *Agricultural Trade, Trade Policies and the Global Food System* (Rome: FAO, 2008).

2. Mark Gehlhar and William Coyle, *Global Food Consumption and Impacts on Trade Patterns* (Washington, DC: USDA Economic Research Service, 2008).

3. USDA Economic Research Service, "Global Food Markets" (last updated May 30, 2012). Available at: http://www.ers.usda.gov/topics/international-markets-trade/global-food-markets.aspx, accessed May 2012.

4. August Sjauw-Koen-Fa, *Sustainability and Security of the Global Food Supply Chain* (Utrecht, The Netherlands: Rabobank Group, 2010).

5. OECD and FAO, *Agricultural Outlook 2010–2019* (Paris: OECD, 2010).

6. Ibid.

7. USDA Economic Research Service, "Wheat: Trade." Available at: http://www.ers.usda.gov/topics/crops/wheat/trade.aspx, accessed May 2012.

8. Ibid.

9. European Commission, Directorate-General for Agriculture and Rural Development, *India's Role in World Agriculture,* MAP Monitoring Agri-trade Policy, no. 03–07, December 2007.

10. European Commission, Directorate-General for Agriculture and Rural Development, *China: Out of the Dragon's Den?*, MAP Monitoring Agri-trade Policy, no. 01–08, May 2008.

11. Food and Agricultural Research Policy Institute, Iowa State University, *2011 World Agricultural Outlook* (Ames, IA: FAPRI-ISU, 2011).

12. Ibid.

13. Richard J. Sexton, "Grocery Retailers' Dominant Role in Evolving World Food Markets," *Choices* (Journal of the Agricultural and Applied Economics Association), 25(2).

14. Ibid.

15. Elizabeth Frazão, Birgit Meade, and Anita Regmi, *Converging Patterns in Global Food Consumption and Food Delivery Systems* (Washington, DC: USDA Economic Research Service, 2007).

16. Bill Vorley and UK Food Group, *Food, Inc.: Corporate Concentration from Farm to Consumer* (London: IIED, 2010).

17. Richard Gilmour, *A Poor Harvest—The Clash of Policies and Interests in the Grain Trade* (New York: Longman, 1982).

18. Timothy J. Sturgeon, "How Do We Define Value Chains and Production Networks?," MIT IPC Globalization Working Paper 00–010 (2000).

19. Torseten Hemme et al., *Dairy Report 2011.* (Kiel, Germany: IFCN Dairy Research Center, 2011).

20. Rabobank, *Global Dairy Outlook: Enter the Giants* (Utrecht, The Netherlands: Rabobank, 2011).

21. UK Department for International Development (DFID), *Concentration in Food Supply and Retail Chains*. Paper produced by the Agriculture and Natural Resources Team and the International Institute for Environment and Development (IIED) (London: August 2004).

22. Ibid.

23. Ibid.

24. Vorley et al., *Food, Inc.*

25. Competition Commission, *The Supply of Groceries in the UK Market Investigation* (London: Competition Commission, 2008).

26. Ibid., ix.

27. Ibid., xii.

28. Institute of Grocery Distribution, *Market Index—Top 12 of 75 Markets* (Herfordshire: IGD, 2011).

29. Sheng Lu, "Understanding China's Retail Market," *China Business Review*, June 2010.

30. Jan-Willem Grievink, Lia Josten, and Conny Valk, *State of the Art in Food: The Changing Face of the Worldwide Food Industry*. Report for Cap Gemini Ernst & Young (London: Reed Elsevier, 2002).

chapter 4

speculation and food prices

What is speculation? Speculation is generally acknowledged to be the practice of engaging in an uncertain financial transaction in an attempt to profit from short-term or medium-term fluctuations in the market value of a commodity, rather than profiting from the normal traders' activity of buying and selling the commodity itself. Speculators tend to ignore the fundamental value of a commodity and are interested solely on profiting from expected movements in its price. As a result, speculators absorb excess risk that other participants do not want and provide liquidity in the marketplace by buying or selling when other participants are undecided. Traditionally, so-called hedging—offering to buy in the future, at a price different from the current or spot price—provided fluidity and transparency in the market, regarded as beneficial to both producers and users of a commodity.

If, for example, the international wheat market had no speculators, then only wheat growers on the one hand and millers, bakers, and other food producers on the other would participate in that market. In such a market, there would be a larger difference—or spread—between the current offer and buying prices of wheat. Any new entrant in the market who wanted to either buy or sell wheat would be forced to accept an illiquid market and market prices wide apart between buying and selling prices. This greater uncertainty could often create a situation where no trade would take place. Farmers often rely on the information provided by such speculative futures markets in deciding whether or not to plant a crop. This greater transparency could thus be argued to contribute to the economists' ideal of the perfect market where both sellers and buyers have full knowledge of market conditions.

But during the first decade of the twenty-first century, the traditional commodities markets have been absorbed into the much wider market for financial instruments. A very much bigger market in commodities trading products has developed, leading to the charge that trading in these instrument has been a major cause of global food commodity price inflation.

main points

- Examination of the thesis that uninformed speculation is a major cause of food price inflation.
- The alternative view that speculation is a necessary component of the price transmission process in international food markets.
- Role of futures and options markets in improving market management for agricultural producers.
- Commodity Index Funds as an important cause of food price and inflating speculative bubble.
- Hedge fund activity going beyond traditional futures trading and becoming a major source of price inflation.
- The trend in prices after the record 2010 harvest tends to support the thesis that speculation is an important inflationary factor.

speculation's impact on food prices

It has been argued that uninformed, or irrational, speculation in agricultural markets exacerbates price fluctuations, and that in 2007–2008 this activity artificially raised prices beyond the levels justified by the fundamental state of the market. In conventional finance theory, the effects of such speculation should be largely offset by the actions of informed speculators, but this assumes that operators in such markets are generally able to distinguish between informed and uninformed trade patterns and that informed speculators have access to sufficient capital. These assumptions may not always be entirely valid, and some have argued that index-based swap transactions by institutional investors may have transmitted distorting price changes across commodity markets and thus amplified the extent of price movements arising from the fundamental facts of the state of the market.

is speculation not a major cause of food price rises?

Contrary to the views of most consumer groups and some food aid charities, according to several notable analysts of the 2008 food crisis, speculation was not a major factor in inflating food prices in this period. Rather this view argues that speculators are likely to have been a significant force in stabilizing markets because they provide an instant connection between buyers and sellers. A study for the OECD indicates that there is no convincing evidence that speculators aggravated price increases that were already on the rise as drought reduced grain production and increasing worldwide demand diminished carryover stocks.[1]

A major conclusion of the OECD study is that the influx of cash from index traders into agricultural commodities markets provided "a deep new pool of liquidity that reduced volatility and helped to reduce the overheating of the world food economy." Professors Scott Irwin of the University of Illinois and Dwight Sanders of the University of Southern Illinois, authors of the OECD report, found the amount of money flowing into commodity index funds increased substantially in the period from 2006 to 2008. But although this increase represents a major structural change in investor participation in agricultural commodities futures, it has not increased price volatility, according to the study.

> **COMMODITY INDEX FUNDS**
>
> The root of the speculative pressure on food prices in 2006–2008, according to the critics, came from commodity index funds, which are financial products whose value is based on an index of commodity futures prices. Commodity exchange-traded funds (ETFs) invest in commodities, such as oil, precious metals, and more recently agricultural commodities. Commodity index funds are sometimes known as commodity mutual funds and are often run by hedge fund companies. They follow the same principles as the funds that track stock exchange indices such as the FTSE 100 and the Dow Jones in New York. They invest money in the commodities listed, in

fixed amounts according to the weightings in the index used. Then, when they are sold, all of the listed commodities are sold at the same time. The value is assessed at the end of each working day according to each commodity's closing price. Index funds do not try to maximize returns via the most lucrative commodities of the moment, nor do they play the market with long and short positions. Instead, they are passively traded; they simply aim to replicate the price movements of the commodities in the index. Among the first commodity ETFs were gold exchange-traded funds, which have been offered in a number of countries. Commodity ETFs are generally index funds, but track non-securities indexes. Because they do not invest in securities, commodity ETFs are not regulated as investment companies under U.S. legislation.

The OECD paper argues that there is "no convincing evidence that positions held by index traders or swap dealers impact market returns. The report states that in agricultural futures markets, "While the increased participation of index fund investments in commodity markets represents a significant structural change, this has not generated increased price volatility, implied or realized." Based on new data and empirical analysis, the study finds that index funds did not cause a bubble in commodity futures prices. Their analysis could find no statistically significant relationship indicating that changes in index and swap fund positions have increased market volatility.

They even go further, admittedly cautiously, to suggest that there is some evidence that increases in index trader positions are followed by lower market volatility. This result must be interpreted with considerable caution, because it is still possible that trader positions are correlated with some third variable that is actually causing market volatility to decline. Nonetheless, this finding contrasts with popular notions about the market impact of index funds, but is not so surprising in the light of "the traditional problem in commodity futures markets of the lack of sufficient liquidity to meet hedging needs and to transfer risk."

The OECD review reinforces the conclusions of other analysts of causes of the food price spirals—most notably experts employed by the UK government to examine the cause of the 2006–2008 phenomenon. Their report to the UK Cabinet Office in 2009 welcomed speculation, the major bogey of the proponents of more protectionist agriculture policies. "Speculation provides liquidity to international agricultural futures and options markets," they argued. "These markets facilitate price discovery and transparency, and improve the management of price risk by agricultural producers and processors (either directly or via intermediaries). They make it easier for producers to lock in price incentives at planting and invest in production with more confidence."[2] They foresaw the importance of futures markets increasing in the context of greater variation of supply caused by climate change and other developments.

Professor Irwin says speculators have been wrongly targeted because the 2008 price spike occurred amid a dramatic surge of index trading that marked a major structural change in commodities futures markets. But research shows the shift was a coincidence, not a contributor to the rise.

The report warned lawmakers on both sides of the Atlantic against trying to limit the operations of commodities futures markets. In particular, the U.S. Congress should rethink planned new limits on speculative trading in futures markets, which are included in a sweeping 2010 financial reform package. "Our policy-makers and regulators should look at the entire body of evidence and make policy decisions based on evidence, not conjecture," Irwin says. "'Do no harm' is the first principle they should adhere to. There needs to be a high standard of evidence before they intervene with any kind of restrictions."

excessive speculation?

Concerned lobby groups, however, allege that excessive speculation by commodity traders outside the normal run of commodity market trading helped to ramp up food prices in the 2006–2008 period and thus increased the number of undernourished people and created commodity market instability. A report by the Institute for Agriculture and Trade Policy (IATP) argues that U.S. deregulation of financial markets opened the door for large financial services speculators to make huge bets that destabilized the structure of agriculture commodity markets.[3]

While commercial speculation in agriculture has traditionally been used by traders and processors to protect themselves against short-term price volatility, IATP argues, the elimination of speculative position limits for financial speculators and the rise of commodity index funds undermined traditional price-risk management. The central IATP argument is that "these funds create a constant upward pressure on commodity prices, alleviated abruptly only when fund contracts are 'rolled over' to take profits."

The IATP report records that in July 2008, $317 billion had been invested in commodities index funds, led by major traders Goldman Sachs and American Insurance Group. "The bundling of agricultural commodities with precious and base metal commodities means that the price movements (and the larger trading weight of the metals in the fund) can trigger the sale of a fund contract, regardless of the supply and demand situation in an agricultural commodity." Large commodity funds now hold about 25–35 percent of all agriculture futures contracts and, with other investors, have become an important source of liquidity to the market, according to the FAO.[4]

The argument that excessive speculation was a major element in the price hike is refuted by the Illinois economists. They say that not only is the allegation that an overblown speculative market was largely responsible for the price rise illogical, but it also conflicts with the observed facts. If what is described as a speculative bubble raises the market price of a storable commodity—that is, wheat or maize—above the true equilibrium price, then stocks of that commodity should increase in much the way that a government-imposed price floor can create a surplus. But, during the 2006–2008 period, stocks were declining, not increasing, in most commodity markets.

relationship between stocks and prices

The relationship between prices and inventories for storable commodities is such that a decline in stocks produces a very significant rise in prices. Therefore, a given reduction in quantity due a to supply and/or demand shock will have a much larger impact on prices when starting with low inventories compared to when starting with a high quantity. This also implies that relatively minor reductions in quantity can result in very large increases in prices when the market supply/demand balance is especially tight. This is in fact what happened as declining stocks, failed harvests, and increased demand all coincided in the 2006–2008 period. The economists point to subsequent movements in the oil market. A series of seemingly small supply disruptions in the spring and summer of 2008 could explain the large increase in crude oil prices during this period in view of the extreme sensitivity of the pricing function for crude oil in the short run.

A further reason why speculation reflected the actual state of the market rather than being any self-propelled inflationary force is that commodity index fund buying is very predictable. That is, index funds widely publish their portfolio (market) weights and rollover periods. Thus, it seems highly unlikely that other large and rational traders would trade against an index fund if they were driving prices away from fundamental values existing in the physical market.

Another important feature of the market at that time, which argues against the overpowering force of speculation, is that if index fund buying drove commodity prices higher, then markets without index fund investment should not have seen price increases. Markets without index fund participation, such as fluid milk and rice futures and commodities without futures markets, notably apples and edible beans, also showed large price increases over the 2006–2008 period. In fact, the figures illustrate that the level of speculation in nine agricultural futures markets from 2006 to 2008 (adjusting for index fund positions) was not excessive—the levels of speculation in all markets examined were within the realm of historical norms. Across most markets, the rise in index buying was more than offset by commercial (hedger) selling.

The Illinois researchers warn against making what they regard as simplistic linkage between hedge fund speculations and the index of commodity prices during the 2008 price hike period: "This type of graphical inspection is commonly presented as establishing an 'obvious' link between index positions and prices. However, it is fraught with statistical complications and begs for a more rigorous test of the linkages, if any." They demonstrate that a simple graphical analysis of index trader positions and market prices can be misleading. For CBOT (Chicago Board of Trade) wheat, for example, there are periods of time—such as mid-2007 through late 2008—where there appears to be a close correspondence between index trader positions and price levels. "Conversely," they argue, "there are periods, such as most of 2009, where any relationship seems remote at best."

The conclusion of the OECD report is that greater than usual speculation in agricultural commodities was not in itself a price inflating factor. As a consequence, policymakers should be chary about legislating to control the operation of index funds, in particular in agricultural commodity markets. The empirical evidence presented in this study does not appear, at present, "to warrant extensive changes in the regulation of index funds' participation in agricultural commodity markets; any such changes require careful consideration so as to avoid unintended negative impacts." It is suggested that limiting the participation of index fund investors could unintentionally deprive commodity futures markets of what is an important source of liquidity and risk-absorption capacity at times when both are in high demand.

hedging is important for efficient commodity markets

Though not as emphatic, the FAO's conclusions are similar. It warns that the installation of mechanisms to intervene in futures markets if prices rise too sharply might divert speculators from trading and thus make less money available for important hedging purposes, which are a vital part of the modern market system, benefiting both traders and producers. For this reason, "proposals to create an international fund to react to price hikes might therefore not be an optimal solution. What is more, such a fund would require exorbitant resources to counteract speculation effectively."[5]

The contrary view on the role of speculators in food price inflation is put by the UN's special rapporteur on the right to food Olivier de Schutter.[6] The 2007–2008 spike in wheat and other agricultural commodity prices, he argues, was caused largely by a speculative boom. The subsequent 2010–2011 rise in prices is further justification for this argument. With stocks rebuilt from the previous eighteen months, and with demand depressed by the global recession and biofuel production static or reduced, this can be the only explanation for the post–June 2010 50 percent rise in wheat and other food commodity prices.

De Schutter argues that while the recent bad harvests in Russia and the other former Soviet Union countries undoubtedly set off the price spiral, the main cause of price rises is a speculative bubble created by the massive growth in financial instruments linked to food commodities. Pension and hedge funds, sovereign wealth funds, and large banks that speculate on commodity markets have been progressively switching into commodities since the early years of the present decade. While most commentators agree that the 2006–2008 crisis was largely created by a combination of depleted stocks, bad harvests, and increased demand, De Schutter would argue that the new financial instruments were a major factor—if not the major factor.

alternative view: role of the speculative bubble

De Schutter argues, "Beginning in 2001, food commodities derivatives markets, and commodities indexes began to see an influx of non-traditional investors." The reason for this was that because other outlets for speculative capital disappeared, they were forced to switch into commodities. According to de Schutter, these other outlets "dried up one by one: the dotcoms vanished at the end of 2001, the stock market soon after, and the U.S. housing market in August 2007. As each bubble burst, these large institutional investors moved into other markets, each traditionally considered more stable than the last. Strong similarities can be seen between the price behaviour of food commodities and other refuge values, such as gold."

The de Schutter thesis is likely to be hotly contested. As already discussed, speculation—and biofuel demand—were regarded as side issues by most analysts, although they might have had some contributory effect on fundamental market conditions. In this period, food prices rose by 83 percent between 2005 and 2008, with maize prices nearly tripling, wheat prices increasing by 127 percent, and rice prices by 170 percent between January 2005 and June 2008–2007.[7]

De Schutter points out that the increase in the involvement of speculation in financial derivatives based on food commodities in this period was massive and influential. A study conducted by Lehman Brothers revealed that the volume of all index fund speculation increased by 1,900 percent between 2003 and March 2008. Morgan Stanley estimated that the number of outstanding contracts in maize futures increased from 500,000 in 2003 to almost 2.5 million in 2008. Holdings in commodity index funds swelled from US$13 billion in 2003 to US$317 billion by more than five times between 2002 and 2008. The value of outstanding over the counter (OTC) commodity derivatives grew from US$0.44 trillion in 1998, to US$0.77 trillion in 2002, to a value of more than US$7.5 trillion in June 2007. The de Schutter argument is that changes in supply and demand were mere catalysts setting off a price escalation caused primarily by "excessive and insufficiently regulated speculation in commodity derivatives."

De Schutter emphasizes that what is important is the difference between traditional commodity futures trading, largely a market facilitating mechanism, and what may be regarded as the new financial instruments. While the traditional speculator may drive up the price of a commodity by hoarding the physical commodity, the index speculator and the fund manager accomplish the same by hoarding futures contracts for those commodities. Such agreements to exchange streams of income, or swaps, are almost always traded on an OTC basis.[8]

The most notable commodity index of these is the S&P GSCI, formerly known as the Goldman Sachs Commodities Index, set up in 1991. Others include the Dow Jones-AIG Index and the Rogers International Commodities Index. Speculative impetus and its inflating effect on prices, it is argued, were largely created by the strategy evolved by the Goldman Sachs managers who ran the GSCI. This was to have nothing but long positions(purchases based on the assumption that prices will continue to rise),[9] to keep on acquiring them, and to roll them over as they expired, no matter how high the price of those futures climbed. The purpose was to accumulate "an everlasting, ever-growing long position, unremittingly regenerated."

Though there is likely to be a large body of opinion disagreeing with De Schutter's analysis and conclusions, his critics may ask themselves why, given that the 2010 harvest was likely to have been one of the largest in recent years, stocks had been rebuilt, and feed demand was heavily depressed, did prices then subsequently continue to rise so much? The sheer volume of new speculative pressure on commodity markets must be at least part of the answer.

summary

Although it is alleged that uninformed speculation was a major cause of recent food price inflation, it can be argued that speculation is a necessary component of the price transmission process in international food markets. It is argued that speculation injected greater liquidity into the market.

Nonetheless, it is difficult to deny that the sheer volume of commodity index funds activity has not been a significant cause of a food price-inflating speculative bubble during the last decade. It is difficult to refute the argument that the massive movement of speculative funds into agricultural commodity markets must have had a price-rising effect. Analysts such as the OECD argue that futures and options markets improve market management for agricultural producers. It is possible that hedge funds have now gone beyond traditional futures trading and in themselves have been a major source of price inflation. It should, however, not be forgotten that in a period of declining commodity stocks—as in 2006–2008—only small changes in stock levels produce inordinately large rises in price. It should also be noted that during this period of food price inflation in sectors where no futures markets existed, the process still rose to exceptional levels. The trend of rising prices after the record 2010 harvest tends to support the thesis that speculation is an important inflationary factor.

notes

1. S. H. Irwin and D. R. Sanders, "The Impact of Index and Swap Funds on Commodity Futures Markets: Preliminary Results," OECD Food, Agriculture and Fisheries Working Paper No. 27 (Paris: OECD Publishing, 2010).

2. Global Food Markets Group, *The 2007/08 Agricultural Price Spikes: Causes and Policy Implications* (London: UK Government, DEFRA, 2010).

3. Institute for Agriculture and Trade Policy, *Commodities Market Speculation: The Risk to Food Security and Agriculture IATP's Trade and Global Governance* (Minneapolis, MN: Institute for Agriculture and Trade Policy, November 2008).

4. FAO, Economic and Social Development Department, *Price Surges in Food Markets: How Should Organized Futures Markets Be Regulated?,* Policy Brief, no. 9, June 2010.

5. Committee on World Food Security, High Level Panel of Experts on Food Security and Nutrition, Price Volatility and Food Security. A Report by the High Level Panel of Experts on Food Security and Nutrition (Rome: FAO, 2011).

6. Olivier De Schutter, "Food Commodities Speculation and Food Price Crises," Briefing Note 2 by the UN special rapporteur on the right to food (September 23, 2010). Available at: http://www.srfood.org/index.php/en/component/content/article/894-food-commodities-speculation-and-food-price-crises.

7. FAO, *Food Outlook* (Rome: FAO, June 2010).

8. *Over-the-counter(OTC) derivatives* are contracts that are traded (and privately negotiated) directly between two parties, without going through an exchange or other intermediary. Products such as swaps, forward rate agreements, and exotic options are almost always traded in this way. The OTC derivative market is the largest market for derivatives and is largely unregulated with respect to disclosure of information between the parties concerned.

9. Conversely, a short position is abstaining from purchasing on the assumption that prices will fall.

chapter 5

the pattern of food consumption

The pattern of world food consumption is continuously changing. Even the once-predictable dietary pattern of the developed countries is changing. Most important, for the future of world food production, the foods consumed in emerging and developed countries are dramatically changing, both in type and quantity. Generalizing very broadly, as people become richer they eat fewer carbohydrates and eat more meat and fats. This is the most fundamental principle in any assessment of the future global demand for the major foods.

While the amount of food consumed in individual countries may increase as their populations become richer, the range of foods eaten will change. At certain points of income increase, the total amount of food will cease increasing and become static, while the range of foods consumed will switch away from carbohydrate staples and toward meat, dairy products, fruits, and vegetables. Dietary preferences and even government policies can also lead to consumption trends away from meat and dairy products and to a more vegetable-dominated diet.

main points

- As people become more prosperous consumption switches from a basic to a more varied diet.
- In developed economies, consumption of fruits, vegetables, and prepared foods increases at the expense of dietary staples.
- Urbanization is a major factor in changing diet.
- Increases in consumption of meat, dairy products, fruits, and vegetables is likely in the period to 2050.
- There is a two-stage change in the consumption pattern—first, increased calories, then a move toward more high quality proteins.

In general it can be safely assumed that food consumption is governed by Engels' law: As people become richer, they spend a decreasing proportion of their income on food.[1] While this is an important principle to keep in mind when assessing the future economic performance of a country—less spending on food means more spent on other consumer goods—it is not overly helpful in determining the global demand for food. What matters here are the factors likely to lead to reductions in the demand for one group of foods and increases in demand for others.

Engels' law is particularly relevant in assessing the food demand picture in developed countries. In the UK, for example, while the most prosperous tenth of the population spend only 7 percent of their household incomes on food, people in the poorest groups spend 15 to 17 percent of their total incomes on food.[2] In the least developed countries of the world the proportion of family income spent on food can range from 30 and 90 percent.

What is most relevant to assessment of the future demand for the different categories of food is the relation of income levels to the different types of food generally consumed. For example, in a prosperous developed country like the UK, one-third of food expenditure goes to meat and dairy products, while the amount spent on fresh meat and dairy levels off with rising income and the proportion spent on fruit, vegetables, and to a lesser extent fish increases. Spending on prepared and processed food also increases, as does spending on food consumed outside the home.[3]

urbanization and food consumption patterns

This latter aspect is a function of urbanization and is therefore highly relevant to any assessment of future demand for different types of foods in emerging and developing countries. It is estimated that more than 60 percent of the world's population will be living in towns and cities by 2020; by 2050 the proportion is likely to exceed 70 percent.[4] As short a time ago as 1960 little more than one-third of the

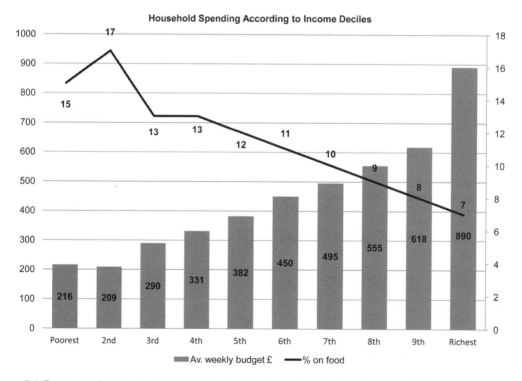

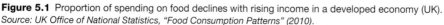

Figure 5.1 Proportion of spending on food declines with rising income in a developed economy (UK).
Source: UK Office of National Statistics, "Food Consumption Patterns" (2010).

world's population lived in urban areas. At that time, one-third of urban population was in developed countries; by the late 1990s the developed world had only one-fifth of total urban population. An ERS analysis says, "Urban population growth in low- and middle-income developing countries has outpaced both the urban population growth in high-income developed countries, as well as the rate of growth of the rural population in developing countries."[5] Growth in the urban population in the LDCs has been at more than 3 percent a year during the past two decades, compared with less than 1 percent in developed countries.

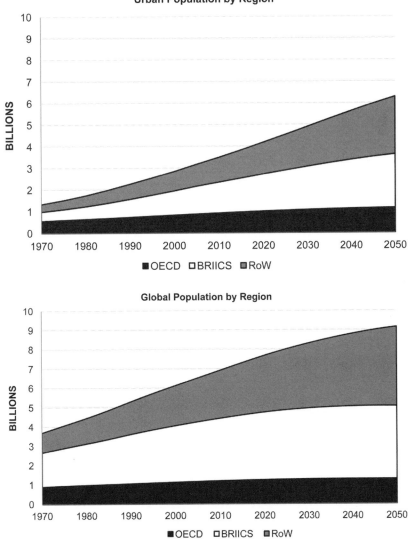

Figure 5.2 Future population growth will be almost totally urban.
Source: OECD, OECD Environmental Outlook to 2050: The Consequences of Inaction, *http://dx.doi.org/10.1787/9789264122246-en (2012).*

There is, however, a wide difference in the rate of urbanization in low- and middle-income countries. Urbanization is itself closely related to economic growth. Most important is the impact on the pattern of consumption; cereal (including rice) consumption declines, and meat, dairy, and fruit and vegetable consumption increases. This is a pattern already clearly present in emerging Asian economies. This change is likely to have a radical effect, particularly in China, where 50 percent of the population grows their own food.

Table 5.1   FOOD CONSUMPTION TRENDS, ANNUAL GROWTH RATES 2007–2012; NOTE HIGH GROWTH RATES FOR PROCESSED FOODS AND READY MEALS IN LESS-DEVELOPED AND EMERGING ECONOMIES

2007–12 CAGR	Cereals	Dairy	Dried processed Food	Oils and fats	Ready meals
China	14.2	11.5	13.8	14.1	10.3
India	27.4	17.4	18.9	17.7	15.6
Indonesia	15.9	12.2	15.1	13.4	7.9
Japan	2.8	1.2	−0.9	0.5	1.4
Philippines	6.0	5.8	7.6	7.4	7.5
Singapore	3.9	4.8	9.2	5.1	2.6
South Korea	6.1	5.3	−0.1	3.4	8.0
Vietnam	18.6	17.6	18.4	16.8	16.4
Bulgaria	7.3	4.9	2.5	2.6	7.2
Czech Republic	3.2	2.8	5.2	2.5	8.7
Hungary	2.3	5.7	5.6	7.0	2.8
Romania	11.4	11.2	5.1	5.5	3.9
Russia	11.9	14.8	11.4	11.3	10.8
Ukraine	16.8	13.2	18.4	14.6	10.1
Brazil	12.2	11.6	3.5	4.7	12.1
Chile	10.3	8.9	6.4	6.1	9.1
Colombia	7.3	7.2	9.6	4.1	7.5
Mexico	7.0	5.3	8.7	5.7	3.6
Morocco	8.5	7.3	6.1	2.9	29.3
South Africa	11.2	9.0	15.2	9.7	12.6
United States	0.9	1.2	3.3	3.5	1.0
France	2.1	1.8	1.5	−0.2	1.5
Germany	0.7	1.2	−2.4	1.1	0.9
Turkey	17.9	5.0	4.6	13.2	4.6
United Kingdom	4.0	4.2	8.0	4.7	3.3

Source: Euromonitor, *Who Eats What: Identifying International Food Consumption Trends*, 2nd ed. (2011).

The increase in the numbers of women working, as inevitably occurs in urban areas, leads to greater consumption of fast foods. Paradoxically, this can lead to an increase in rice consumption in some Asian and west African countries because rice forms an important component of such meals. This illustrates the important point that urbanization will affect diet differently in different regions: while rice consumption declines in Asian countries, it could increase in sub-Saharan Africa.

In developed countries there is a tendency for patterns of consumption to be similar. With the globalization of the food industry and food marketing, it is likely that developing countries will follow the same trends. "The presence of U.S.-style fast food restaurants in other countries has greatly affected food consumption in these countries," says the USDA's Economic Research Service.[6] Age cohorts are also important in this development. Significantly, the outline of food consumption in developed countries has tended to converge over time; the OECD points that by the mid-1980s the types of food consumed had become similar in all developed countries.[7]

relationship between income and dietary change

To obtain a clear picture of the pattern of demand for food it is necessary to quantify the relationship between food demand, composition of diet, and income levels. There is, for example, a preference for higher value processed foods as income increases. It is estimated that 85 percent of the increase in global demand for cereals and meat over the 1995–2020 period is likely to occur in the less-developed countries, with demand for meat in these regions doubling in the same period.

Analysis by the ERS of food consumption trends in fifty-one countries indicates that less than 16 percent of household budgets on average is spent on food in the developed countries, whereas in the developing countries people spend an average of 55 percent of their income on food.[8] This survey also indicated that rising incomes inevitably result in a more diversified diet. It therefore follows that there will be a greater change in the dietary pattern in the LDCs than in the developed countries in the 2012–2050 period.

There is little doubt that the global pattern of food consumption is in a phase of radical change. Major alterations in the matrix of consumption of the main foods is occurring, with consumption moving away from basic staples toward more diversified diets comprising more meat, dairy products, and vegetable products. Populations in developing countries undergoing rapid economic transition are exhibiting radical nutritional transition. This transition is likely to take different forms due to differences in race, sociodemographic factors, and other consumer characteristics. In addition to urbanization and food industry marketing, trade liberalization policies of the past two decades are facilitating this nutrition transition.

In the developing countries there were large increases in consumption of calories from meat (119 percent), sugar (127 percent), and vegetable oils (199 percent) between 1963 and 2003. In contrast, in developed countries only vegetable oil consumption was seen to increase appreciably (105 percent) in this period. With rapidly increasing wealth, China, the prime example of a populous developing country, showed the most dramatic changes in this forty-year period, especially in the consumption of vegetable oils (680 percent), meat (349 percent), and sugar (305 percent). In both developing and industrial countries, but most notably in the former, and again notably in China, there were significant reductions in the consumption of pulses, roots, and tubers between 1963 and 2003.

two stages of dietary change

The process of changing dietary composition tends to follow two main stages. In the first expansion stage, the main change is in terms of consumption of increased energy supplies, with extra calories being obtained from cheaper foodstuffs of vegetable origin. This occurs in both developed and developing economies. The second substitution stage results in a change in the range of foods consumed, but with no major change in the overall energy supply. In this second stage the shift is primarily from mainly carbohydrate staples—cereals, roots, tubers—to vegetable oils, animal products—meat and dairy foods—and sugar. In contrast to the first stage, this is country-specific and is influenced by culture, beliefs, and religious traditions, where such traditions can influence the extent to which animal products are substituted for vegetable products and the specific types of meat and animal products consumed.

In developing countries in sub-Saharan Africa and parts of Asia, cereals can form as much as 70 percent of total energy intake, while in developed countries they are likely to provide only about 30 percent of energy intake and 50 percent of total carbohydrate consumption. It is expected that in the period to 2050 the share of cereals in total global calorie intake will fall slowly from around 50 percent in 2011 to 49 percent in 2030 and 46 percent in 2050.[9]Global rice consumption remains static. This is largely due to declining consumption in countries where rice has been the diet staple—China and other east Asia countries.

On the other hand, global wheat consumption continues to increase faster than all other cereals. This growth is largely due to increased consumption in developing countries—particularly in China and India—where the technological advances of the last decades of the twentieth century allow increased domestic production. It is likely that growth in wheat consumption will continue to be greatest in developing countries as a more varied diet leads to substitutions for rice and tubers. Maize consumption, steadily increasing in line with improved food consumption levels in developing countries, will continue to increase to 2050. However, it is probable that much of the increase will be in developed countries as a manufactured substitute for sugar such as high fructose corn syrup (HFCS),particularly in North America and the European Union, with removal of production restrictions under the EU sugar market regime.

meat consumption to increase

A major feature of the global pattern of food consumption is likely to be the increase in meat consumption. Meat has always been a major component of diet in northern European and subsequently North

America; only more recently has it become important in Asian diets. Poultry meat has, in recent decades, tended to become the dominant meat protein source. Significantly, more than half of total developed country meat consumption is in processed products: sausages, burgers, pork pies, and so forth.

Globally, meat consumption has increased 62 percent in the past half century—mainly because of a threefold increase in developing countries—much of it in Asia generally and China in particular. China has experienced a stunning ninefold increase in consumption, while Brazil has seen a threefold increase. It is, however, unlikely that other developing countries such as India and those in Africa will experience anything like these increases in meat consumption.

In many European countries meat consumption is declining due to perceived health considerations. The UK, for example, is one of the lowest per capita consumers of red meat in Europe, with consumption declining steadily over the past thirty years. Recently, this trend has been accelerated by food health scares, such as the bovine spongiform encephalopathy (BSE) or mad cow disease crisis of the 1990s. Globally, both in developed and undeveloped countries, a considerable proportion of the increase in meat consumption has been in the form of poultry meat. Beef consumption, alone among meats, remains static. This is because while beef consumption has risen modestly in some developing countries and emerging economies (such as China and Brazil), it has tended to fall in most industrial countries in North America, Oceania, and Europe. Most projections of meat consumption to 2050 indicate that it will increase only moderately, due principally to increases in pork and particularly poultry meat consumption.

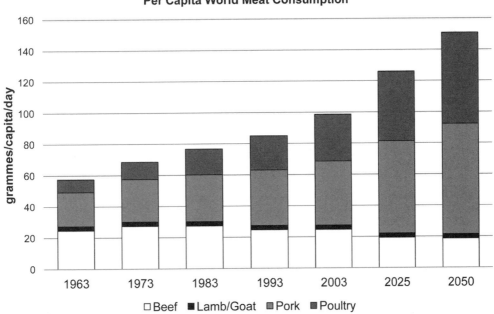

Figure 5.3 Pork and poultry meat dominate increasing world meat consumption.
Source: FAO Food Balances Monthly Reports (2012).

Table 5.2   REGIONAL MEAT CONSUMPTION TRENDS

		Meat consumption patterns in specific regions (gr/capita/day)						
		1963	1973	1983	1993	2003	2025	2050
China	Total	16.44	27.4	43.84	90.41	147.95	201.53	283.03
	Beef	0	0	0	2.74	10.96	19.98	26.23
	Lamb/Goat	0	0	0	2.74	5.48	13.47	16.97
	Pork	13.7	21.92	35.62	65.75	95.89	129.77	181.77
	Poultry	2.74	2.74	2.74	13.7	27.4	29.51	44.51
Brazil	Total	73.97	87.67	104.11	169.86	221.92	288.48	382.98
	Beef	43.84	52.06	57.53	76.71	90.41	117.83	147.33
	Lamb/Goat	0	0	0	0	0	0	0
	Pork	19.18	16.44	16.44	41.1	35.62	59.24	73.74
	Poultry	5.48	13.7	27.4	46.58	90.41	127.13	177.88
India	Total	8.22	8.22	8.22	10.96	13.7	21.69	25.19
	Beef	5.48	5.48	5.48	5.48	5.48	5.48	5.48
	Lamb/Goat	0	0	0	0	0	0	0
	Pork	0	0	0	0	0	0	0
	Poultry	0	0	0	0	2.74	0	0
Sub-Saharan Africa	Total	32.88	30.14	32.88	30.14	30.14	38.65	37.4
	Beef	13.7	13.7	13.7	10.96	10.96	13.61	11.61
	Lamb/Goat	5.48	5.48	5.48	2.74	5.48	4.595	3.92
	Pork	0	0	0	0	2.74	0	0
	Poultry	2.74	2.74	2.74	2.74	5.48	5.48	5.48
Eastern Europe	Total	117.81	164.38	183.56	186.3	189.04	229.56	270.56
	Beef	27.4	30.14	38.36	35.62	21.92	38.11	36.86
	Lamb/Goat	2.74	5.48	2.74	2.74	2.74	2.74	2.74
	Pork	71.23	101.37	109.59	106.85	106.85	137.07	156.32
	Poultry	8.22	19.18	30.14	30.14	49.32	63.29	86.54
Western Europe	Total	153.43	194.52	221.92	232.88	246.58	311.11	367.36
	Beef	54.8	60.27	60.27	54.8	52.06	50.83	48.08

		Meat consumption patterns in specific regions (gr/capita/day)						
		1963	1973	1983	1993	2003	2025	2050
	Lamb/Goat	8.22	8.22	8.22	8.22	8.22	8.22	8.22
	Pork	63.01	82.19	104.11	112.33	117.81	159.85	194.85
	Poultry	16.44	30.14	38.36	46.58	54.8	73.15	96.4
UK	Total	194.52	194.52	189.01	197.26	227.4	219.19	236.19
	Beef	71.23	60.27	57.53	46.58	54.8	29.42	17.67
	Lamb/Goat	30.14	21.92	19.18	16.44	13.7	11.45	1.95
	Pork	71.23	73.97	71.23	65.75	68.49	58.31	54.81
	Poultry	16.44	32.88	38.36	63.01	79.45	108.57	147.57

Data from: Food and Agriculture Organization of the United Nations (2009) Food balance sheets: FAO

Source: FAO Food Balance Sheets (2009). Data for 2025 and 2050 are the author's own.

Consumption of dairy products and eggs shows a variable pattern in different regions of the world. The levels of egg consumption worldwide have shown the greatest increases—doubling since the 1960s. Increases have been more marked in developing countries than in the industrial countries, but with considerable variability. In some developing countries such as India and most of sub-Saharan Africa there has been little or no increase, while in others such as Brazil and China there have been significant increases in egg consumption. A similar picture of variability exists for the consumption of eggs in the industrial countries, with a modest rise in Europe, especially eastern Europe, a modest decline in North America, and a sharper decline in Oceania.

While milk and dairy product consumption has increased in developing countries, it has generally declined in the developed world. In the United States, for example, milk has been replaced with carbonated beverages and juices. Future outlook for consumption to 2050 indicates that, globally, consumption of eggs will continue to rise and the consumption of milk will continue to fall (at least in developed countries). Butter and cheese consumption is predicted to remain static.

the impact of food price increases on poorer consumers

Given the predominance of the daily cost of food in the budgets of the poorest people, it is obvious that food price rises will affect the poor a great deal more than the rich. Rising prices affect the poor directly, as both producers and consumers, and, ultimately, through the impact on the economies of poorer countries. The greatest effect is likely to be on levels of food consumption. Because the poor generally spend most of their budgets on food, rising prices are likely to reduce food consumption. Calorie intake is often maintained by diversion of spending to cheaper, calorie-rich staples and away from foods rich in protein and vitamins, such as meat, fish, dairy, fruits, and vegetables, thereby reducing the quality of their diets.[10] "The short-term impacts are alarming," according to the International Fund for Agricultural Development (IFAD): "Incomes fall by more than 25 percent, and food consumption by almost 20 percent. Medium-term prospects remain bleak, with incomes and food consumption down by 11 percent and 8 percent respectively." In other words, for the poorest people in the least prosperous countries, there is not only a reduction of food consumption when food prices rise, but also a deterioration in the quality of their diets.

The impact of a rise in price of food on poor rural people is painful. Households have to spend a larger proportion of limited income on food needs and as a result consume smaller quantities, less frequently. while eating usually less-nutritious foods. In the extreme where households are dependent on one main staple food the impact is most crippling. Most obviously, an increase in the price of rice is most serious in those poorer regions where the population is dependent on rice for its main food. A rice price increase thus has a special significance for the poverty and income distributional impacts of price increases in Asia. This is because of the predominant share of rice in household expenditures—not just food expenditures but total expenditure—in Asian economies, especially among their poor.[11]

While rice can easily account for roughly 20–35 percent of total expenditure for the bottom 20 percent of the population across countries, it can account for as little as 5–10 percent of total expenditure for the top 20 percent. It is therefore obvious that a sharp rise in the price of rice, and its more general impact on food prices, across Asian countries can be expected to have an impoverishing effect among lower-income groups. It will affect most seriously those who are already living below the poverty line and can be expected to drive others into poverty.

Food price increases reduce the average standard of living. Estimates by the Asian Development Bank (ADB) suggest that if food prices rise by 10 percent, the average standard of living of the people in the Philippines and Pakistan are likely to decline by 4.16 percent and 4.84 percent, respectively.[12] But rising food prices affect people with varied income levels differently. Higher prices put upward pressure on the cost of living and thus lower the overall standard of living. ADB suggests that a food price increase will reduce the average standard of living of the poorest 10 percent of the population more than that of the richest 10 percent of the population in both countries.

In Africa, IFAD surveys record that food price increases in the late 2000s resulted principally in reductions in daily food intakes:

In Cameroon, some eat only once a day, while others eat only what they can afford to buy, irrespective of quality. In Ghana, people are reducing both the quality and quantity of their food intake. In Togo, many households cook with cheaper foods, and cook only one meal (dinner) at home, a practice that also reflects the high cost of wood and charcoal. In Kenya most households are limiting their food intake to one or two meals a day and leaving out the more costly, but nutritious, food items (meat, dairy, poultry, fruits and vegetables). In Senegal, rural people are no longer eating bread, and they are switching to eat only twice per day; while in Ghana it appears that more people are buying local cassava-based and other similar products (sweet potato, yams) rather than bread and imported rice.[13]

Similar patterns of privation are noted by IFAD in Asia. In China, households have reduced their nonstaple foods (meat, oil, etc.), while in Pakistan households are devoting a greater proportion of their income to acquiring food and reducing consumption of other essentials. In the Philippines the response to food price hikes in the late 2000s has been to cut down both the quantity and quality of food and the frequency of meals. These impacts have already been seen in increased levels of malnutrition and undernutrition. In Pakistan the number of food insecure people increased from 60 million to 77 million in 2007–2008, with increased levels of malnutrition.

Other, often extreme measures that poor rural households are obliged to take in response to rising food prices also have to be taken into account. In Egypt, families are spending less on other essentials, such as health and education, while in Yemen, households are taking their children out of school and sending them to work. In Ghana, affected populations are forced to sell their farm animals to purchase food, while in Senegal, rural families are sending their children to the cities or abroad to look for work in ever greater numbers.

Undoubtedly, while a large proportion of the world's population will still be stuck in the rut of poverty, which allows them little freedom to choose what foods they eat, the majority will have increasing choices as their prosperity increases. In developed countries there will be increasing refinement of the diet away from basic food commodities toward fruits, vegetables, and more processed foods. In the emerging and developing countries the traditional staples of rice, maize, and other cereal foods will be abandoned in favor of more meat and dairy products. These countries will also be booming markets for new processed, packaged, and takeaway foods. Globally, farmers will need to be producing larger quantities of meat, dairy products, fruits, and vegetables. Demand for cereals staples, with the probable exception of rice, will have to be increased to meet the rising demand for food in general, but also to feed the livestock needed to supply increased quantities of livestock products.

summary

Food consumption pattern is governed by Engel's law: As people prosper, a smaller proportion of income is spent on food. As people become more prosperous, consumption switches from a basic to a more varied diet. In developed economies, consumption of fruits and vegetables and prepared foods increases at the expense of dietary staples, while in developing countries, consumption of carbohydrate food staples increases with rising incomes, and, at a later stage, these are replaced by higher consumption of meat and dairy products. It is likely that 85 percent of the increase in global demand for cereals and meat will occur in the less-developed countries, with demand for meat in these regions doubling in the same period. Urbanization is likely to be a major factor in changing diet, with a distinct trend toward processed foods. Increase in fast-food consumption is closely linked to the numbers of women working. Dietary trends are also likely to be influenced by globalized food marketing and consequent increasing harmonization of dietary patterns. It is important to note the regional nature of changes in dietary makeup. with increases in income still leading to different patterns of change in different emerging and developing countries. There will likely be substantial increases in consumption of meat, dairy products, fruits, and vegetables in the period to 2050. Increases in meat consumption is likely to be dominated by increased poultry meat consumption. It is important to note the impact of food price rises on consumption in most food-needy countries. Food price rises in LDCs reduce standards of living.

notes

1. Engel's law (Ernst Engel, 1821–1896) states that as income rises, the proportion of income spent on food falls, even if actual expenditure on food rises. In other words, the income elasticity of demand of food is between 0 and 1. It is important to note that Engel's law does not mean that food spending remains unchanged as income increases. It suggests that consumers increase their expenditures for food products proportionately less than their increases in income.

2. UK Government, Cabinet Office, The Strategy Unit, *Food: An Analysis of the Issues. Report to Government* (London: Cabinet Office, January 2008; updated and re-issued August 2008).

3. Ibid.

4. Anita Regmi, ed., *Effects of Urbanization on Global Food Demand: Changing Structure of Global Food Consumption and Trade*, WRS-01–1 (Washington, DC: USDA Economic Research Service, 2001).

5. Ibid.

6. Ibid., iii

7. OECD and FAO, *Agricultural Outlook 2009–2018* (Paris: OECD, 2009).

8. USDA Economic Research Service, *Cross-Country Analysis of Food Consumption Patterns: Changing Structure of Global Food Consumption and Trade* (Washington, DC: USDA Economic Research Service, 2010).

9. N. Alexandratos, ed., *World Agriculture: Towards 2030/50, Interim Report: An FAO perspective* (Rome: FAO, 2006).

10. International Fund for Agricultural Development (IFAD), *Soaring Food Prices and the Rural Poor: Feedback from the Field* (Rome: IFAD, 2007). Available at: http://www.ifad.org/operations/food/food.htm, accessed January 2012.

11. Asian Development Bank, *Food Prices and Inflation in Developing Asia: Is Poverty Reduction Coming to an End?* Special Report (Manila, Philippines: Asian Development Bank, 2008).

12. Ibid.

13. Ibid., vi.

chapter 6

---

population growth and the demand for food

Population increase or decline is influenced by a number of factors. Most obviously, if the birthrate exceeds the death rate then population will increase. The one thing we can be certain about is that, looked at globally, population is increasing because births exceed deaths. For the purposes of assessing future world food needs, it is necessary to know where the population is increasing, remaining static, or decreasing. While it is obvious that population will increase in the key areas where more food will be needed, it is necessary to estimate with some accuracy the magnitude of future increases.

main points

- Population estimates are not a matter only of arithmetic.
- Asia will dominate population increase to 2050.
- There are wide regional differences in population increase.
- Population increase is governed by several major factors: fertility, age structure, mortality, demographic transition, education, and urbanization.
- UN population statistics are open to interpretation.
- There are arguments supporting the conclusion that global population will peak in 2070.

not a matter of mere arithmetic

As in answering all economic questions, it is important to remember that we are dealing with human behavior, which can change radically from current patterns. This is most true in relation to the impact of behavioral change on the trend of population increase or decrease.

To answer the population increase question is not a matter of simple mathematics—the mere projection of present trends into the future. Rather, it is necessary to examine such factors as the number of women of childbearing age at any given time, family size, infant mortality rates, and life expectancy in order to discover how population trends may change. Government policies are also important (e.g China). Health and living conditions obviously affect these main factors; urbanization may be a positive or negative influence. Education, particularly of women, also plays an important part in determining such factors as family size and infant mortality. It is also necessary, as far as is possible, to build in such external considerations as disease, political unrest, and even natural disasters. Immigration and emigration clearly affect the population levels of individual nations or regions.

Achieving reliable estimates of population change is thus extremely difficult, as one of the major agencies providing population data, the International Institute for Applied Systems Analysis (IIASA) admits:

Only truly probabilistic population projections can serve this purpose. The conventional high, medium, low variants (based on alternative fertility assumptions) can greatly underestimate the uncertainty in the future number of elderly because they disregard old-age mortality uncertainty. A larger set of scenarios also does not fully serve this purpose, if it makes no reference to a probability range. But what should these assumptions be based on? Mechanistic trend or error extrapolations without substantive reasoning are not enough. Science-based projections require a better knowledge base. We need more hypotheses and theories with predictive power that also can be tested. This requires nothing less than a reorientation of the currently dominant demographic research agenda.[1]

The once traditional method of producing population projections of simply taking current total population size and using these to project future growth rates has been superseded by a much more sophisticated approach that takes into account the different growth rates of different sectors of populations—the age-specific, so-called cohort-component method. To obtain the national population projections on which any world population must be built, age-group based projections have to be used. Such assessments allow differentiation between the major behavioral components—fertility, mortality, and migration—and inherent changes that originate in age structural effects. This is particularly important for assessing population changes in countries that have gone through significant fluctuations in fertility and mortality trends and hence have irregular age structures. Even for high fertility countries that traditionally had very stable and regular population patterns, so-called age pyramids, the assumed future fertility decline will be partly compensated in terms of population by larger numbers of potential mothers coming of reproductive age. The number of births will continue to increase.

reliable population estimates vital for food demand projections

Reliable estimates of future population growth, both on a regional and a global basis, are vital to any assessment of future demand for food. Whatever the imperfections of current forecasting methods, certain current trends can be identified. Because average well-being of the human race is increasing, total global births now substantially outnumber deaths, 134 million births a year against 57 million deaths. As a result, the world's population is increasing at the rate of around 1.1 percent a year. Although this is half the annual increase of the peak years of the 1960s and the rate of increase is falling, the world's total population could still increase by nearly 30 percent by the middle of the twenty-first century.

More important, most of this increase is expected to take place in those areas where the food supply–population conflict is most acute: Africa and south Asia. According to the United Nation's most recent estimates, the population of Africa is likely to very nearly double between now and 2050, while that of Asia will increase by at least 20 percent. Between them, these two regions will contribute almost all of the expected 2 billion increase in population over the next four decades. The only solace to be gained from these figures is that it is expected that the rate of increase is likely to steadily decline and, consequently, world population is therefore likely to reach its peak sometime between 2050 and 2100.

It has been estimated that there is an 80–90 percent chance that the world's population would reach a peak before 2100 and then begin to decline in subsequent years.[2] The accuracy or otherwise of these estimates is heavily dependent on assumption of long-term fertility levels in different key regions of the world. For the purposes of this work, it can safely be assumed that the population will continue to increase up to and beyond 2050.

Exactly how much it will increase in this period is very much a matter of expert speculation. Estimates of the world's population in 2050 vary by as much as 2 billion, that is between 8 and 10 billion. As already stated, practically all the increase will happen in the developing world. When it is considered that to feed an extra billion people (at current levels of per capita consumption) requires an additional 375 million tonnes of wheat, rice, and animal feed grains—about 17 percent of current production—it is clear that to get any clear idea of future food demand and needed supply it is necessary to examine closely the reliability of any population estimates used in this calculation.

While the picture of future population growth is undoubtedly heterogeneous—with some countries and regions likely to increase substantially while others have declining growth rates—all countries and regions are experiencing growth in their aging population. At the moment, approximately 8 percent of the total world population is above the age of 65. This proportion is expected to double over the coming twenty years and by 2040 reach the level of 16 percent—equal to the current European level. The most rapidly aging region is Asia, where the current population proportion above the age of 65 is likely to increase by three times from 7 to 21 percent by 2050. China is expected to rapidly catch up with Europe and reach about 27 percent above the age of 65 by mid-century. Currently, Asia's proportion of elderly is only half that of the European one.

Even in Africa, which has a very young population structure, with only 3 percent of the population above age 65, the projected increase in life expectancy together with declines in fertility will result in a significant shift in the average age. But it is not just the crude global figures that are important. Changes in the distribution of population and prosperity will have an important effect on the larger population's demand for food.

factors affecting population levels and changes

Fertility

The current growth of population is driven mainly by fertility, or more accurately natality—the number of surviving infants born to each female of childbearing age. Such total fertility is a strong function of regional factors. The more developed countries have lower natality rates than the least developed countries, while the most rapidly developing countries tend to have declining fertility rates. While fertility rates in the developed world are close to replacement levels and therefore these countries have relatively stable population, rates in the developing world are much higher and their population is rapidly expanding. It is therefore clear that the level of development and the pattern of population growth are closely coupled.

The natality level is heavily influenced by economics and social motivation. The high birthrate of the developing countries is to a major extent explained by the need for large numbers of people to perform manual agricultural tasks. Families with large numbers of children in these conditions are likely to be better off than those without. As technology improves and production of essentials becomes more efficient, parents realize that having more children becomes a handicap in achieving an improved standard of living. An outstanding example of this phenomenon was the recent shift in population growth in Thailand; when parents realized that future economic status and well-being was linked to education (expensive in Thailand), the birthrate dropped from about six to two within ten years.

Age structure

The rate at which a particular society will grow is basically dependent on the number of people and, in particular, females of childbearing age. Developing countries typically have a larger proportion of their female population in the childbearing age group of 15 to 40 than do developed countries, where the age distribution is much more even. Anywhere near accurate assessments of future population growth therefore have to take into account the distribution of different age groups in key regions and to gauge the likelihood and timing of any significant change in this pyramid of population age groups.

In developing countries, not only are there many females able to reproduce but also many younger females likely to be potential mothers. Thus, the distribution of the age groups for the developing world indicates that the population growth will be highly positive in the immediate future as the cohort of fertile females enlarges each year, replenished from the larger lower sections of the age pyramid. There has to be a redistribution upward in age groupings before the rate of increase can lessen or, indeed, the population becomes stable. In some countries (e.g., Thailand) this takes place because of a change in social attitudes; in others it occurs as a result of government policy as well as social attitudes. In China, for example, the one-child family policy is achieving remarkable change to the age structure and therefore in population size.

Mortality

Mortality, or the death rate per individual, is the other major basic factor determining population growth. In the developed world, the death rate has dropped, more or less continuously, since the industrial revolution. Improved hygiene and better sanitation and modern medicine and health care have all influenced the trend of declining mortality rates.

Demographic transition

The combination of decreasing death rate coupled with a decrease in birthrate due to changes in economic conditions, leads to a profound change in the population growth curve. The point where low death rates and lower birthrates coincide to bring about a stable population, where replacements equal losses, is generally regarded as the point of demographic transition.

The stage of demographic transition will determine the likely future pattern of development of a country's population size and makeup. The process is generally regarded as having four separate phases or stages. In the first stage, birthrates and death rates are both high due to poor nutrition and low health standards; both fluctuate according to physical circumstances. In stage two improved physical conditions begin to drive the death rate down, leading to a significant upward trend in population. The birthrate remains high in economies based on agriculture. In the third stage increasing urbanization tends to decrease the economic incentive for large families and the birthrate falls. At stage four the population stabilizes with increased urbanization and industrialization. Birth and death rates are both relatively low and the standard of living becomes much higher.

All of these transitional stages clearly make different demands on the food supply. The one thing that is clear is that in countries most needing increased food supplies, it is likely to be some considerable time before they move through all stages of demographic transition. The countries where the food need is greatest are unlikely to reach the fourth stage of transition before 2050.

Global fertility rate declining

What is encouraging however is that the global fertility rate has declined faster than most of the population monitoring authorities were expecting two decades ago. In particular, the total fertility rate (TFR) of the developing countries has fallen to 3.1 children per female (this calculation does not include China). In the world's poorest least developed countries the TFR has fallen to 4.5, compared to between 6.1 and 6.6 in the 1950s. As a consequence, the UN population projections have been significantly revised downward. The projection for 2050 is now 8.9 billion (medium variant), compared with the 1996 projection of 9.4 billion.

Overall, the main reason for the lower projection is global fertility rates declining more rapidly than expected, as health conditions have improved more than expected and an unexpected trend to smaller families in some countries. However, it should be borne in mind that the HIV/AIDS epidemic has played an important part in slowing population increase in sub-Saharan Africa and parts of the Indian subcontinent. About a third of the reduction in long-range population projections is due to this factor alone.

A major factor in assessing future population growth in the developing countries is likely to be the attitude of women to the size of their families. In the UN Demographic and Health Surveys, a global program examining aspects of reproductive health, it is significantly shown that the answer to this question may change over time in some developing countries.[3] In others it does not change. In most countries the declared ideal is rarely 2.0 or less. In Egypt, for example, women gave 2.9 children as their ideal in the 1988 survey and exactly the same figure during five subsequent surveys up to the most recent in 2008. The actual recorded TFR in Egypt is currently about 3.0. In Indonesia, the TFR has been below 3.0 since the early 1990s but is still only 2.4. The number of children given as ideal in Indonesia declined from 3.2 in 1987 to 2.8 in 2007. In Bangladesh, the ideal number of children was 2.5 in 1993–1994 and

2.3 in 2007. Undoubtedly, the desired number of offspring is slowly changing, but that any early overall further decline to European-like fertility levels is unlikely.

What these figures emphasize is that populations in certain regions will continue to grow, while elsewhere human numbers will stabilize or even decline in the most developed countries. Most importantly for the assessment of food supply and patterns of food consumption, within countries populations will continue to shift from rural to urban areas while becoming increasingly older and better educated.

What is obvious is that the largest increases in population will be in the developing countries. In 1960, 70 percent of the global population lived in less-developed regions. By late 1999, the less-developed region population had grown to comprise 80 percent of the global total. Of the projected growth of the world population by 2025, 98 percent will be in these countries, most in sub-Saharan Africa and south Asia.

Africa, with a TFR of more than 5 during the entire 1960–2008 period, has grown the fastest among regions. There were almost three times as many Africans alive in 2011 (767 million) than in 1960. Asia, by far the most populous region, with one-half to two-thirds of the world's total population, has more than doubled its population to more than 3.6 billion, as has Latin America and the Caribbean. In contrast, the population of North America has grown by only 50 percent in the past fifty years, while Europe has increased its numbers by only 20 percent and is now roughly stable.

In the long run, the level of fertility has the greatest effect on population growth because of its multiplier effect; additional children born today will have additional children in the future. Fertility projections are made by projecting the course of the TFR over time, and translating this total fertility rate into age-specific fertility rates. In general, the projection of TFR is divided into assumptions regarding a level at which fertility eventually becomes constant in the country or region, and the path taken from current to eventual levels. Once fertility reaches its eventual constant level, assuming mortality and migration rates also stabilize, the population will eventually reach a stable age structure and constant growth rate. Population is likely to be stable when deaths are replaced by the same number of births; in most developed economies this occurs when the birthrate is in the region of 2.1 to 2.5.

Urbanization

What is as important for calculation of food supply needs as gross population figures is the degree of urbanization. The world's urban population is growing by 60 million a year, about three times the increase in the rural population. The movement of people toward cities has accelerated in the past forty years, particularly in the less-developed regions, and the share of the global population living in urban areas increased from one-third in 1960 to 47 percent in 1999 and is currently (2012) approaching 55 percent. The trend of increasing urbanization is the product of a combination of urban births and migration of people from rural regions. By 2030, it is expected that nearly 5 billion (61 percent) of the world's 8.1 billion people will live in cities.[4]

Significantly for economic and social development, most of what have been described as new mega-cities with 10 million or more inhabitants are in the less-developed regions. In 1960, only New York and

Tokyo had more than 10 million people. By 1999, there were seventeen megacities, thirteen of them in less-developed regions. It is projected that there will be twenty-six megacities by 2015, twenty-two of them in less-developed regions (eighteen will be in Asia); more than 10 percent of the world's population will live in these cities, up from just 1.7 percent in megacities in 1950.

Clearly population forecasting cannot be an exact science. This is why the United Nations population estimates are presented in high, medium, and low variants (and further variants of each of these variants). Such variations, it is stressed, are intended to allow analysts to interpret the figures intuitively.

THE UN POPULATION ESTIMATES

The preparation of each new revision of the official population estimates and projections by the United Nations Population Division involves two distinct processes: (a) the incorporation of all new and relevant information regarding the past demographic dynamics of the population of each country or area of the world; and (b) the formulation of detailed assumptions about the future paths of fertility, mortality, and international migration.

On the current revision, the future population of each country is projected starting with an estimated population for July 1, 2010. Not unexpectedly, problems arise because population data are not necessarily available for that date. The 2010 estimate will have been derived from the most recent population data available for each country, obtained usually from a population census or a population register, projected to 2010 using all available data on fertility, mortality, and international migration trends between the reference date of the population data available and July 1, 2010. In cases where data on the components of population change relative to the past five or ten years are not available, estimated demographic trends are projections based on the most recent available data.

To project the population until 2050, the Population Division uses assumptions regarding future trends in fertility, mortality, and international migration. Because future trends cannot be known with certainty, a number of projection variants are produced. The following paragraph summarizes the main assumptions underlying the derivation of demographic indicators for the period starting in 2010 and ending in 2050.

The 2008 revision includes eight projection variants. The eight variants are low; medium; high; constant-fertility; instant-replacement-fertility; constant-mortality; no change (constant-fertility and constant-mortality); and zero-migration. The UN population analysis of public reports centers on the medium variant of the most recent revision. The first five variants, namely, the low, medium, high, constant-fertility, and instant-replacement-fertility variants, differ among themselves exclusively in the assumptions made regarding the future path of fertility. The sixth variant, constant-mortality, differs from the medium variant only with regard to the path followed by future mortality. The seventh variant, denominated no change, has constant mortality and constant fertility and thus differs from the medium variant with respect to both fertility and mortality. The eighth variant, zero-migration, differs from the medium variant only with regard to the path followed by future international migration. Generally, variants differ from each other only over the period 2010-2050.

The UN's three main population variants are calculated on the assumption of three alternative fertility projections, combined with identical mortality and migration trends. The UN argues that this method provides a plausible range of future population trends. Critics argue, however, that it is not explained what is meant by plausible—100 percent of all possible cases, 80 percent, or only 50 percent?[5] An additional major flaw in the UN method is that it only covers the uncertainty of future fertility trends while not including the uncertainties of future mortality or migration.

Undoubtedly, fertility is the most important determinant of long-term population growth. The UN approach is therefore an acceptable simplification if we are primarily concerned with only total population size. But it is likely that such an approach is inadequate to deal with the age structure of future population growth in key regions of the world; this is particularly true in relation to future food demand. There is also the additional problem created by the aggregation of calculations of national populations to arrive at a world population total. This is because the global high variant of the UN projections is calculated as the sum of all national level high variants, thereby assuming correlation among all national trends. It is argued by critics of the UN method that such perfect correlation is highly unlikely. A higher than expected population growth trajectory in one part of the world could be partly offset by diverging trends in other regions.

IIASA analysts argue: "Only 'fully probabilistic' projections can avoid such problems. These are based on pre-defined uncertainty distributions over time for each of the three components which are stochastically [randomly] combined in large numbers (typically several thousands) of cohort-component projections with the individual random draws being subject to assumed autocorrelations and, in the case of multi-regional projections, correlations among the regions. In most projections, the components are assumed to be uncorrelated between each other."[6]

There is also the problem of source data on current population levels and the conditions that will determine future developments. Statistics on the population size and structure, as well as the levels of fertility and mortality in a given country in the starting year of any projections, can often be unreliable. In those areas that matter most in any calculation of future food needs, Africa and parts of Asia, there are major holes in the fabric of information.

Assessing the future relationship between population and food is not only a matter of biology. Levels of education have a profound influence on the stage of human development and therefore on population increase. The IIASA has produced population projections for most countries in the world differentiated by age, sex, and four levels of educational attainment up to 2050.[7] The baseline scenario in these projections deviates from the UN medium variant in assuming different future fertility levels throughout Europe on the basis of Eurostat projections, as well as variations in some east Asian countries. IIASA has also calculated a so-called UN scenario to compare with its own education-influenced scenarios.

Education

The inclusion of trends in changing educational composition over time in the calculation results in differences compared with the UN projections even if education-specific fertility and mortality assumptions are defined to be as close as possible to the UN assumptions. This IIASA approach suggests the total world population increasing from an estimated 6.9 billion in 2010 to 7.6 billion in 2020, 8.2 billion in

2030, and around 9 billion by 2050. An important feature of these estimates is that they clearly show the likely decelerating speed of world population growth. While the decadal increase in world population is estimated by the UN to be 760 million between 2000 and 2010, it is projected to decline to 616 million for the decade 2020–2030 and 322 million for 2040–2050. The distribution of this growth over continents shows that the population of Africa is still expected to roughly double, while that for Europe is already on a declining trajectory.

peak in 2070?

Whichever projection of population change is considered, it can be concluded that the actual eventuality will be somewhere close to the UN median projection and its conclusion that world population will peak in the early part of the second half of the present century. The view of the IIASA is that the period during which the median of the projections reaches a peak will be around 2070 and that the level of this peak will be around 9 billion people. It points out that by the middle of the century, the 80 percent certainty range for world population is 7.8 to 9.9 billion. By 2100 it further broadens to 6.2–11.1 billion. In other words, there is a more than a 10 percent chance that the world population in 2100 will be smaller than it is today and an equal chance it could be more than 11 billion. However, a further near doubling of world population from currently 7.7 to 13.2 billion is seen as extremely unlikely (a less than 2 percent chance) from today's perspective.

What matters however is that the aggregated global picture is likely to hide several important regional shifts. Continued very low fertility or further fertility declines in regions that already had low fertility, such as eastern Europe and China, (the IIASA World Population Program [POP] research) means that population growth is expected to be lower than originally projected ten years ago. This is likely to be offset at the global level by higher anticipated population growth in sub-Saharan Africa. Two important recent developments in this region have critically changed earlier assumptions of all international forecasting agencies. First, fertility decline seems to have stalled in a number of important African countries. This coincides with an actual decline in the level of schooling of young adults and worsening health care and family planning services.

Second, fewer people than anticipated are dying of AIDS. This arises from a significant downward correction of the estimates made by the United Nations Programme on HIV/AIDS (UNAIDS) of the numbers of people infected with the virus.[8] Put together, a higher starting level of fertility plus a lower level of mortality result in higher population growth, even when the long-term assumptions are left unchanged.

Africa's population will almost certainly more than double from its current level of around 740 million. Because of the great longer-term uncertainties on the future rate of fertility decline and possible new health crises expected under the anticipated very poor development conditions, the 95 percent range by the end of the century is very broad, from a low 1.1 billion to a very high 3.3 billion. The central 20 percent range is 1.9–2.2 billion by 2100. Two factors are likely to mean that Africa will remain at the bottom of the world development scale, unless some trends change radically in the near future: continued very rapid population growth combined with stagnant or declining educational attainment (partly as a

Table 6.1   EXPECTED POPULATION INCREASE (IN MILLIONS): WHILE POPULATION OF AFRICA AND ASIA WILL CONTINUE TO INCREASE, CHINA SHOWS SIGNS OF A DECLINING FERTILITY RATE

	World	Africa	SS Africa	Asia	China	India	Nile Catchment
2000	6124	821	680	3705	1270	1046	225
2010	6885	1032	867	4145	1330	1220	285
2020	7617	1271	1081	4546	1371	1379	354
2030	8233	1518	1308	4846	1374	1506	424
2040	8699	1765	1540	5024	1324	1579	492
2050	9021	1998	1761	5095	1238	1658	555

Source: Data compiled by the author from IIASA and UN sources.

consequence of rapidly increasing numbers of children), and the likely additional environmental and agricultural problems caused by climate change.

China is the oddball in the population development pattern of developing countries. While its population is likely to increase in the immediate future, it is likely to experience almost certain population decline in the longer run. Its history of quite high fertility followed by a very steep fertility decline has resulted in an age structure where the age groups of people of reproductive age are still increasing. Currently, this implies some further population growth to around 1.5 billion in the 2020s before a lasting population decline will begin. The China situation is uncertain because there is no clear picture of the country's current level of fertility. In 2001 the consensus was that its fertility rate was around 1.9 children per family. Subsequently, there has been increasing evidence to suggest that even at the time of the 2000 census it was already much lower, probably somewhere in the 1.2 to 1.8 range, with the best guess at around 1.5.

To cope with this uncertainty regarding the world's most populous country, the UN population forecasters chose to expand the probabilistic approach to include not only uncertain future paths, but also uncertain starting conditions above the range just indicated. But as the median of this range is still 0.4 children lower than the earlier assumptions, the new outlook for China shows more rapid population aging and shrinkage than just a few years ago, again under the same long-term assumptions. After an initial increase, China's population is likely to be back down to its 2000 level during the 2040s and then, by the end of the century, possibly almost down to half the 2000 level.

There is a growing doubt about the tendency of population projections to assume that all countries of the world, post-demographic transition, will converge demographically. The UN forecasters' assumptions that all countries would converge to replacement-level fertility and eventually even to the same level of life expectancy and the consequent conclusion that demographic differentials around the world would disappear, has come under increasing scrutiny.

On a global level, the demographic trends have seen little convergence over the past decades. In fact, over the past few years there has been outright divergence. Regions with already low fertility have seen further declines, and regions with high fertility have shown lower than expected declines. The high level of path dependency inherent in population growth has already produced a more heterogeneous demographic picture for the twenty-first century. Based on these trends, it is probable that analysts will have to rethink, among other things, some of the longer-term socioeconomic scenarios used for the analysis of climate change. A world where there is little international cooperation may not necessarily be a world with a higher population; it may be a world with rapid population shrinkages in some areas and explosive growth in others.

summary and conclusion

It is clear from examination of varying approaches to projection of future population growth that, certainly for the purpose of estimation of future food demand, a regional approach is essential to any useful forecast of demographic change. In particular, it is necessary to look at the effects of migration. As has been stressed by more than one expert in this area, economic differences are likely to stimulate the future migration from less-developed to developed countries.[9] Most obviously, there is likely to be increased migration from Asia and Africa to Europe and North America. A very critical view has to be maintained on projections of fertility levels. Only relatively small deviations in fertility levels are needed to have a major effect on future population growth—particularly if they are sustained.

To take an extreme example, the fertility rate in the UN low variant projection to 2300 is only 0.25 of a birth lower than the figure for the medium variant, and yet this results in the world population falling to only 2.3 billion by 2300 rather than remaining at around the actual medium variant estimate of 9 billion—a highly unlikely development. It is also important to note that in the UN medium variant there will be a significant change in the age pattern of the world population. Most of the increase will be in the above fifteen year groups. It should also be noted that under the UN median variant the average TFL will reach 2 by 2050, suggesting that if this projection is anywhere near the eventual mark, population must level off after 2050.

There is also the problem of feedback. If there are inadequate supplies of food, water, or energy in any given region, its death rate will increase and its birthrate decline. Conversely, improved supplies of any of these essentials will have the opposite effect. There is also the major question of future mortality levels. It is expected by all estimators that life expectancy will rise in all world regions by mid-century with one exception—southern Africa. It is assumed that female life expectancy in the more developed regions will increase from 79 to 85 years in the period between 2000–2005 and 2045–2050, while rates for the less-developed countries will be at 64 to 75 years in the same period.

All of these projections could of course be disrupted by climate change, sudden regional famines, war, or disease outbreak. In order to provide a reasonably sound basis for future population/food supply calculations it is reasonable to assume that a consensus of the available projections will provide a relatively safe foundation.

It has to be accepted that, however that imperfect though they may be, the UN estimates need to be the basis for any calculations on the relationship between population and food supply. All international organizations, particularly the UN Food and Agriculture Organization, use these as the basis for their projections (the famous FAO claim that world food production needs to increase by 70 percent by 2050 is based on the UN medium population increase variant). There is in fact an institutional agreement to use only these projections in order to avoid technical complications arising from using different numbers in different sections of the UN.

As the IIASA admits: "Despite the shortcomings of the UN projections, particularly in the way they deal with uncertainty, there is no doubt that virtually all groups and agencies dealing with food security and agriculture expect to see the UN medium variant as their population projection of choice. For this reason and with the only exception of China [our] review also recommends using the UN medium variant in terms of population size and the age and sex structures that come with it."

It will form the basis for the main calculations and projections on population and food supply used in this book.

notes

1.   "Towards a Food Secure World," IIASA *Options* (Winter 2007): 16.

2.   Wolfgang Lutz et al.,"The End of World Population Growth," *Nature* 412 (August 2, 2001).

3.   United Nations Population Division, "Population Reference Bureau World Population Data Sheet," Available at: http://www.prb.org/Publications/Datasheets/2012/world-population-data-sheet/worldmap. aspx#/map/population, accessed December 2011.

4.   United Nations, *Demographic Yearbook: Data on Population of Capital Cities and Cities of 100,000 and More Inhabitants* (New York: United Nations, 2011).

5.   Wolfgang Lutz and K. C. Samir, "Dimensions of Global Population Projections: What Do We Know about Future Population Trends and Structures?," *Philosophical Transactions of the Royal Society* 365B (2010): 2779–2791.

6.   Ibid.

7.   International Institute for Applied Systems Analysis (IIIASA), *Probabilistic World Population Projections & Research Themes & Research Plan 2006–2010*, 2007 update (Laxenberg, Austria: IIIASA).

8.   United Nations Programme on HIV/AIDS, *UNAIDS Report on the Global AIDS Epidemic* (New York: United Nations, 2010).

9.   Timothy Dyson, "Why the World's Population Will Probably Be Less than 9 Billion in 2300," in United Nations Department of Economic and Social Affairs Population Division, *World Population to 2300* (New York: United Nations, 2004).

chapter 7

the production response

Food production needs to increase in all parts of the world if a population of 9.5 billion is to be adequately fed. While there are few serious obstacles to the increase in production of grains and animal products in the developed countries or even in the emerging agricultural growth areas of Brazil and some parts of Asia, the major global challenge is to raise agricultural productivity and production in the most food needy areas of the world. The problems of increasing food production are concentrated largely in sub-Saharan Africa. If we accept the FAO assumption that world food production needs to increase by at least 70 percent (more if higher population estimates prove to be accurate), then an annual global total factor productivity (TFP) increase of at least of 1.75 percent will need to be sustained.

main points

- An increase in agricultural productivity of at least 25 percent is needed to meet increased global food need by 2050.
- Africa and some other LDCs will increasingly fall behind global productivity.
- Inadequate spending on agricultural development by both aid agencies and LDC governments threatens productivity increase targets.
- Falling yield growth rates is a challenge.
- Effort has to be concentrated on increasing yields.
- More financial inputs are needed in agricultural development and production in LDCs.
- Biofuel production is unlikely to affect food supply in developed countries but indirect land use change (ILUC) will affect cropping in emerging agricultural exporting countries.

The Global Agricultural Productivity[1] index[2] showed that the annual growth in world total factor productivity (TFP) in agriculture was until recently running at 1.4 percent a year—suggesting that a 25 percent increase in the TFP growth would be needed to close the potential food supply gap in 2050 (see Chapter 11). If, however, the figure for the most recently calculated year (2010) of 1.74 percent annual rate were to be maintained, this would be more than high enough to ensure adequate nutrition for a 9.5 billion population in 2050. The problem is that this aggregate figure for world production increase does not guarantee adequate production increases in the most vulnerable regions of the world.

low productivity growth in africa

Currently, TFP growth for sub-Saharan Africa is averaging only approximately 0.85 percent, in sharp contrast to growth rates for Brazil and China of more than 2 percent. To provide adequate output to meet projected food needs without imports sub-Saharan Africa would need to double its TFP growth. It is therefore clear that while some of the region's growing demand for food may be met by input intensification, reduction in post-harvest loss, and increased imports, the challenge of achieving such an increase demands policy changes vigorously supporting agricultural development.

It is in the least prosperous and currently least agriculturally productive countries where TFP growth is most needed. There has been an almost continuous decline in agricultural productivity during the last two decades in these least prosperous nations. This has meant that although during the Green Revolution of the 1970s and 1980s food production increased faster than population, agricultural output has subsequently failed to keep up with population growth. As the Green Revolution has run out of steam, hunger and malnutrition have increased. The least developed of the LDCs have faced increasing food import bills, exacerbated by recent falls in the production and exports of the major exporting countries. With the international food price index rising by 54 percent in 2008, for example (compared with 2000), the food import bill for sub-Saharan Africa is estimated to have increased by close to 20 percent.

While many Asian countries are likely to remain heavily dependent on imports, because of their basic lack of agricultural resources, this is not necessarily true of large parts of sub-Saharan Africa. Many countries in this region have substantial untapped reserves of agricultural productive capacity. Why do these resources remain unexploited?

A major reason is that development assistance from both national governments and overseas agencies to agriculture and its related infrastructure has seriously declined. Overseas development aid fell 58 percent to $3.4 billion between 1984 and 2004. To take the example of only one African government, Uganda, expenditure on agriculture as a share of total government spending declined from 33 percent to 4.2 percent in the same period. Climatic factors, reduced global food stocks, and worsening terms of trade further compounded the cost of food supplies for the least prosperous developing countries (LLDCs). Increasing reliance on thin and volatile international markets for a significant proportion of their supplies is clearly a major problem.

Some of these are short-term influences, but there are clearly longer-term obstacles that have to be overcome if the food supply problem of these countries is to be solved. The most obvious obstacle is the lack of political will of too many governments to support agriculture. Other obstacles are the lack of structural adjustment (both social and physical), the lack of physical infrastructure (roads, communications, transport networks), poorly developed markets for agricultural produce, and the economic bias against developing country products in international markets.

the problem of falling yield growth rates

What is now worrying governments is that yield growth rates have slowed in many countries and for major commodity crops. What is most worrying is that the growth rates of cereal yields have been falling since the Green Revolution years, falling from 3.2 percent a year in 1960 to 1.5 percent in 2000. The hopeful aspect of this analysis is that the capacity to increase growth rates exists. In sub-Saharan Africa, in particular, according to the FAO, there are indications of yield gaps that could be exploited with given varieties and with known practices. In other words, it is the husbandry skills and knowledge that are missing.

It is pointed out that cereal yields in Africa have grown little and are still stuck at around only 1.2 tonnes per hectare, compared to an average yield of some 3 tonnes a hectare in the developing world as a whole (for comparison, in western Europe yields currently average over 7.5 tonnes per hectare). But the production and productivity gap can be put down very clearly to poverty: resources are not available for agricultural education, or for vital production inputs. For example, fertilizer consumption is little more than 13 kg per hectare in sub-Saharan Africa, compared with 73 kg in the Middle East and North Africa and 190 kg in east Asia and the Pacific.

Broadly, there are many reasons why the yield gap persists. Too often, farmers and smallholders do not have sufficient economic incentives to adopt yield enhancing seeds or cropping techniques. These arise from such factors as lack of access to information, inadequate provision of extension services, and, as a result, lack of technical skills. Poor infrastructure, weak institutions (such as market structures and communications), and inappropriate government farm policies are all likely to obstruct the adoption of improved technologies at farm-level. There is also the frequent problem of attempts to apply inappropriate technologies to specific local conditions.

Crop production can be increased in four ways: by increasing yields, by expanding the cultivated area (arable land), by a combination of the two, or by increasing cropping intensity, that is, by multiple cropping or shortening of fallow periods (effectively an increase in the effectively harvested area).

A detailed investigation by the FAO of present and future land-yield combinations for thirty-four crops under rain-fed and irrigated cultivation conditions for 108 countries and country groups indicated that approximately 80 percent of likely growth in crop production in developing countries could come from intensification in the form of yield increases (71 percent) and greater cropping intensity (8 percent).

in land-scarce regions growth has to come from greater intensity

In the land-scarce regions of south Asia, unsurprisingly, the bulk of any increases in output has to come from increased cropping intensity—probably by more than 95 percent. In the Near East and North

Africa, increases in yield would also have to compensate for the likely decline in the available arable land area. Nonetheless, arable land expansion will remain an important factor in increased crop production in many countries of sub-Saharan Africa and Latin America, although in lower proportions than in the recent past.

availability of land

It is generally assumed that worldwide there is limited additional high-quality land available for food production. Marginal land is available for increased production, but could only be brought into production with difficulty and at higher cost.[3] In summary, to meet future food, feed, and fuel needs the current area of agricultural land needs to be maintained in production, with possibly some slight increase in cropped area, but scientific effort will have to be concentrated on increased, but sustainable, production on the current agricultural land. In addition, nonforested land not currently or extensively farmed would need to be considered for agricultural production. A rapid development of second-generation feed stocks and processing technology will be needed to avoid increased conflict between bioenergy and food production.

In developed countries like those of the European Union, it is inevitable that prime land available for food production is likely to diminish significantly under pressure from urban development, amenity and environmental uses, and biofuel production. Unfortunately, it is likely that it will be the most fertile agricultural land area that will be reduced by these demands. At the same time, however, there are substantial reserves of lesser quality and marginal land that could be brought into the production of food and fuel.

A study by experts at the Netherlands Wageningen University estimates that 20 million hectares of Europe's agricultural area is expected to be absorbed by nonagricultural development by 2030—or some 11percent of the currently cultivated area of the EU-27.[4] But it is probable that a significant part of land to be used for biomass/ biofuel production in the future would come from areas not currently included in the EU-27 total of 182.3 million hectares of cultivated land. Population increase and prosperity growth are likely to be the most important cause of reduction in available good agricultural land. The United States experience suggests that urban land development will take place on the most fertile land and will therefore have a disproportionately large overall negative impact on food production capacity.

more marginal land needs to be cultivated

Globally, similar pressure will force the cultivation of much more marginal and underutilized land. The Wageningen study says that by 2080, 100 to 250 million hectares of additional cultivated land will be needed—even at best attainable productivity levels—to cope with increased world demand for food, even though demographic growth can be expected to taper off from the mid-century. This refers to food and feed purposes only. According to the study, "The demand for additional cultivated land for food and feedstock comes mainly from population growth and shifts in lifestyle." In the most extreme demand scenario, 12 percent of the share in growth of agricultural production from 2000 to 2050 could be met from an increase in the agricultural land area. The remaining growth in agricultural production would have to come from an increase in crop yield (75 percent) and husbandry improvement (13 percent).

It is estimated that globally, from a total land area of 13.1 billion hectares, not including Antarctica and Greenland and excluding current cultivated land, forests, built-up land, water, and desert, there are 4.5 billion hectares that are not cultivated. If very low potential and unproductive areas such as tundra and arid land are also excluded, then there is a remaining area of 2.1 billion hectares of grassland and woodland that could be cultivated. The Wageningen researchers estimate that, currently, about 60–70 percent of this available land is needed for animal feeding (grazing). This leaves, with current use unchanged, 600–800 million hectares of the world's land area potentially available for additional production.

climate change will affect production

Inevitably, climate change prognostications have to be taken into account in any calculation of future European and global food production. Expected climate change would affect the availability and productivity of prime agricultural land; in northern Europe there is expected to be a beneficial effect—at least initially. Rising temperatures and increased rainfall are likely to increase productivity in the first half of this century, which should allow increased production of wheat, potatoes, and dairy products on the same or a smaller area of land.

According to a report by the American Economic Association and Universidad de Politécnica de Madrid "Up to 2050, agriculture will be able to adapt to climate change by changing crop varieties, planting dates, moisture conservation tillage, efficient irrigation, but in the second half of the century, climate change will have a clearly negative impact. In the EU27, sufficient extents of agricultural land could become available for biomass production while satisfying food and feed demand."[5]

Land-use scenarios for developed and emerging economies show that by 2030, an extra 22 to 30 million hectares of cultivated land will be available in the EU-27 and another 20 million hectares in Ukraine. In addition, some 15 million hectares of pasture could be used for energy crops. By 2030, with larger areas likely to be used for bioenergy feedstock production, the efficiency and sustainability of production will be crucial.

Current targets for the use of biofuels in the EU's total energy consumption, for example, would if fulfilled certainly put significant pressure on the use of the best land. To manufacture bioethanol and biodiesel prime arable land has to be diverted from food production. The production of biomass for the production of heat and power is another matter, because the process is able to utilize crops that can be grown on marginal land and land that is currently unproductive. Environmental pressure does however increase with increased biomass production.

Overall, what the land use estimates suggest is that there is sufficient flexibility in Europe's current utilization of its land to allow production of both food and fuel to be increased without excessive impact on the price of food. Politically, however, the question is, Can increases in output be achieved without additional environmental stress? The answer undoubtedly lies with the scientists.

The crude figures suggest that, globally, there is enough uncultivated land still available in the world to allow a considerable increase in production. It is estimated by the FAO that currently more than 1.5 billion hectares of land or approximately some 12 percent of the world's total 13.4 billion hectares of land surface is cultivated for crop production. This farmed area represents slightly more than a third (36 percent) of the land estimated by the FAO to be capable of growing crops.

These figures would suggest that there could be about 2.7 billion hectares with crop production potential. But it is argued by more pessimistic analysts that very little of this land can be brought into production without considerable economic or environmental cost.

land use expansion will be significant

It is likely that pressure to increase food supplies in emerging and developing economies will stimulate further exploitation of currently uncultivated land. Land use expansion will continue to be significant, say FAO experts, "in those developing countries and regions where the potential for expansion exists and the prevailing farming systems and more general demographic and socioeconomic conditions favour it."[6] One of the frequently asked questions in the debate on world food futures and sustainability is: How much land is there that could be used to produce food to meet the needs of the growing population?

An indication of the availability and use of the world's used and potentially usable land can be gained from the Global Agro-Ecological Zone (GAEZ) study published in 2002.[7] This survey combined soil, terrain, and climate characteristics with crop production requirements, estimates of land extent, and attainable yield levels in each region for crop production at three input levels (low, intermediate, and high).

On the basis of the GAEZ survey combined with assessment of technology levels, it is estimated that about 30 percent of the world's land surface, or 4.2 billion hectares is suitable to some extent for rain-fed agriculture. Of this area some 1.6 billion hectares are already under cultivation. Significantly, the developing countries have some 2.8 billion hectares of land of varying qualities that is potentially capable of growing rain-fed crops at yields above what is regarded as an acceptable minimum level. Of this area nearly 970 million hectares are already under cultivation. Therefore it can be calculated that the gross land balance of 2.6 billion hectares (4.2 less 1.6 billion, equals 1.8 billion hectares for the developing countries) would allow significant further expansion of crop cultivation.

To avoid accusations of oversimplification, it is necessary to consider the very real constraints in reaching a realistic assessment. These global figures include areas of human occupation, including infrastructure such as roads, reservoirs, forest, and uncultivable land. It is therefore likely that the net available land balance for developing countries could be only around 40 percent of the indicated gross balance. There will be significant regional differences. In south Asia where land is scarce and heavily populated, probably 45 percent of the land with apparent crop production potential is in fact occupied by human settlements.

It is therefore obvious that continuing increases in population in these areas and the pressure of expanding urbanization will put even more limitation on the amount of land that could be brought into cultivation. It has been estimated that urban areas probably occupy some 60 million hectares of the world's gross land balance, protected areas some 200 million hectares, and forests 800 million hectares.[8] This means that the real net land balance is actually in the region of 1.5 billion hectares.

As important in identifying available land is to decide how productive the land available after these various deductions is likely to be for crop production. There are large tracts of land in areas such as North Africa that can be utilized only for certain and often permanent crops such as olive trees. It is therefore necessary to assess land suitability on the basis of its potential ability to produce major food crops.

There is also the problem of the geographical disposition of suitable underused land—land defined as having crop production potential but not cultivated. An estimated 90 percent of the remaining 1.8 billion hectares said to be available in developing countries is likely to be in Latin America and sub-Saharan Africa, with half of the total concentrated in only seven countries: Brazil, Democratic Republic of the Congo, Angola, Sudan, Argentina, Colombia, and Bolivia. In contrast, there is virtually no spare land available for the expansion of cropping in south Asia, the Near East, and North Africa. In several countries in these regions, a significant proportion of the land is not suitable for cultivation in its present state. Some of this land could be made productive through investment in terracing of sloping land or irrigation of arid and hyper-arid land. Even within the apparently land-abundant regions, there is great diversity of land availability, in terms of both quantity and quality, among countries and subregions.

There are also problems of ecological fragility, low fertility, toxicity, high incidence of disease, or lack of infrastructure; in fact, some land that is probably not farmable under any conditions. Such land requires high application of fertilizer, trace elements, and other inputs, plus new husbandry skills to bring it into sustainable usefulness, or requires disproportionately high investments. It is likely that more than 70 percent of the land with rain-fed crop production potential in sub-Saharan Africa and Latin America suffers from one or more soil and terrain constraints.[9]

Factors arising from natural causes as well as human intervention have also led to deterioration of the productive potential of land in important areas—for example, through soil erosion or salination of irrigated areas. Not taking such factors into account in any evaluation of suitability will also result in overestimation.

problem of soil degradation in developed countries

The major challenge in improving world food security is the state of the food-producing land in the least prosperous and most vulnerable countries. The problem is without doubt concentrated in sub-Saharan

Africa and south Asia. In these areas are concentrated the world's most degraded soils.[10] In a swathe across the northern part of the sub-Saharan region—through Mali, Niger, Chad, and northern Sudan—are soils classified as very degraded and where over the past thirty years, it is estimated, there has been the loss of the equivalent of 22 kg of nitrogen, 2.5 kg of phosphate, and 15 kg of potash per hectare through erosion and other causes of structure breakdown. Indeed, it is estimated that 83 percent of all the land in sub-Saharan Africa is problematic for agriculture, with 55 percent unsustainable for crop production and 28 percent of only medium or low potential.

In India the vast proportion of the country's soil is classified as very degraded, with, in the worst areas, the estimated loss of the equivalent of 80 kg of the three main plant nutrients per hectare every year.

regional productivity trends

As the FAO points out in its "How to Feed the World in 2050" report, the world's farmers have been able to meet the rapidly increasing global demand for food, feed, and fiber, between the end of World War II and the turn of the millennium at falling real agricultural prices. This, however, was only due to significant agricultural productivity growth. The important question is, Will productivity growth keep up with increasing food demand during the next half century? Another important question is, How will productivity match increasing need in the less-prosperous regions of the world?

What there is little doubt about is that yields of the major arable crops in the developed and developing countries of the world increased enormously in the second half of the twentieth century. Average yields of wheat in the UK rose for example from 3 to 8 tonnes a hectare; there were similar increases in France, Germany, and the Low Countries. The average world wheat yield increased from 1.08 to 2.7 tonnes a hectare. In the world's major grain exporter, the United States, average yields of eleven crops increased by between 1 and 3 percent a year during the half century to 2000. Significantly, the increase trend was linear or exponential, showing no sign of deceleration. A large study of national average yields of wheat, rice, and maize in 188 countries showed that they were mostly increasing, that the increases had been predominantly linear, and that the biggest producers' yields had increased at more than 33.1 kg per hectare a year.

It is essential that these increase rates be maintained if per capita consumption is to remain at current levels, never mind be increased, by 2050. What has to be emphasized is that both in the developed and developing countries a large proportion of this increase was achieved by the use of nitrogen fertilizer, the application of crop-protection chemicals, and the provision of the suitably responsive varieties.

A major problem pointed out by a group of scientists at the UK's Rothamsted Research Institute, working on the future development of new crop varieties, is that only one of the several factors responsible for the major past yield increases can be relied on for the future: varietal improvement.[11] They argue that the advantage gained from the other production increasing factors in the past cannot be repeated in the future because optimizing the use of nitrogen fertilizer and controlling pests, disease, and weeds can only be achieved once. If a disease is controlled and yield increases, this cannot be repeated to achieve another yield increase.

They therefore postulate the vital question, Are yield increases in the past any guide to increases in the future? The probable answer is no, for the reasons already given. It puts the emphasis for the future very much on improvements in crop plant varieties. At the same time, it has to be remembered that the levels of fertilizer application and pest and disease control in many developing countries has been far from optimal. In these countries it is probable that factors other than varietal potential will be as important in boosting food output.

There is a particular warning for developed countries' approach to increasing yields from the Rothamsted researchers: "In addition to concentrating on raising the potential yield, plant breeders will have to continue or even increase the attention they give to breeding crops for resistance to pathogens in order to increase the obtainable yield and its stability. This is especially important in the developed countries, many of which are restricting the types and amounts of pesticide permitted to be applied. Increased effort to breed for resistance to pests and pathogens is likely to divert resource applied to breeding for yield potential, reducing the pace at which yield can be improved."

The pessimistic scenario that the world is reaching a crop yield ceiling is not generally accepted by plant breeders and other agronomists. As the Rothamsted researchers point out, there is "every reason to expect that yields will increase as new varieties are introduced that are adapted to the changed, CO_2-enriched environment. A large proportion of the yield increases that will be required to feed the world's population must be delivered via plant breeders."

The need is quite clearly to make advances as quickly as in the past, if not faster. But to do so "all the tools that biotechnology can provide" will have to be applied. Genomics and bioinformatics are likely to be of paramount importance. Will there therefore be a second Green Revolution? Too heavy reliance on potential biotechnological breakthroughs will not necessarily meet the yield increase challenge.

possible productivity scenarios

So what is possible? What has to be assessed is not the maximum yield that can be achieved under laboratory and field trial conditions, but that which can be attained on the farm under normal conditions. There is usually a significant difference between the two. To fully maximize the potential of improved crop varieties, on-farm husbandry techniques also have to be improved so as to replicate as near as possible the conditions under which the crops were developed. Closing this gap would have massive effects on yields and production as well as the efficiency of input utilization. The question posed by the scientists is, "How can real-world farmers today achieve yields closer to the potential of current crop varieties, given that they cannot modify soil texture or increase the water supply?"[12]

To demonstrate the potential gains from closing this gap, the Rothamsted scientists used yield statistics from the FAO for 1961 to 2007 for a selection of major crops to calculate linear trends as the yield changed over time for each country in significant developed and developing country regions. The linear trends were converted to relative yield changes: the future change in yield was calculated from the relative change at the end of the observation period—between 2006 and 2007. Possible yields of various

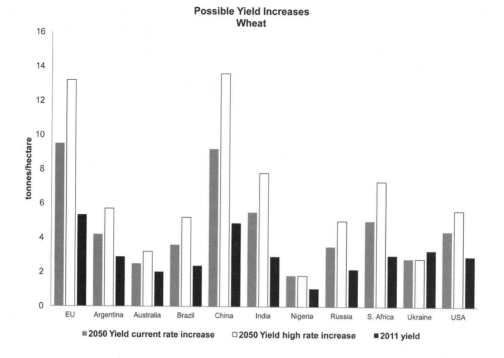

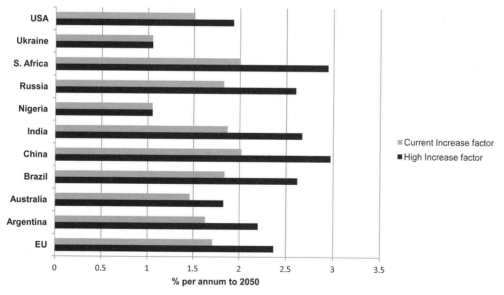

Figure 7.1 Future possible yield increases.
Source: K. W. Jaggard, Aiming Qi, and E. S. Ober, "Possible changes to arable crop yields by 2050, Philosophical Transactions of the Royal Society *365 (B 2010): 2835–2851.*

crops were calculated by assuming three future yield improvement scenarios. The first assumed that potential yield continues to improve at 1 percent each year (i.e., current yield trends are maintained). The second case assumed that yield trends are modified to 70 percent of the recent annual gain, while the optimistic third scenario assumed that the present trends are increased to 2 percent per year.

The achievable yield in relation to the theoretical level achievable under research conditions (i.e., the yield gap) was assumed to be 55–80 percent and was assumed to increase by 10 percent. In the first, conservative scenario the assumptions for most crop-country combinations provide 50 percent more yield per unit area in 2050 than in 2007 (Figure 7.1). The exceptions to this pattern tend to be in Russia and Ukraine, where recent political factors have obstructed and continue to obstruct agricultural development.

prerequisites for production increase in LDCs

The improvement in the infrastructure of needy but potentially productive areas is as important as increases in crop and livestock productivity. At ground level, the major objective has to be increased productivity of staple food crops—both through improved varieties and improved husbandry. The wider use of input subsidies, not only to stimulate the use of improved plant varieties, but also to increase the use of fertilizers, is clearly going to be required. Seed breeding and production to meet the specific needs of particular geographical areas is also clearly a priority. Small farmers also need financial aid in order to become more productive: commercial banks need to be encouraged into agriculture. Adaptation to climate change is likely to become increasingly important. Probably most important, there is an overall need for the state to take a stronger part in the stimulation of agricultural growth and the development of markets. Improvements in infrastructure are also essential to agricultural development.

A major, if not the major, obstacle to increased production at the farm level in Africa is the low level of fertilizer use. On average, fertilizer use is less than 10 kg per hectare—about a fifth of the average use in Europe for example—despite the need often being very much greater. The low, undoubtedly inadequate, usage is due to a number of factors. Most important are probably the poverty of too many landholders and the unavailability of the money to purchase adequate supplies. There is also the problem of supply. Inadequate transport and market structures prevent the delivery of the plant food to where it is most needed, which is exacerbated by too often a heavy dependence on imports. To make matters worse, rather than subsidizing the use of fertilizers, governments often tax imports, thus making them more expensive for users. There is also the problem of lack of knowledge on the most efficient application techniques. More information dispersal and advisory systems are needed to improve the efficiency of fertilizer use.

There is a wide variation of conditions among countries. The actual combination of the factors used in crop production—land, labor, and capital—in the different countries will be determined by their relative prices. Land use expansion is most likely to take place where land is cheap in relation to other factors; the less scarce it is, the greater the role land can be expected to play in crop production increase. For the forty-two developing countries that at present use less than 40 percent of their land estimated to have some rain-fed crop production potential, arable land expansion is projected to account for as much as one third of any growth in crop production. On the other hand, the group of nineteen land-scarce countries—countries with more than 80 percent of their suitable land already in use—the part to be played by further land expansion in crop production growth is likely to be very small, no more than 2 percent.

In contrast, in the developed countries the area of arable land used to produce crops reached a plateau in the late 1960s, then remained unchanged before declining starting in the mid-1980s. Therefore, the growth in crop yields has accounted for most of the recent increases in crop production and compensated for declines in arable land area. This trend is expected to continue to 2050. As a result, intensification—principally higher yields and more intensive use of land—is expected to provide more than 90 percent of the likely growth in global crop production.

Due to land shortages, the necessary growth in the production of rice in developing countries will have to come almost entirely from yield gains. Yield increases are likely to have to compensate for a slight decline in the area devoted to the crop. In the developing countries, most of the wheat and rice crop is produced in the land-scarce regions of Asia, the Near East, and North Africa. Maize is the major cereal food crop in sub-Saharan Africa and Latin America. Both of these regions encompass many countries that are still able to expand their tilled area. The FAO expects that the expansion of cultivated land will make the major contribution to increased maize production.

the biofuel / food supply conflict

Achievement of biofuel mandate targets in both the European Union and the United States is likely to increase the area of cropland in both areas. It is unlikely to reduce food production in either of the two major biofuel producers and users and could increase the profitability of ruminant livestock production. While expansion of bioethanol and biodiesel production is unlikely to reduce livestock production in Europe and America, it could lead to reductions in livestock production in other regions, as well as increased cereal and protein crop production in emerging agricultural exporters such as Brazil, due to the impact of European and American biofuel production on world animal feed markets.

Overall, it is concluded that official biofuel mandates, if fully achieved, will encourage crop production in both biofuel and non-biofuel producing regions, while reducing livestock and processed livestock production in most regions of the world outside the EU and the United States. These two regions are projected to reduce their coarse grains exports, while increasing imports of oilseeds and vegetable oils. While all livestock industries are expected to use more biofuel by-products in animal feed rations, the dairy and other ruminant industries benefit most from the greater availability of by-products. It is likely that the nonruminant industry will reduce production more than other livestock industries because it is less able to take advantage of biofuel by-products.

What is not in doubt is that, at least initially, food prices will rise because of the increased demand for crops by the biofuels industry. Consumers consequently are expected to be likely to reduce their demand for food, to some extent, in response to the higher prices. But fulfillment of the biofuel mandates is likely to generate smaller percentage changes in the prices of crops, but output of the major crops rises more in the United States and EU than if food consumption were unaffected by biofuel production-induced food price rises. This is due to the trade effect of biofuel mandates. If the full effect of price rises, consumption reductions, and increased trade are taken into account, the U.S. and EU cropland areas are estimated to rise by 1.2 and 2.5 million hectares, respectively.

biofuels and the indirect land use change (ILUC) issue

Apart from the effect on international grain and oilseed markets, it is likely that certainly in the case of the EU there will be a significant biofuels policy impact on the demand for oilseeds and feed grain from other exporting countries—the so-called indirect land use change (ILUC).

Certainly, the actual pattern of EU biofuel production and use will be more complex than the pattern suggested in a report by the Center for Global Trade Analysis (CGTA).[13] A European Commission analysis suggested that a considerable proportion of the biofuel needed to fulfill the EU mandate target will come from imports.[14] It estimated that 16 percent and 14 percent of EU demand, respectively, for ethanol and biodiesel would come from imports. Ethanol imports are estimated to peak in 2015 at 43 percent of EU ethanol use and then fall, partly due to the assumption that second-generation (i.e., non-cereal or sugar source) ethanol will be phased in after 2015. The increase in production of so-called second-generation biomass sources would result in reduced competition with food crops for arable land because much of these new crops could be grown on marginal land currently used for neither arable crops nor high output pasture.

The commission's assessments of the impact on EU land use are significantly less dramatic than that suggested by some analysts. Cereal production is estimated to increase by only 1.4 percent, but because EU policies are more encouraging for domestic biodiesel, oilseed production is expected to be 12.3 percent higher.

For this reason, price differences for the main cereal energy crops (+10.2 percent) are less marked than for oilseed energy crops (+19.5 percent). This reflects the fact that, compared with oilseeds, demand for cereals as a feedstock is a much smaller share of total demand. By contrast, on the demand side, total demand for cereals is higher by 6.9 percent (slightly lower for human consumption but much higher for biofuel processing), whereas total oilseed demand is only 0.3 percent higher. This is explained largely by the expected much higher level of imported vegetable oil likely to be used as feedstock (especially palm oil).

The commission's assessment of the impact on land use is much lower than that suggested by GTAP. Cereal production area is hardly affected, being only 0.05 percent higher, whereas oilseeds area is projected to be 10.5 percent higher as a result of the expected pattern of production and imports needed to meet the mandated biofuel policy targets. The commission believes that the higher rates of land use for energy crops will be largely at the expense of land currently devoted to fodder production and fallow—lower by 0.2 percent and 5.6 percent, respectively.

Table 7.1 EUROPEAN COMMISSION'S PROJECTION OF IMPACT OF BIOFUEL MANDATE ON LAND USE IN THE EUROPEAN UNION. NOTE THAT A SUBSTANTIAL PROPORTION OF THE EXTRA LAND NEEDED IS PROVIDED BY THE TAKEUP OF SET-ASIDE AND FALLOW

Cereals	Area (million hectares)	Yield (tonnes/hectare)	Production (million tonnes)
Soft wheat	0.05	1.37	1.42
Durum wheat	4.07	1.12	5.23
Rye/meslin	−0.08	0.27	0.19
Barley	−4.05	−0.57	−4.59
Oats	−4.41	0.2	−4.23
Grain maize	3.18	1.65	4.88
Other cereals	−7.34	−0.4	−7.7
Paddy rice	−1.23	0.02	−1.2
Sugar beets	−1.09	0.08	−1
Oilseeds	10.51	1.6	12.27
Rapeseed	23.05	0.33	23.46
Sunflower	6.07	0.41	6.5
Fodder	−0.23	0.07	−0.15
Set-aside and fallow	−5.65		

Land use pressure is expected to be moderated by greater productivity in arable cropping. Yields for the main energy crops, according to the Commission, are expected to be higher, "[r]eflecting a shift from lower- to higher-yielding crop varieties and a greater degree of intensification of production systems."

Where GTAP and the European Commission clearly agree is on the impact of achievement of biofuel targets on the pattern of cereal trade. The commission expects that increased demand for ethanol will affect the EU's cereal trade balance. Europe could be expected to increase cereal imports in order to satisfy increasing demand for ethanol (marginal effect of 0.46 percent) and reduce its exports (marginal effect of −0.16 percent). Supply is reckoned to be relatively inelastic, increasing by 0.02 percent for each demand increase of 1 percent. The resulting marginal changes in the net trade position of the EU-27 for cereals are that net trade declines at the rate of −1.4 percent for each 1 percent increment in ethanol demand.

What both of these studies clearly illustrate is the extreme complexity of any attempt to calculate the effect of increased biofuels production on the total crop and animal production systems of Europe and America. What is also clear from both studies is that in the medium term, the in-built productivity potential of the agricultural industries will be able to absorb the impact of increased biofuel production without serious longer term effect on food supplies or prices. But a large question mark remains over the indirect land use change likely to be brought about by increasing imports of oilseeds for biodiesel production.

summary and conclusion—achieving the 70 percent production increase

There is very little serious dispute with the assumption that an increase in agricultural productivity of at least 25 percent globally is needed to meet the world's increased food needs by 2050. Nor is there any doubt that Africa and other LDCs are falling behind current global productivity increase levels. While land available for cropping can be increased, urbanization will take up more land and therefore effort has to be concentrated on increasing yields. Inadequate spending on agricultural development by aid agencies and LDC governments threatens productivity and production increase targets. While the FAO says that increased output can be achieved by increased yields and more intensive cropping, the challenge of falling yield growth rates in LDCs can only be met by intensified research.

Rice production is most under pressure from urbanization—yield increases are therefore crucial to maintain supply. Maize production will need to increase to meet rising demand for livestock products. Biofuel production is unlikely to affect food supply in developed countries, but independent land use change will affect cropping in emerging agricultural exporting countries. While it is clear that the developed countries will be able to absorb any increased demand for crops for biofuel production without serious impact on either domestic food supply or prices, the problem of raising production is concentrated in the developing countries. What matters is the ability of the world food production system to increase output to cope adequately with a likely 35 percent increase in population over the next forty years.

Such a target can be met, but not without difficulty, as the Rothamsted scientists quoted earlier warn: "Our assumptions and calculations indicate that it will be possible to increase food production by 50 percent by 2050." However, this relies heavily on improved technology: "While large increases in crop yields have been achieved in recent decades, similar advances cannot be repeated without major changes in crop genetics. It will be necessary to introduce novel or foreign genes with large effects on yield."

To meet productivity and production targets the world will be reliant on the maintenance of soil fertility and control mechanisms for pests, diseases, and weeds, but will be especially reliant on successful plant breeding. "So long as plant breeding efforts are not hampered and modern agricultural technology continues to be available to farmers, it should be possible to produce yield increases that are large enough to meet some of the predictions of world food needs, even without having to devote more land to arable agriculture."

None of this can be achieved without the devotion of money and other resources to scientific research and agricultural development in the most hungry countries. Unfortunately, during the past twenty years the developed countries have not met this need. Over this period there has been a serious decline in the proportion of foreign aid going to agriculture—from 17 percent in 1980 to 3 percent in 2006.[15] Total aid spending on agriculture fell 58 percent in real terms over the same period. Increased spending on agriculture by developing country governments themselves is also vital. In Africa, for example, governments currently spend on average only 4.5 percent of their budgets on agriculture, largely ignoring an African Union target of allocating 10 percent of total public spending on agricultural development.

Agricultural development aid and LDC national government spending will have to be invested in development of a new Green Revolution. This requires not only increasing yields, but also developing methods with less dependency on water, fertilizers, pesticides, and energy. This is likely to involve de-velopment and promotion of new husbandry techniques, including such such fertility preserving and cost-reducing methods as integrated pest management, minimum tillage, drip irrigation, and integrated soil fertility management.

notes

1. Defined as the amounts of total inputs used per unit of output, including comparisons of the growth of output to growth of input use. To illustrate, a 1 percent increase in TFP would mean that 1 percent fewer agricultural resources are required to produce a given output of crop and livestock products so that if prices were unchanged, the average cost of production would decline by 1 percent.

2. Compiled by Global Harvest Initiative established by four major agri-business concerns: Archer Daniels Midland Company, DuPont, John Deere, and Monsanto plus IBM.

3. Generally defined as marginal because at present market prices it does not pay to bring it into production.

4. Simone Verzandvoort, René Rietra, and Mirjam Hack Alterra, *Pressures on Prime Agricultural Land in Europe* (The Netherlands: Wageningen UR, November 2009).

5. American Economic Association: Energy & Environment and Universidad de Politécnica de Madrid, *Adaptation to Climate Change in the Agricultural Sector*, AGRI-2006-G4-05, Report to European Commission Directorate-General for Agriculture and Rural Development, ED05334 (December 2007).

6. Jelle Bruinsma, "The Resource Outlook to 2050: By How Much Do Land, Water, and Crop Yields Need to Increase by 2050?" FAO Expert Meeting on How to Feed the World in 2050, June 24–26, 2009.

7. Günther Fischer, Harrij van Velthuizen Mahendra, and Shah Freddy Nachtergaele, *Global Agro-ecological Assessment for Agriculture in the 21st Century: Methodology and Results* (Luxembourg: IIASA and FAO, January 2002).

8. Freddy Nachtergaele, Riccardo Biancalani, Sally Bunning, and Hubert George, *Land Degradation Assessment: The LADA Approach* (Rome: FAO Land and Water Division, 2010).

9. Ibid., iv.

10. Prabhu Pingali, "Malthus Is Still Wrong." Presentation to the 7th International Conference of the Asian Society of Agricultural Economists, Hanoi, Vietnam, October 13, 2011.

11. Keith W. Jaggard, Aiming Qi, and Eric S. Ober, "Possible Changes to Arable Crop Yields by 2050," *Philosophical Transactions of the Royal Society* 365B (2010): 2835–2851.

12. bid.

13. J. R. Stevenson, N. B. Villoria, D. Byerlee, T. Kelley, and M. Maredia, "Green Revolution research saved an estimated 18 to 27 million hectares from being brought into agricultural production." *Proceedings of the National Academy of Sciences* (West Lafayette, IN: Center for Global Trade Analysis, Agricultural Economics Department, Purdue University, 2012).

14. María Blanco Fonseca et al., *Impacts of the EU Biofuel Target on Agricultural Markets and Land Use: A Comparative Modelling Assessment* (Seville, Spain: European Commission Joint Research Centre Institute for Prospective Technological Studies, 2010).

15. Alex Evans, *The Feeding of the Nine Billion: Global Food Security for the 21st Century* (London: Chatham House, 2010).

chapter 8

impact of energy supply on food production and food prices

Energy, particularly in the form of oil, is essential to modern agricultural production. While its use as the primary source of motive power to cultivate, harvest, and transport crops and animal feed is crucial, oil and other fuels are also important in the manufacture of machinery and pesticides. The major source of energy for the production of artificial fertilizer (principally nitrogen) is natural gas. Production of the large quantities of nitrogen essential to intensive crop production is heavily dependent on natural gas in most developed countries but on coal in China. The price of all energy sources are clearly interlinked and most strongly influenced by the price of oil. It is therefore clear that if the price of oil rises, so does the cost of producing food. While much has been made of the issue of "peak oil," with its suggestion of the world's oil resources running dry, the current expert view is that production will reach a plateau that will persist into the second half of the 21st century. What is certain is that the production of conventional oil and energy generally will continue to cost more.[1] Food will inevitably therefore become more expensive.

main points

- Oil is the predominant energy source in food production.
- Natural gas is of major importance in fertilizer production.
- Rising energy prices threaten food production in some areas.
- Natural gas supply is likely to increase with new exploitation.
- The world surplus of nitrogen fertilizer is increasing.
- The oil price–agricultural production relationship: Food prices are likely to rise with rising oil prices.
- Oil prices are likely to rise by 35 percent or more in real terms by 2035—leading to a long-term rise in the price of food.

First, a definition is needed for what is meant by the *food system* in the context of energy use. It includes all the processes and facilities needed to feed a population: the cultivation, planting, harvesting, processing, packaging, transporting, marketing, and dispersal of food and food-related items. In energy use, assessment of the considerable power used in processing and preparing food by consumers is highly significant. In various developed countries, the percentage of total energy consumption used by the food system has been estimated to range between 10 percent and 14 percent.

It has also been calculated that about one-third of the energy needed to produce, process, and distribute food comes from oil. The obvious reason for this is that these processes, including mechanization of production and the transportation of raw materials, raw food, finished food products, and waste, are carried out by fuel-powered machines. Oil provides around 20–25 percent of the energy needed to produce a crop of wheat. The remaining energy requirement, principally in the form of natural or coal gas, is required to produce the necessary fertilizers and pesticides.

Typically, in the production of wheat in developed countries 50 percent or more of the energy use will be for fertilizer production, 25 percent for fuel (diesel), 10 percent for machinery manufacture, 5 percent for pesticide manufacture, and the remainder for post-harvest handling. This means that because the manufacture of nitrogen fertilizer, which forms the bulk of fertilizer use, is mainly dependent on natural gas, the actual oil requirement is very much less than some analysts claim.

According to the U.S. Department of Agriculture (USDA) 13 gallons (150 lbs) of diesel oil is needed (global average) to produce one tonne of wheat or maize.[2] On average, the world produces 13 tonnes of grain for each tonne of fertilizer used. But the figure varies widely among countries. For example, in China a tonne of fertilizer yields 9 tonnes of grain, in India it yields 11 tonnes, and in the United States, 18 tonnes. This means that the actual world demand for oil for field crop production, on the basis of an annual global production of 2.3 billion tonnes of grain, will be in the region of 172 million tonnes of oil annually. In addition, 340 million tonnes of natural gas will be required for fertilizer manufacture, plus a further 200 million tonnes of oil-equivalent energy to produce farm machinery and pesticides.

Therefore, at 2012 levels of world cereal output, the annual global energy requirement for crop production will be in the range of 600 to 650 million tonnes of oil equivalent. Clearly, a substantial additional amount will be needed to fuel world livestock production. It is, however, unlikely that the total energy requirement of the world agricultural industry would exceed 1 billion tonnes of oil equivalent—25 percent of 2012 estimated global consumption of oil (or 7.5 percent of estimated total world energy consumption of 13.3 billion tonnes of oil equivalent). The total food chain energy requirement up to the point of delivery to the consumer would be around 2.2 billion tonnes of oil equivalent (16.5 percent of total, if the food delivery industries share of transport usage is included).

Future oil and energy resources and their cost will be fully explored later in this chapter. First, it is necessary to be clear why agriculture is so dependent on oil. There are three main needs in the food system: motive power, fertilizer production, and the processing and transport of crops and food products.

power for agriculture

Since the 1940s, agricultural productivity has increased dramatically, due largely to the increased use of energy-intensive mechanization, fertilizers, and pesticides. The vast majority of this energy input comes from fossil fuel sources. Between 1950 and 1984, the Green Revolution transformed agriculture around the globe, with world grain production increasing by 250 percent as world population doubled. Modern agriculture's heavy reliance on petrochemicals and mechanization has raised justifiable concerns that oil shortages could increase costs and reduce agricultural output, threatening future food supplies.

The growth in agricultural productivity has come from a tenfold increase in fertilizer use, a near tripling of land irrigation, and the development of high-yielding crop varieties. This modern industrialized agriculture is driven by the large amount of fossil energy needed to manufacture and power petroleum-fueled farm machinery and to produce fertilizers and pesticides.

Alongside the increases in productivity of modern crop plants have come significant gains in the productivity of husbandry techniques. Crops are now grown with far less expenditure of power and labor than they were a generation ago. It is also arguable that modern mechanized techniques are more ecologically sound than those used half a century ago. Where once European and American famers would have applied at least four separate operations to the planting of a crop of grain—plowing, cultivating, fertilizing, and sowing—all of these operations are now carried out in a single operation. In addition, the once traditional heavy, often environmentally unsound, deep plowing has been replaced by minimal surface scarring, which ensures that the remains of the previous crop provide moisture-retaining humus for the new crop. Because of the speed and ease of modern minimal and no-tillage cultivation techniques, the land is without crop cover for a very short time—minimizing erosion and nitrogen leaching.

Even the leading critic of modern industrialized agriculture, Lester Brown, has to admit that as a consequence of new methods the energy used in agriculture has been substantially reduced.[3] In the United States the combined use of gasoline and diesel fuel in agriculture has fallen from its historical high of 7.7 billion gallons in 1973 to 4.6 billion in 2002, a decline of 40 percent. To illustrate this increase in fuel efficiency, the gallons of fuel used per tonne of grain produced dropped from 33 in 1973 to 13 in 2002, a decrease of 59 percent. There have been similar reductions in western Europe.

One reason for this was a shift to minimum and no-till cultural practices on roughly 40 percent of U.S. cropland. No-till cultural practices are now used on roughly 95 million hectares worldwide, nearly all of them concentrated in the United States, Brazil, Argentina, and Canada; they are also extensively practiced in the intensive arable farming areas of Europe. The United States—with 25 million hectares of minimum or no-till farming—leads the field, closely followed by Brazil.

Clearly any calculation of the energy requirement of global agriculture has to take account of the fact that while European and U.S. agricultural use of gasoline and diesel has been declining, in many developing countries it is rising, as the shift from draft animals to tractors continues. A generation ago, for example, cropland in China was tilled largely by animals. Today much of the plowing is done with tractors.

Modern industrialized agriculture depends on fossil fuels in two fundamental ways: 1) direct consumption on the farm; and 2) indirect consumption to manufacture inputs used on the farm. Direct consumption includes the use of lubricants and fuels to operate farm vehicles and machinery, and use of gas, liquid propane, and electricity to power dryers, pumps, lights, heaters, and coolers. American farms directly consumed about 1.2 exajoules (1.1 quadrillion BTU) in 2002, or just over 1 percent of the country's total energy.

Indirect consumption is mainly oil and natural gas used to manufacture fertilizers and pesticides, which accounted for 0.6 exajoules (0.6 quadrillion BTU) in 2002. The energy used to manufacture farm machinery is also a form of indirect agricultural energy consumption, but it is not included in USDA estimates of U.S. agricultural energy use. Together, direct and indirect consumption by U.S. farms

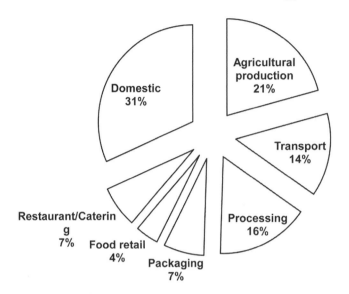

Shares of Total Food Chain Energy Use %

Figure 8.1 Energy in the U.S. food system—comparable with most developed countries.
Source: M. Heller and G. Keoleian, Life-Cycle Based Sustainability Indicators for Assessment of the U.S. Food System
(Ann Arbor: Center for Sustainable Systems, University of Michigan, 2003).

accounts for about 2 percent of the nation's energy use. Direct and indirect energy consumption by U.S. farms peaked in 1979 and has gradually declined over the past thirty years. Food systems encompass not just agricultural production, but also off-farm processing, packaging, transporting, marketing, consumption, and disposal of food and food-related items. On-farm production of primary commodities accounts for less than one-fifth of food system energy use in the United States.

Given the heavy dependence of the food production sector on oil and other sources of energy, it is clear that it is highly susceptible to fluctuations in energy supply and the likelihood of rising prices. In an era of increasing oil shortage, the real price of food will rise. Increasing scarcity of energy can be expected to have five main impacts on the global food production sector:

- Increasing oil prices will directly affect the price of diesel used for cultivation, and for the transport of crops from fields, and from storage to processing and delivery to the consumer.
- Increasing natural gas prices will increase the price of the major fertilizer component, nitrogen.
- In those areas of the world, most notably China, where coal is still used for nitrogen production, there will be serious strain on coal reserves.
- Increased costs for direct and indirect energy inputs into agriculture may lead to reduced cultivation efficiency and lower fertilizer applications with consequent lower yields for major agriculture crop commodities.
- Less-intense husbandry could lead to the expansion of land areas under these crops, leading to increased environmental pressure and increased prices because of less-efficient production.

high energy prices will stimulate technology improvements

The rising price of energy, however, will also have a stimulatory effect on technological development, which is likely to reduce energy dependency. According to a group of scientists writing in a recent UK Royal Society paper, there could be substantial gains in efficiency of energy use and reductions in greenhouse gas (GHG) emission in all areas of food production and supply.[4] In particular, farmers are likely to be spurred into adopting new cultivation and land management techniques that will reduce energy consumption. In addition, new natural gas exploitation techniques could be expected to increase the supply available for fertilizer production. The development of novel drilling technologies in the United States is already enabling access to what had been regarded as tight gas reserves; this may delay a switch to coal and reduce inflationary pressures on nitrogen fertilizer prices.

"While increasing fossil fuel prices could pose a major risk to agriculture as production costs increase, and also cause increased volatility in prices between the different major agricultural commodities, there is substantial scope for technological and management innovations to occur, decreasing the dependence on fossil energy supplies and creating opportunities for new markets. The opportunities and threats will vary substantively between the different crops and a careful review on a crop-by-crop basis is necessary to understand and manage these threats and the risks to future production posed by increasing fossil fuel prices."[5]

fertilizers

The biggest fossil fuel input to agriculture is the use of natural gas as a hydrogen source for the Haber-Bosch fertilizer-creation process. Natural gas is used because it is the cheapest currently available source of hydrogen. If oil becomes more costly, as it will, it is likely that natural gas will become a partial replacement in some uses. While this will tend to raise the price of gas, current prospects for natural gas production suggest that it will still remain the major, but probably more expensive source of energy for the Haber-Bosch fertilizer production process.

Nitrogen is one of the most important elements in fertilizers. In the most common method of production, the Haber-Bosch process, hydrogen is combined with nitrogen to form ammonia. It requires high temperatures and strong atmospheric pressure, therefore needing a great deal of energy. The nitrogen is taken from the atmosphere and the hydrogen is obtained from natural gas. Worldwide use of commercial fertilizers more than doubled between the late 1960s and early 1980s.

In most of Europe, nitrogen fertilizer production mostly uses natural gas. In China, coal currently provides about 80 percent of the energy inputs into nitrogen fertilizer production, rising from 71 percent in 2004. Diesel comes from crude oil. Electricity, generated through various sources, is used either directly (e.g., cooling or drying grain) or indirectly in machinery manufacture. The dominant energy used in wheat production is thus natural gas, but in China it is likely to be coal. The energy embodied in machinery is equal to about 40 percent of the energy used in diesel, reflecting the heavy wear of cultivating and harvesting equipment and the high power demand on engines, compared with road transport.

Without fertilizers it is impossible fully to maximize the genetic potential of modern crop varieties. The experimental evidence supporting this conclusion is comprehensive and unquestionable. Rather, the question is, can we afford to reduce fertilizer use under pressure of rising energy prices and thus risk falling production? Given the population and economic pressures described elsewhere in this book, this is clearly not an option. Comprehensive experimental evidence indicates that in the extreme situation of no nitrogen, average maize yields would likely decline by 41 percent, rice by 37 percent, barley by 19 percent, and wheat by 16 percent.[6] Eliminating nitrogen from the production of leguminous crops such as soybeans and peanuts would of course have no effect on yield because such plants manufacture their own nitrogen. However, elimination of potash and phosphate from fertilizer treatment would reduce substantially the yield of such crops, probably more than in the case of nonleguminous crop plants.

The essential role of fertilizers in modern agriculture has been demonstrated in long-running experiments on both sides of the Atlantic. The Broadbalk Experiment at Rothamsted Research Station in the UK is the oldest continuous field experiment in the world. Winter wheat has been grown continuously on the Broadbalk field since 1843. Application of nitrogen fertilizer with phosphorus and potassium over many decades has been responsible for 62 to 66 percent of wheat yield compared to phosphorus and potassium applied alone. From 1970 to 1995, high-yielding winter wheat continuously receiving 96 kg nitrogen/hectare was grown; omitting phosphates decreased the yield an average of 44 percent, and omitting potash reduced yields by 36 percent. This and other long-term studies from temperate climates demonstrate convincingly how essential fertilizer is in cereal productivity, accounting for at least half of the crop yield.

The use of fertilizer is even more crucial to crop production in tropical countries. Without fertilizer, the world would produce only about half as much staple foods and more forested lands would have to be put into production. What is incontrovertible is that inorganic fertilizers are essential to the world's food security. They cannot be replaced by organic manurial sources or by organic growing techniques.[7]

U.S. fertilizer efficiency is high because U.S. farmers routinely test their soils to precisely determine crop nutrient needs and because the United States is the leading producer of soya beans, a leguminous crop that fixes nitrogen in the soil. Soya beans, which rival maize for area planted in the United States, are commonly grown in rotation with maize and, to a lesser degree, with winter wheat. Since maize has a voracious appetite for nitrogen, alternating maize and soybeans in a two-year rotation substantially reduces the nitrogen fertilizer needed for the maize.

Whatever its raw material supply problems, it is likely that the world's fertilizer industry will be able to meet any foreseeable demand from the agriculture industry. According to the May 2011 forecast of the International Fertilizer Industry Association (IFA), global fertilizer demand is projected to expand at an average annual rate of 2.4 percent between 2010 and 2015.[8] Despite this, production of all three major plant nutrients, nitrogen, phosphate, and potash, remain at well above potential demand. World fertilizer consumption is projected to be close to 190 metric tonnes of nutrients in 2015. The strength of this growth exceeds the historical growth rate of the past decade, of 2.2 percent per annum. But global fertilizer production capacity is expected by the IFA to continue to increase with close to 250 production-increasing projects being carried out worldwide, combined with a large number of expansions at existing production sites. IFA estimates that about US$88 billion will be invested by the global fertilizer industry between 2010 and 2015.

Most important, production of the major plant nutrient, nitrogen, is expected to more than meet likely demand. Countries with a heavy consumption of nitrogen are increasing their production capacity—several of these countries are expected in time to become net exporters.

The IFA expects that global ammonia capacity will increase by 19 percent over 2010, reaching 229.6 million tonnes in 2015. It is likely that as many as sixty-seven new plants under construction in 2011 will be completed and operating by 2015. A third of these new plants will be in China. The main additions to capacity would occur in east Asia, Africa, west Asia, Latin America, and south Asia. As a result of this expansion, the IFA predicts a world nitrogen surplus in the latter half of the second decade of the twenty-first century. It also expects that global nitrogen production will increase at an annual rate of 3.7 percent between 2010 and 2015, compared with a growth in demand of 2.3 percent per year in the same period. This will mean that the global nitrogen supply/demand balance will move from a moderate potential surplus in 2010 of 3.8 million tonnes to 6–7 million in 2012–2013 and probably accelerating to 15 million in 2015.

transport and handling needs for energy

Although calculation of the food industry's fuel use commonly focuses on energy use on the farm, this accounts for only 20 to 25 percent of total food system energy use in most developed economies. Transport, processing, packaging, marketing, and kitchen preparation of food account for nearly 80 percent of food system energy use.

Packaging and freight services are energy intensive but still use considerably less energy than other sections of the food industry. Energy use by packaging and freight service firms in the United States from 2001 to 2005 increased 22 and 24 percent, respectively.[9] These figures are indicative of the trend toward fewer and larger firms and processing plants, leading to greater use of freight services and substantial increases in the average distance per domestic shipment of all foods between 1997 and 2002. Longer shipping distances inevitably mean greater use of transport fuel per unit of food produced.

In contrast to all the other food-related industries, energy use by wholesalers and retailers decreased over the same period, according to the USDA. Food-service industry growth may have cut into the demand for retail services. At the same time, rapid consolidation of grocery store chains in 1997–2002, resulting in fewer stores with larger areas of retail space, coupled with more energy-efficient lighting, heating, and cooling equipment, also may have contributed to declining energy use by food retailers.

Food staples, such as wheat, have traditionally moved over long distances by ship, traveling from the United States to Europe, for example. What is new is the shipment of fresh fruits and vegetables over vast distances by air. This is probably the most energy-intensive development in the modern food industry. With the expanding world trade in food, so-called food miles—the distance food travels from producer to consumer—have inevitably increased. Among the longest hauls are the flights during the Northern Hemisphere winter that carry fresh produce, such as salad vegetables and fruit, from east Africa and New Zealand to the United Kingdom and other parts of western Europe.

Packaging is also surprisingly energy-intensive, accounting for 7 percent of food system energy use. With modern food presentation methods, it is not uncommon for the energy invested in packaging to exceed that of the food it contains. But the most energy-intensive segment of the food chain is handling and processing by the consumer. More energy is said to be used to refrigerate and prepare food in the home than is used to produce it in the first place. While the use of oil dominates the production end of the food system, electricity (usually produced from coal or gas) dominates the consumption end.

the energy cost and food price relationship

The impact of higher oil prices on the level of production of major food crops depends on the price paid for the output. In plain terms, if fuel, fertilizer, and pesticide costs rise due to higher oil and other energy prices and the price paid for the crop remains unchanged, production will fall. If, on the other hand, prices rise sufficiently to compensate the farmer, production will remain unchanged. Again, to simplify, in the short term—one production cycle—production could fall, but this would likely stimulate a rise in price for agricultural commodities, with production rising in the following seasons in response to higher prices. In the medium and longer term, the price of agricultural commodities will rise to absorb the higher cost and this in turn will inevitably raise the shop price of food.

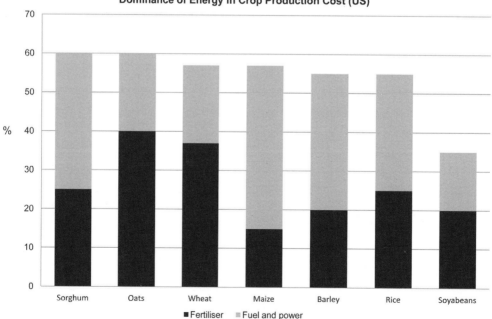

Figure 8.2 The importance of energy costs in total crop production costs.
Source of Data: R. Sands et al., Impacts of Higher Energy Prices on Agriculture and Rural Economies *(Washington, DC: USDA Economic Research Services, 2011).*

Analysis by the USDA Economic Research Service shows the impact on the production of major food crops of different energy-related production costs.[10] In a study on this relationship in the period 2012 to 2018, on a per-acre basis, maize and rice were shown to have the highest energy-related costs of the seven major food crops (corn, sorghum, barley, oats, wheat, rice, and soybeans), while soybeans have the lowest. With a rise of energy-related expenses (fuel up an average of 2.6 to 5.3 percent; fertilizer up 4 to 10 percent), total acreage for these seven crops would decline by an average of 0.2 percent to 0.4 percent. Planted area would decline for six of the seven crops, the exception being soybeans.

oil prices and the cost of food production

The current and future cost of food is highly dependent on the price of oil and other energy sources. In the growing of the major feed grains wheat and maize the total energy cost is between 50 and 60 percent of the cost of production. For rice the proportion is less—probably around 30 percent for commercially grown rice. These figures include not just the fuel needed for motive power to cultivate and harvest crops, but also the cost of fertilizers and pesticides, which are heavily dependent on natural gas for their production. It is likely that synthesis of nitrogen and other fertilizer production represent at least 30 percent of the total cost of wheat production.

On the basis of the production cost of five wheat-producing countries producing an average of 5 tonnes a hectare, the current total cost of production is US$149.50 a tonne, of which more than half is the cost of energy in one form or another.

It is therefore obvious that increases in the prices of oil and other energy sources are likely to have a profound effect on the cost of producing cereals and on food production costs in general. In the short run, of course, the price of food is dependent upon what the market is prepared to pay. In the longer run, with which we are concerned here, the price paid will have to cover this cost of production or production will fall. Rising energy prices will therefore mean rising food prices.

The questions are, How much will the price of oil increase? What effect will this have on the longer run price of food? How far will technical developments moderate the impact of energy cost rises over the next forty years?

Table 8.1   AVERAGE COST OF WHEAT PRODUCTION IN SIGNIFICANT PRODUCING COUNTRIES

	Average
Yield (tonne/hectare)	5.02
Variable costs (US$ per hectare)	278.33
Fixed costs (US$ per hectare)	446.67
Cost per tonne (US$)	149.50

Source of Data: Bidwells Consultants (UK), "Farm Management." Available at: http://www.bidwells.co.uk/services/rural/farm-management.

While oil prices are volatile, the trend is likely to be steadily upward. Sudden reductions, such as that provoked by the OPEC decision to raise production in 2009, are unlikely to recur and certainly are not likely to be sustained. Oil price predictions for the next decades vary widely. According to the U.S. Energy Information Administration (EIA), by 2035, international oil prices will be the equivalent of $125 per barrel—a somewhat optimistic view given that in 2011 the price was already $111 per barrel.[11] The forecast is based on the assumption that2010–2011 conditions will be preserved, particularly the OPEC share in global oil production and the prospect of recovery in global economic growth. The major oil companies, who not only know the state of the world's oil and gas reserves, but also can be expected to have a sound view on the costs of exploration and extraction, tend toward moderation in their expectation of future price increases. BP's most recent estimate is for a 17 percent increase in price up to 2030.[12] Projecting this level of increase to 2050 would suggest a price of $155 per barrel—an increase of close to 40 percent from 2011.

Other estimates are more pessimistic. The International Energy Agency's worst case prediction is that if there is a higher pace of economic growth in the emerging and developing economies and a consequent increased growth of demand for oil in these countries, as well as limitation of oil production by the largest oil-producing countries and a fall of OPEC share in global oil production to 37 percent, the oil price trend will be steeper—certainly to 2035. It predicts that under such conditions, oil prices could rise to $146.03 per barrel in 2015, $169.12 per barrel in 2020, $185.79 per barrel in 2025, and $200 per barrel in 2035. This would suggest a price of beyond $230 per barrel by 2050.

If the price of oil were to increase only modestly, in line with the BP estimate, then the cost of producing a tonne of wheat would increase by about 20 percent, from current $149.50 a tonne to $180 a tonne in 2050. If, on the other hand, the oil price rise follows the IEA's most pessimistic estimate, the increase in the cost of producing wheat would be more than 50 percent, at $224 a tonne.

These estimates assume that there are no technical advances that could reduce the quantity of fuel and fertilizer required to produce each tonne of grain. Hopefully, new crop varieties and husbandry

Table 8.2   WHEAT PRODUCTION COST INCREASES ON BASIS OF TWO ENERGY COST ASSUMPTIONS (AUTHOR'S CALCULATIONS)

	2010	2015	2020	2025	2030	2035	2040	2045	2050	%+2050/2011
Production cost-modest oil price increase $/tonne	149.5	151.7	154.7	158.3	163.2	165.3	169.4	174.1	180.0	20.4
Per cent increase in production cost		1.5	1.9	2.3	3.1	1.3	2.5	2.8	3.4	
Oil price (US$barrel)	111.0	114.0	118.0	123.0	130.0	133.0	139.0	146.0	155.0	39.6
Per cent increase in oil price		2.7	3.5	4.2	5.7	2.3	4.5	5.0	6.2	
Production cost-worst case oil price increase? $/tonne	149.5	175.4	190.7	201.0	205.3	209.4	212.9	222.6	226.4	51.4
Per cent increase in production cost		17.4	8.7	5.4	2.1	2.0	1.7	4.5	1.7	
Oil price (US$barrel)	111.0	146.0	169.1	185.8	193.0	200.0	206.0	223.0	230.0	107.2
Per cent increase in oil price		31.6	15.8	9.9	3.9	3.6	3.0	8.3	3.1	

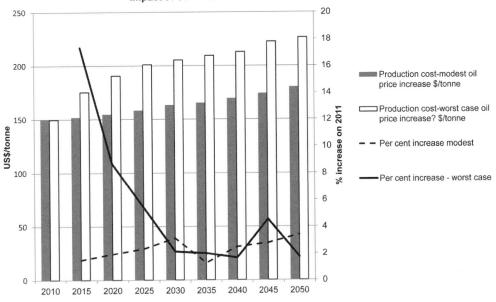

Figure 8.3 Impact of rising energy prices on the cost of wheat production.
Source of Data: R. Sands et al., Impacts of Higher Energy Prices on Agriculture and Rural Economies *(Washington, DC: USDA Economic Research Services, 2011).*

methods—particularly the extension of minimum tillage systems—will lead to further reductions in energy requirement.[13] Without such innovation substantially higher food prices are inevitable.

oil quantity and price—future scenarios

It is clear that agricultural and food production are highly vulnerable to adverse developments in the energy sector. What is the outlook for the supply and price of the major energy sources in the period to 2050?

While it has been argued many times over the past decades that the world would reach the point of peak oil, where production would reach a plateau and then decline, this theoretical point in world oil production appears to move forward with each rise in energy prices. Higher prices stimulate fresh exploration and increased production. It also leads to some substitution of one energy resource for another as new resources are discovered. Oil industry analysts disagree on almost all aspects of the future supply-and-demand pattern. What is indisputable is that global demand for crude oil increased an average 1.76 percent a year from the mid-1990s to 2004–2005. Projections for future demand vary widely. One leading source estimates that largely because of global rise in consumption, mainly in emerging Asian economies, total world demand for crude oil will increase by 37 percent by 2030 compared with 2006.[14]

While some analysts have predicted that consumption will exceed supply by the middle of the second decade of the twenty-first century, others are more optimistic. Oil is expected to be the slowest-growing fuel—both in production and consumption terms—over the next twenty years, according to BP's 2011 outlook.[15] Rising supply to meet expected demand growth should come primarily from OPEC, where output is projected to rise by 13 million barrels per day (Mb/d) in the period to 2030. The largest increments of new OPEC supply will come from natural gas liquids (NGLs), as well as conventional crude in Iraq and Saudi Arabia. Non-OPEC supply will continue to rise, albeit modestly. A large increase in biofuels supply, along with smaller increments from Canadian oil sands, deep water Brazil, and the former Soviet Union is expected to offset continued declines in a number of mature producing areas.

Global demand for liquid fuel (oil, biofuels, and other liquids), according to BP estimates, is likely to rise by 16.5 Mb/d, exceeding 102 Mb/d by 2030. Growth comes exclusively from rapidly growing non-OECD economies. Non-OECD Asia accounts for more than three-quarters of the net global increase, rising by nearly 13 Mb/d. Demand from the Middle East, South America, and Central America will also grow significantly. OECD demand is likely to have peaked in 2005, and consumption is expected to decline by just over 4 Mb/d.

A little more than a cursory glance at energy production statistics indicates that the peak of conventional crude oil production—as distinct from other sources of energy—was probably reached around 2009–2010. Latest International Energy Agency figures indicate that production of conventional crude oil is likely to decline steeply during the next two decades. What is important is that the production of other sources of energy, some directly substitutable for oil, is likely to increase. Thus, while the cost of the main motive power source for agriculture is likely to increase due to falling production, the cost of natural gas, the major source of energy for fertilizer production, is unlikely to suffer the same supply limitations.

For the fertilizer supply outlook, the Energy Information Administration says: "Contributing to the strong competitive position of natural gas among other energy sources is a strong growth outlook for reserves and supplies. Significant changes in natural gas supplies and global markets occur with the expansion of liquefied natural gas (LNG) production capacity and as new drilling techniques and other efficiencies make production from many shale basins economical worldwide. The net impact is a significant increase in resource availability, which contributes to lower prices and higher demand for natural gas in the projection."[16] But even with improvements in the supply of natural gas, it is inevitable that it will cost more.

prices

Despite the 2008 economic downturn and the continuing oscillations into the second decade of the twenty-first century, oil and other energy sources have become more expensive. Most analysts agree that they will continue to become more expensive. The reason is we have certainly passed the point of peak oil, if by this is meant availability of oil that is easily accessed. Whatever the level of demand, maintaining oil consumption at current and future levels can only be achieved through more costly resources.

Liquid fuels—mostly petroleum-based—remain the largest source of energy and of primary interest to world agriculture. According to the U.S. Energy Information Administration, the liquids share of world marketed energy consumption is likely to fall from 34 percent in 2008 to 29 percent in 2035, as projected high world oil prices lead many energy users to switch away from liquid fuels when feasible.

The EIA points out that the impacts of world oil prices on energy demand are a considerable source of uncertainty in all projections. Oil prices have been exceptionally volatile in the recent past, reaching a high of $145 a barrel in July 2008 (daily spot price in nominal dollars) and a low of $30 in December 2008, as the global recession substantially dampened demand and thus prices. Improving economic circumstances, especially in the developing economies, strengthened liquid fuel demand, and prices rose in 2009 and 2010. More recently, growing demand and unrest in many oil-supplying nations of the Middle East and North Africa have supported price increases through 2011 and into 2012. Prices rose from an average $62 per barrel in 2009 to $79 per barrel in 2010, and they are expected to have averaged about $100 per barrel in 2011. The EIA, like the International Energy Agency, forecasts that world oil prices will continue increasing, to $108 per barrel in 2020 and $125 per barrel in 2035.

The EIA has three price scenarios:

1. **The Reference case.** World oil prices are $95 per barrel in 2015 (real 2009 dollars), increasing slowly to $125 per barrel in 2035 ($200 per day in nominal terms). The Reference case represents EIA's best judgment regarding exploration and development costs and accessibility of oil resources outside the United States. It also assumes that OPEC producers will choose to maintain their share of the market and will schedule investments in incremental production capacity so that OPEC's conventional oil production represents about 42 percent of the world's total liquids production. To retain that share, OPEC would have to increase production by 11.3 million barrels per day from 2008 to 2035, or 43 percent of the projected total increase in world liquids supply. Non-OPEC conventional supplies—including production from high-cost projects and from countries with unattractive fiscal or political regimes—account for an increase of 7.1 million barrels per day over the projection, and non-OPEC production of unconventional liquid fuels provides the remaining 8.2 million barrels per day of the increase.

2. **The High Oil Price case.** World oil prices are about $200 per barrel in 2035 ($320 per barrel in nominal terms), with the higher prices resulting from the combination of an outward shift (greater demand at every price level) in the demand schedule for liquid fuels in the non-OECD nations and a downward shift (reduced supply at every price level) in the supply schedule. The shift in the demand schedule is driven by higher economic growth relative to the Reference case in the non-OECD region, with non-OECD growth rates raised by 1.0 percentage point relative to the Reference case in each projection year, starting with 2015. The downward shift in the supply schedule is a result of the assumption that several non-OPEC producers further restrict access to, or increase taxes on, production from prospective areas, and that the OPEC member countries reduce their production substantially below current levels. High oil prices encourage the expansion of unconventional production relative to the Reference case.

3. **The Low Oil Price case.** The available supply is higher at all price levels. The low prices result from the combination of a shift to lower demand at every price level in the demand schedule and a shift to increased supply at every price level in the supply schedule. The shift in demand is driven by lower economic growth in the non-OECD region relative to the Reference case, with non-OECD growth rates lowered by 1.5 percentage points relative to the Reference case

in each projection year starting with 2015. The upward shift in the supply schedule in this case results from greater access and more attractive fiscal regimes in prospective non-OECD areas, as well as higher levels of production from OPEC members. But the lower prices make it uneconomical to expand production of unconventional resources. The OPEC countries increase their conventional oil production to obtain a 52 percent share of total world liquid fuel production, and oil resources are more accessible and/or less costly to produce (as a result of technology advances, more attractive fiscal regimes, or both) than in the Reference case. With these assumptions, conventional oil production is higher in the traditional Low Oil Price case than in the Reference case, but low prices constrain the expansion of unconventional resources. Oil consumption is higher solely as a result of the lower prices (which are the same as in the Low Oil Price case), reflecting a movement downward and to the right along the demand curve.

summary and conclusion

The world's food system is heavily dependent on oil. If the price of the agriculture industry's primary energy sources, fuel oil and natural gas, rise, the price of food will also rise. It is almost certain that the price of these energy sources will rise, but so too will their production. Oil is the predominant energy source in food production, while natural gas is of major importance in fertilizer production. Fortunately, modern agriculture is becoming more energy efficient: New agricultural techniques have cut fuel usage by nearly 50 percent in the last half century. However, rising energy prices threaten food production in some areas. On a more optimistic note, the supply of natural gas is likely to increase with new exploitation and there is an increasing world surplus of nitrogen fertilizer.

Provided that prices for agricultural commodities also rise, the trend in energy costs will not restrict the necessary increase in world food production. The outlook for the heavily energy dependent fertilizer supply is less clear. Production is rising to a state of incipient surplus, but world demand will increase as agricultural production in China and other Asian countries expands. Much depends on the post-crisis world economy; increased growth in the emerging economies will increase the demand for agricultural commodities and therefore for oil and other energy resources. This combination of circumstances suggests that fertilizer prices will tend to stabilize in the medium term but increase more in line with rising energy prices in the longer run.

The most important conclusion for the energy production and prices outlook comes from a recent International Monetary Fund report: "After decades of substantial spare capacity, demand largely caught up with capacity early on in the current oil price cycle. However, the supply response to robust demand growth and high prices has been sluggish, and there is now widespread consensus that the production and distribution capacity will be slow to build up reflecting soaring investment costs, technological, geological, and policy constraints. High oil prices along the entire futures price curve now partly reflect expectations that only sustained high prices will induce the investment required to satisfy demand going forward."[17]

notes

1. D. Yergin, *The Quest—Energy Security and the Remaking of the Modern World*, rev. ed. (London: Penguin Books, 2012).

2. Patrick Canning, Ainsley Charles, Sonya Huang, Karen R. Polenske, and Arnold Waters, *Report: Energy Use in the U.S. Food System*, ERR-94 (Washington, DC: USDA Economic Research Service, 2010).

3. Lester R. Brown, *Plan B 2.0: Rescuing a Planet under Stress and a Civilization in Trouble* (New York: W. W. Norton, 2006).

4. Jeremy Woods et al., "Energy and the Food System." *Philosophical Transactions of the Royal Society,* 365B (2010): 2991–3006.

5. Ibid.

6. Canning et al., *Report: Energy Use in the U.S. Food System*.

7. Ibid.

8. Patrick Heffer and Michel Prud'homme, *Fertilizer Outlook 2011—2015* (Paris: International Fertilizer Industry Association [IFA], May 2011).

9. USDA Economic Research Service, *Impacts of Higher Energy Prices on Agriculture and Rural Economies,* Economic Research Report No. 123 (Washington, DC: USDA Economic Research Service, 2011).

10. Ibid.

11. U.S. Energy Information Administration, *International Energy Outlook 2011* (Washington, DC: EIA, 2011).

12. British Petroleum (BP), *Energy Outlook 2030* (London, January 2011).

13. Woods et al., "Energy and the Food System."

14. U.S. Energy Information Administration, *2007 International Energy Outlook* (Washington, DC: EIA, May 2007).

15. British Petroleum (BP), *Statistical Review of World Energy* (London, June 2011). Available at: www/bp.com/statistical review, accessed November 2011.

16. U.S. Energy Information Administration, *Annual Energy Outlook 2012* (Washington, DC: EIA, 2012).

17. International Monetary Fund, *Food and Fuel Prices—Recent Developments, Macroeconomic Impact, and Policy Responses* (Washington, DC: IMF, 2008).

chapter 9

climate change and world food supply

Any assessment of the world's future supply of food has to take account of the impact of rapidly rising levels of carbon dioxide and other greenhouse gases (GHGs) in the atmosphere, their role in raising global average temperatures, and their effect on agricultural production. The main expected (even already apparent) effects resulting from increased carbon dioxide and ozone levels are seasonal changes in rainfall and temperature, as well as modified pest, weed, and disease populations. The main longer term manifestations of this change in agro-climatic conditions are likely to be alterations of the length of growing seasons, and the necessary change in timing of planting and harvesting. Climate change is also likely to affect water availability and water usage rates.

main points

- Climate change will not seriously affect agriculture globally until after 2050—but will affect the most-vulnerable regions sooner.
- Warming will tend to increase agricultural production in the Northern Hemisphere and reduce it in the Southern Hemisphere.
- Food export capacity of Northern Hemisphere developed countries could rise, while food deficit in the south will increase.
- Carbon fertilization resulting from temperature rise will moderate negative effects of warming on agricultural production.
- Almost all of the world's 1 billion food-insecure people will be negatively affected by climate change.

likely timescale of global warming

In its 2007 assessment report, the Intergovernmental Panel on Climate Change (IPCC) reported: "Projected warming in the 21st century shows scenario-independent geographical patterns similar to those observed over the past several decades. Warming is expected to be greatest over land and at most high northern latitudes, and least over the Southern Ocean and parts of the North Atlantic Ocean. Eleven of the last twelve years (1995–2006) rank among the 12 warmest years in the instrumental record of global surface temperature (since 1850)."[1]

The *Stern Review on the Economics of Climate Change* stated in October 2006 that "on current trends, average global temperatures could rise by 2–3percent within the next fifty years."[2] This could particularly harm agricultural yields in Africa. Reduced water availability could also threaten productive capacity in some regions. On the other hand, agricultural productivity in other areas could benefit from increased levels of carbon dioxide in the atmosphere (carbon fertilization) and modest increases in temperature (1 degree C). On balance, higher temperatures could reduce global cereal production by 5 percent, with a production shift from developing to developed countries. Higher prices are likely to boost supply, but they also affect the purchasing power, and hence nutritional intake, of people in poorer countries.[3]

The term "global warming" is commonly used to refer to surface air temperature changes that are believed to be a response to increasing atmospheric greenhouse gas concentrations. But the warming is not expected to be uniform over the globe, nor is it expected to be the same during all seasons of the year. Computer model simulations conducted at the National Oceanic and Atmospheric Administration (NOAA) Geophysical Fluid Dynamics Laboratory (GFDL) and elsewhere project that GHG-induced warming will be more rapid over landmasses than over oceans.[4] The greatest warming is expected during the winter over northern North America and north-central Asia. Warming over oceans tends to lag warming over large landmasses in part due to water's high heat capacity and its ability to mix heat vertically.

major impact of global warming likely to be serious after 2050

What is clear from most of the evidence and computer modeling is that apart from serious—too often disastrous—disconnected climatic events in sub-Saharan Africa and south Asia, the effect of global warming on agriculture does not become serious until the second half of the twenty-first century. Food production in some of the most vulnerable regions could be affected much sooner. The International Food Policy Research Institute (IFPRI) says in its 2010 study *Food Security, Farming, and Climate Change to 2050*, "Our analysis suggests that to 2050, the challenges from climate change are 'manageable,' in the sense that possible investments in land and water productivity enhancements may partly, or even substantially, mitigate the negative effects from climate change. But the challenges of dealing with the effects between 2050 and 2080 are likely to be much greater, and possibly unmanageable. Starting the process of slowing emissions growth today is critical to avoiding a calamitous post-2050 future."[5]

The International Food Policy and Research Institute (IFPRI) synthesis confirms that the climate change threat will become much more severe after 2050. It points out that in 2050, the increases in mean surface air temperature relative to the late twentieth century across all scenarios are relatively modest, of the order of 1 degree C, but diverge dramatically in the following decades, with figures for increase ranging from 2 degrees C to 4 degrees C by 2100. Temperature increases over land are likely to be higher than these averages, because they include ocean areas. Yields of many more crops will be more severely threatened in the 2010 to 2050 period.

Climate change is generally expected to have an increasingly insidious and significant effect on farm productivity from the present time onward. Rising temperatures, changes in the pattern of rainfall, and more extreme weather events, such as severe thunderstorms or hurricanes, could affect crop production in a number of ways, and there are many additional and countervailing effects. The actual impact of these phenomena will depend on adaptations by humans and natural systems, the physical and chemical composition of soils, and may other variables—some not even yet identified. One generalization can be made: The various climate models indicate that if warming is modest— no more than a few degrees—climate change will produce higher crop yields in northern latitude areas because of longer growing seasons and the availability of additional carbon dioxide to enhance photosynthesis.[6]

In the United States—responsible for 25 and 30 percent of respectively of current world wheat and maize exports—climate change could mean 15–20 percent higher yields for commercial crops like wheat, rice, barley, oats, potatoes, and most vegetables. This assumes a doubling of atmospheric carbon dioxide and sufficient nutrients and water. These calculations do not take into account the possible negative side effects of climate change, including increases in pests and diseases, increased soil erosion due to heavier rainfall, and rising levels of ozone (smog).[7]

serious impact on tropical agriculture

Most threatening to future global food security, tropical and subtropical areas could face a general reduction in crop yields. In Africa, according to IFPRI, climate change could worsen an already bleak food outlook, given the continent's heavy reliance on rain-fed agriculture, its vulnerability to frequent droughts and floods, and the fact that many African crops are already near their maximum temperature tolerance. A lack of economic resources and technology also limits Africa's capacity to adapt to climate change through the use of better weather forecasting, new crop varieties, and improved water supply and drainage systems.

Climatic change will also influence important plant physiological functions including evapotranspiration, photosynthesis, and biomass production. It could also be expected to change the pattern of agricultural land suitability. In general, research indicates that the overall effect of a rise in global temperature will tend to reduce global crop and animal production, although there will be considerable regional variation. In some areas a rise in the average temperature will foster increased output. Unfortunately, those areas of the world that can least afford it will suffer most from the expected reduction.

Many studies have been carried out about the possible effect of climate change on crop production, and there are considerable variations in the results. A recent analysis and synthesis of these studies[8] demonstrates the probable impact of temperature and carbon fertilization on changes in global cereal yields. There is likely to be a wide range of variability in yield. This assessment indicates that in mid- to high latitudes, increases in temperature could be expected to produce increases in yields, but with diminishing effect when temperature changes are greater than 3 degrees.

The most yield depressing effects, too often making an already bad situation worse, are likely to be seen in tropical and subtropical regions for all crops, reflecting the lower growing temperature threshold capacity in these areas. Assessment of the carbon fertilization effect suggests that a 16 percent decline in global agricultural production capacity can be expected if carbon fertilization is not considered, compared with a 3 percent reduction if it is taken into consideration.

Unfortunately, these studies suggest that agricultural productivity in developing countries is likely to decline by 9–21 percent due to global warming. Meanwhile, agricultural productivity in industrialized countries is estimated to decline by up to 6 percent or increasing by up to 8 percent, depending on whether or not the carbon fertilization effect is included in the calculation.

To assess the likely impact on food production over the next four decades, it is important to define what level of global warming can be expected and over what time period.

scenarios differ on timing and scale

Most climate change scenarios project that greenhouse gas concentrations will increase through 2100 with a continued increase in average global temperatures. How much and how quickly the Earth's temperature will increase remains unknown, given the uncertainty of future greenhouse gas emissions and the Earth's response to changing conditions. In addition, natural influences, such as changes in the sun and volcanic activity, will also influence future temperature fluctuations. The extent of such impacts is unknown because the timing and intensity of natural influences cannot be predicted.

More sophisticated model simulations, combined with more data on observed changes in climate, have led to increased confidence in projections of future temperature changes. In its 2007 assessment, the Intergovernmental Panel on Climate Change (IPCC) for the first time was able to provide good estimates and likely ranges for global average warming under each of its emissions scenarios.

Inevitably, due to uncertainties about the future level of anthropogenic (i.e., human-induced) greenhouse gas (AGHG) emissions and consequent concentrations of greenhouse gases, the net atmospheric warming effect and the reaction of the climate system, estimates of future temperature change are uncertain. Bearing in mind these reservations, the IPCC has made the following projections of future warming:[9]

- The average surface temperature of the Earth is likely to increase by 1.1–6.4 degrees C by the end of the twenty-first century, compared with the 1980–1990 period. Its best estimate is an increase in the range of 1.8–4.0 degrees C. In simple terms, its calculations indicate that the average rate of warming over each inhabited continent is very likely to be at least twice as large as that experienced during the twentieth century.
- Warming will not be evenly distributed around the globe. Land areas will warm more than oceans because of water's ability to store heat.

- High latitudes will warm more than low latitudes, in part because of positive feedback effects from melting ice.
- Temperatures in most of North America, all of Africa, Europe, northern and central Asia; and most of Central America and South America are likely to rise more than the global average. Projections suggest that the warming will be close to the global average in south Asia, Australia, New Zealand, and southern South America.
- The warming will differ by season, with winters warming more than summers in most areas.

According to several recent studies, even if the composition of today's atmosphere was fixed, which it certainly is not and never has been, surface air temperatures would continue to warm (by up to 0.9 degree C). The IPCC's studies suggest that some of the warming arising from past human activity has not yet been realized due to heat being stored in the oceans. It reasons that the earth will therefore continue to warm whatever changes eventuate. At the same time, greenhouse gases that have already been emitted remain in the atmosphere for decades or longer, and will continue to contribute to warming.[10]

So far, only one economic model has been used to predict impacts on food security, under differing crop impact models. FAO researchers Josef Schmidhuber and Francesco N. Tubiello have concluded that an additional 5 to 170 million people will suffer from malnutrition as a result of global warming, depending on which production impact scenario is used.[11] Africa will inevitably be the region with the highest population most vulnerable to increased food shortages, accounting for up to 75 percent of the world total by 2080.

Other researchers maintain that population increase is likely to have a much greater effect than climate change on the scale of malnutrition. Martin Parry, one of the most experienced agro-climatologists, and his colleagues began examining the impact of climate change on world agriculture in the 1980s.[12] Their subsequent work has consistently shown that regional variation in the number of food-insecure people is better explained by population changes than climate impacts on food availability.[13]

According to Parry, the main effects on agriculture will be warmer conditions in northern Europe and drier conditions in the south, with intensification of rainfall and increased frequency of extremely hot days or seasons. In agricultural terms, this would benefit northern farming while disadvantaging southern agriculture, but there will be costs in both north and south. There could be more water shortage and heat stress in the south and more flooding in the center, north, and in mountainous areas. Current environmental problems such as desertification in the south and soil leaching in the north may be aggravated. Overall there is, according to Parry's analysis, "likely to be a south-to-north geographical shift of climate resources in Europe, increasing the difference in resource endowment between north and south of Europe." Economic and other development policies remain paramount in influencing food supply and future human well-being. What is clear is that 95 percent of the models predict that climate change will to some extent depress yields for vital food crops in vulnerable regions: wheat in South Asia, rice in Southeast Asia, and maize in sub-Saharan Africa.

warming will change cropping patterns

It can be concluded that, on the assessment of the most comprehensive calculations, climate change is a likely probability and will significantly affect the world's crop distribution, pushing the margins of crop production further north and allowing crops more tolerant of high temperature to be produced in the south. The major problem will be in water availability and biodiversity. The future pattern of water demand will depend on the profitability of crop production, more efficient use of irrigation techniques, the cost and returns from building reservoir storage, and policy measures aimed at controlling water use. An increased research effort will be needed to develop drought-tolerant strains of crop plants.

In summary, the likely effects on crop production fall under four main categories:

- Seasonal changes in rainfall and temperature, altering growing seasons, planting and harvesting timing, water availability, and pest, weed, and disease population levels.
- Alteration of evapotranspiration, photosynthesis, and biomass production.
- Alteration of land suitability.
- Increased carbon dioxide levels leading to a positive growth response.

The main conclusions to be drawn from the many computer-model predictions are:

- Important risk disparities exist between developed and developing countries.
- For temperature increases of only 1–2 degrees C, developing countries without adaptation will likely face a depression in major crop yields.
- In mid- to high latitudes, increases in temperature of 1–3 degrees C can improve yields slightly, with negative yield effects if temperatures increase beyond this range,
- Stronger yield-depressing effects will occur in tropical and subtropical regions for all crops, which reflect a lower growing temperature threshold capacity in these areas.
- Cereal imports will increase in developing countries by as wide a range as 10 to 40 percent by 2080.
- Africa will become the region with the highest population of food-insecure people, accounting for up to 75 percent of the world total by 2080.

The International Assessment of Agricultural Knowledge, Science, and Technology for Development (IAASTD), a multi-institutional project established to assess the impacts of past, present, and future agricultural knowledge, science, and technology on world food supply, has devoted a considerable proportion of its efforts to assessing the likely impact of climate change on agriculture. In a recent report the IAASTD said climate change "is taking place at a time of increasing demand for food, feed, fibre and fuel, which has the potential to irreversibly damage the natural resource base on which agriculture depends."[14] It stresses that the relationship between climate change and agriculture is a two-way street, in which agriculture contributes to climate change in several major ways as well as experiencing the effects of climate change.

regional impacts of climate change

Europe

The major likely impacts on the European climate have been identified by Professor Parry:[15]

- Annual temperatures will increase at the rate of 0.1 to 0.4 degree C each decade.
- Hot summers will double in frequency by 2020 (but increase five times in southern Spain); hot summers will be ten times as frequent by 2080.
- Summers will become drier in southern Europe.
- Winters will become wetter in northern Europe and intensity of rainfall increases.
- Additional risks are possibility of change in the Gulf Stream; at present little known about this.

The major implications for agriculture in Europe are:

- Warmer in the north; drier in the south; intensification of rainfall; increased frequency of extremely hot days or seasons.
- More benefits to the north; more "disbenefits" to the south;
- Worsening of current resource issues, such as more water shortages and heat stress in the south and more flooding in the center, north, and mountains.
- Aggravated current environmental problems (e.g., desertification in the south, soil leaching in the north).

Taken together, these imply a south-to-north geographical shift of climate resources in Europe, increasing the difference in resource endowment between the north and south of Europe.

The consensus of most of the climate change models is that warming is the most likely probability. This being so, there will be important implications for crop distribution in Europe, pushing the margins of crop production further north and allowing more high temperature–tolerant crops to be produced in the south. In both north and south there are likely to be problems with water availability and, possibly, the maintenance of biodiversity.

One of the most important aspects of climate change is its effect on water availability. In the north the main effect may be too much water at certain seasons, with increased risk of flooding, and water shortages in the south. There is also likely to be increased flood risk in mountainous areas. For example, it is estimated that there would be a 20 percent increase of flood risk in the Alps.

Globally, the expected pattern of climate change could be beneficial to European agriculture. Seen from the point of view of the worldwide impact of climate change, Europe is likely to face fewer negative effects than most other regions. This suggests that there may be an opportunity to increase Europe's share of world food production and, from the global viewpoint, it may be necessary to increase food production in Europe in order to maintain world food security.

The change in Europe's climate as a result of an expected rise in global temperature over the next seventy plus years is expected to provide advantage to some of Europe's farmers, have a significant damaging effect on others, while increasing the variability of the factors governing crop and livestock production for everybody.

A report by UK consultants AEA Energy and Environment and Madrid's Polytechnic University assessed likely climatic change in the period to 2080 and analyzed its likely impact on Europe's main farming regions.[16] They agreed with the Parry conclusion that temperatures will rise across Europe, especially during winter, and that rainfall will increase, but with increased interseasonal variability and evapotranspiration. Summer rainfall is likely to decrease over much of Europe, with periods of intense rainfall becoming more common and less winter precipitation falling as snow. Extreme weather events are more likely to occur, bringing more flooding, higher winds, destructive precipitation events, and longer periods of drought. Sea levels are predicted to rise by as much as 5 meters with greater incidence of salination of water resources and soils in coastal areas.

The report also indicates that the harmful effects of climate change will affect the extreme north and the extreme south of the European continent, while the greatest benefit will be felt in the central west to east belt of the main farming areas. But all areas will suffer the problems of greater variability of seasonal weather patterns.

It should be kept in mind that certain regions of some countries will move from a least favored to a more favored climatic region due to the changes over the projected period. For example, southern Norway, parts of south-central Sweden and southwestern Finland will, by 2080, no longer be classified as part of the boreal agro-climatic region but will likely be experiencing weather patterns currently found in the central Atlantic zone.

In summary, the main threats and challenges for Europe from climate change in the period to 2080 are likely to arise from:

- changes in water resources and irrigation requirements
- agricultural pests and diseases
- soil fertility, salinity, and erosion
- crop growth conditions, crop productivity, and in crop distribution
- optimal conditions for livestock production
- land use
- increased expenditures on emergency and remedial actions

What is likely to be the response to these changes? The AEA report suggests that farmers are likely to adjust automatically and adapt their husbandry methods as they become aware of the changing climate: "Changes at the level of an individual farmer, relating to tillage practice, cultivar variety, planting date and the use of external inputs have been widely studied and demonstrate that adaptation to climate impacts can occur autonomously to some degree with little or no external support."

At the individual farm level, climate change may on balance be beneficial, particularly in the most favored regions. "While climate change is often perceived as having negative consequences, there may be regions where increased average temperatures have the potential to increase the yield of current crops, the area over which those crops may be grown, or allow the cultivation of new crops. All of which could increase farm incomes. Hence, in some parts of the EU, farmers may benefit if they have access to capital or knowledge that will enable them to adapt their farming practices to take advantages of these potential opportunities."[17]

Impact on food-insecure developing countries

Significant changes in seasonal weather patterns are likely to have their most serious effects in tropical areas where the agricultural production system is already seriously under stress. Broadly speaking, higher temperatures and reduced rainfall—or at the other extreme increases in excessive seasonal rainfall—will exacerbate existing obstacles to increased agricultural production and development of improved husbandry systems.

Researchers at the CGIAR Research Programme on Climate Change, Agriculture and Food Security (CCAFS) have identified what they believe are the most food supply–vulnerable areas of developing countries.[18] Their latest work has matched future areas of significant climate change with regions already suffering chronic food shortages. The aim is to identify highly vulnerable countries, where the prospect of more restricted growing seasons could affect many millions of people. The CCAFS researchers identified populations as chronically food insecure if more than 40 percent of children under the age of five were stunted, falling well below the World Health Organization's height-for-age standards.

The researchers highlighted areas of potential vulnerability by examining a variety of climate models and indicators of food shortages to create a series of detailed maps. By overlaying the maps, the team was able to pinpoint which parts of the tropics would be most affected. The study shows regions around the world at risk of crossing certain climate thresholds, such as temperatures too hot for maize or beans that over the next forty years could lower food production. Regions that may be sensitive to such climate shifts due to having large areas of land devoted to crop and livestock production were also identified.

The report states: "These are areas highly exposed to climate shifts, where survival is strongly linked to the fate of regional crop and livestock yields, and where chronic food problems indicate that farmers are already struggling and they lack the capacity to adapt to new weather patterns."

Use of IPCC data shows that the length of growing period declines by 5 percent or more across a broad area of the global tropics, including heavily cropped areas of Mexico, Brazil, southern and west Africa, the Indo-Gangetic Plains, and Southeast Asia. This indicates that most of the tropics will experience a change in growing conditions that will require rethinking current agricultural systems in order to compensate for climate change. High temperature stress (above 30 degrees C) will be widespread in east and southern Africa, north and south India, Southeast Asia, northern Latin America, and Central America.

As a consequence, the length of the growing period is estimated to shrink to fewer than 120 days in a number of tropical regions, notably in Mexico, northeast Brazil, southern and west Africa, and India. The CCAFS warns that this is a critical threshold for certain crops and rangeland vegetation.

The CCAFS report concludes that in large parts of south Asia, including almost all of India, and parts of sub-Saharan Africa, chiefly west Africa, there are 369 million food-insecure people living in agriculture-intensive areas that are highly exposed to a potential 5 percent decrease in the length of the growing period. Higher temperatures could also take a heavy toll. At present, there are 56 million food-insecure and crop-dependent people in parts of west Africa, India, and China who live in areas where, by the mid-2050s, maximum daily temperatures during the growing season could exceed 30 degrees C. This is close to the maximum temperature that beans can tolerate, while maize and rice yields may suffer when temperatures exceed this level. For example, a 2011 study in the journal *Nature* found that even with optimal amounts of rain, African maize yields could decline by 1 percent for each day of the growing season that is above 30 degrees C.[19]

There are clear signs that farmers are already adapting to variable weather patterns by changing their planting schedules or moving animals to different grazing areas. The CCAFS study suggests that the speed of climate changes and the magnitude of the changes required to adapt could be much greater. In some places, farmers might need to consider entirely new crops or new farming systems. For some regions, however, this still might not meet the problem. In parts of east and southern Africa, for example, temperatures may become too hot to maintain maize as the staple crop, requiring a shift to other food crops, such as sorghum or cassava, to meet nutrition needs.

In addition, farmers who now focus mainly on crop cultivation might need to integrate livestock and forestry as a way to maintain and increase food production. For example, the Republic of Congo will plant 1 million hectares of trees by 2020 to restore degraded forest and provide wood for paper and fuel. Researchers have also identified regions of potential concern extending way beyond those considered most at risk. They found, for example, that by 2050, prime growing conditions are likely to drop below 120 days per season in intensively farmed regions of northeast Brazil and Mexico.

Growing seasons of at least four months are considered critical not only for the maturing of maize and several other staple food crops, but also for vegetation crucial to feeding livestock. In addition, parts of Latin America are likely to experience temperatures too hot for bean production, a major food staple in the region. With many areas in Africa predicted to become drier, countries such as South Africa that predominately farm maize may have the option to shift to more drought-resistant crops. But for countries such as Niger in western Africa, which already supports itself on drought-resistant crop varieties like sorghum and millet, there is little maneuvering room.

Impact on sub-Saharan Africa

The IPCC expects the following impacts of climate change to be seen in Africa:

- Decreased grain yields
- Decreased average runoff and water availability on major rivers

- Exacerbated desertification
- An increase in droughts, floods, and other extreme events
- Significant extinction of plant and animal species
- Coastal erosion and inundation caused by rises in sea levels

---

IIPC MOST "AT-RISK" COUNTRIES OF SUB-SAHARAN AFRICA

Central Africa: Angola, Cameroon, Central African Republic, Chad, Congo, Democratic Republic of Congo, Equatorial Guinea, Gabon

West Africa: Benin, Burkina Faso, Gambia, Ghana, Guinea, Guinea Bissau, Ivory Coast, Liberia, Mali, Mauritania, Niger, Nigeria, Senegal, Sierra Leone, Togo

East Africa: Burundi, Djibouti, Eritrea, Ethiopia, Kenya, Madagascar, Malawi, Mozambique, Rwanda, Somalia, Tanzania, Uganda, Zambia, Zimbabwe

---

Some critics, such as the World Bank,[20] argue that climate change and its links to human activity are subject to wide margins of error and that economist Nicholas Stern and other analysts have taken the most extreme scenarios and low discount rates to estimate high costs in the future and to increase the present value of very long-term benefits. Although the direct link between the increase in disasters and climate change is still debated, the links between climate change and certain categories of disasters, particularly hydrometeorological events, are being more closely scrutinized. Even if it is accepted that the links between climate change and economic activity are subject to wide margins of error, it can be observed that some of the changes can be seen in the increased intensity and number of disasters, particularly in sub-Saharan Africa.

If Stern's projections, which incorporate the impact of more severe climate change, are correct, the World Bank's analysts deduce that the possibility of a sharp drop in income and consumption must be expected in sub-Saharan Africa.[21] On these assumptions, increased poverty, malnutrition, and even mass famines, as well as serious disruption to development can be expected. Whatever estimates are used, sub-Saharan Africa is likely to be one of the most adversely affected regions in the world. The World Bank warns: "The continent is highly exposed to climate change, and its structural weaknesses result in lower resilience."

With 40 percent of its population living on arid, semi-arid, or dry subhumid areas, Africa is one of the areas of the world most exposed to global warming.[22] It has experienced a warming of approximately 0.7 degree C during the past century, and the temperature is expected to increase by between 0.2 degree C and 0.5 degree C in each future decade. The situation is already bad; in the 25 years up to 2000, the decline in rainfall observed in the Sahel was the most substantial and sustained recorded anywhere in the world since instrumental measurement began.

It should be noted that a large proportion of the population of sub-Saharan Africa lives in coastal areas; one-quarter of the population lives within 100 kilometers of a seacoast. The combination of increased climate variability and rising sea levels means that this population will be increasingly vulnerable. The forecasted rise in sea levels could increase the number of people in Africa at risk from flooding from 1 million in 1990 to 70 million by 2080 (this assumes that the global sea level will rise by the predicted 38-centimeters during this period).

Africa's ability to deal with climate change

In addition to being the area of the world most liable to harmful climatic developments, most of the regions of sub-Saharan Africa face structural difficulties that threaten to exacerbate the effects of climate change and hamper effective countermeasures. Most obviously, more than half of the African population lives in rural areas and is therefore highly vulnerable to natural hazards and is heavily dependent on local food production. The reality is that food production has been declining in key parts of Africa for the past two decades, contrary to the global trend. Continuing high population growth will put more strain on limited land resources. Most countries of sub-Saharan Africa are also highly vulnerable to economic and political disruption (for example, terms of trade variability or aid volatility).

For all of these reasons, sub-Saharan African nations are the most at risk, according to an FAO Interdepartmental Working Group on Climate Change.[23] The working group found that in Africa, 1.1 billion hectares of land have a viable crop growing period of fewer than 120 days per year. By 2080, the team estimates, climate change could extend this area at risk by 5–8 percent, or between 50 and 90 million hectares. The report states: "In some 40 poor, developing countries, with a combined population of two billion, including 450 million undernourished people, production losses due to climate change may drastically increase the number of undernourished people, severely hindering progress in combating poverty and food insecurity."

Projections by Cranfield University for the UK's Department for International Development indicate that implications for crop growth resulting from global warming could show contrasting results in east Africa.[24] While east African maize will benefit from climate change in west and central Kenya (+30 percent productivity) by the 2020s, in southern and eastern Kenya maize yield is forecast to be reduced by 2 percent and 12 percent, respectively. Productivity of rice could increase by as much as 11 percent, with reduced yields for sugarcane, wheat, and cassava of around 10 percent. Maize growth could be favored by climate change, but Kenyan maize productivity is likely to fall in the southern regions. Wheat output could be cut by amounts of as much as 60 percent in the 2050s, but maize could increase from 1 to 9 percent in the eastern region. Maize productivity is forecast to increase in the central (+100 percent) and western (+20 percent) areas of the country, while it may decrease by around 40 percent in the southern and eastern areas.

The Cranfield forecasts for central Africa suggest that in Cameroon by the 2020s climate change could have beneficial effects on maize (up to 25 percent), but negative effects for sorghum (–7 percent). The predictions for the central African region by the 2030s indicate yield reductions for sorghum, wheat, cassava, yams, and maize, with millet suffering the worst productivity reduction (as much as 21 percent). Productivity of wheat is forecast to fall by 80 percent in western Africa in the 2050s, with average maize productivity remaining stable. The productivity of maize in Cameroon, Central African

Republic, Chad, Democratic Republic of Congo, Congo, Gabon, and Tanzania is expected to be reduced by between 10 and 20 percent. Figures for impact on crops in Cameroon are negative for sorghum (–40 percent) and for maize (about –15percent) by the 2080s. In the case of a temperature increase of 2 degrees C and a precipitation reduction of 20 percent, maize productivity could fall by 11–14 percent.

In the west African region rice is likely to be the crop most affected (–8 percent) by climate change because of its importance in the area. Wheat productivity is expected to decrease by 9 percent in western Africa in the 2080s, while maize productivity will have a smaller response to climate change, with productivity reduced by 1 to 7 percent. In contrast, the productivity of maize is forecast to increase slightly (by 1.6 percent) in Ivory Coast and decrease in Liberia and Mauritania (–1.5 percent). Reductions of 15–30 percent are expected in Benin and Burkina. Predictions for the 2020s show a negative effect on cassava in Ghana (–3 percent) and on millet in Niger for several scenarios by up to –26 percent. Small variation is predicted for the 2030s in Faso, Equatorial Guinea, Gambia, Ghana, Guinea, Guinea-Bissau, Liberia, Mali, Mauritania, Niger, Nigeria, Senegal, Sierra Leone, and Togo. Cassava production is forecast to decrease by 13 percent in Ghana, and by the 2080s by about 53percent. Other studies predict a yield decrease in west African sorghum (11–17 percent), millet (6–11 percent), and maize (11–13 percent).

The effects of climate change on southern African crop productivity by the 2030s are forecast to be negative except for rice (+8 percent). The most-negatively hit crops will be maize (–35 percent) and wheat (–22 percent). South African maize could be reduced by 8 percent. Probably most serious, given the importance of these crops in the food supply pattern, maize and wheat productivity could be halved. Maize yield is expected to be reduced by 10–35 percent in Angola, Botswana, Madagascar, Malawi, Mozambique, Namibia, South Africa, Zambia, and Zimbabwe, and increased by 26 percent in Lesotho. Sorghum in Botswana is forecasted to decrease by 10 percent and 36 percent in the Hard Veldt and the Sand Veldt regions, respectively. In Swaziland sugarcane productivity is expected to increase by 15 percent if crop water requirements are satisfied.

In contrast to sub-Saharan Africa, north Africa is likely to largely benefit from global warming, although some important crops could be negatively affected, but not to the extent as regions to the south of the Sahara. The Cranfield study indicates that by the 2030s an increase of 50–56 percent in average maize productivity is likely. Average maize productivity by the 2050s is expected to have risen even further—by about 50 percent. Wheat yields on the other hand are predicted to fall by 10–14 percent. In Sudan, maize productivity could fall by 17 percent. Variation forecast for the Mediterranean coastal countries—Algeria, Tunisia, Libya, and Egypt—is predicted to decrease by 5–10 percent for 2031–2060 while in Morocco, there could be a positive impact (+70 percent) for the 2050s, or a reduction of 10 percent. Climate change effects on wheat productivity in the 2050s are expected to be positive in Algeria, Tunisia, and Egypt (4–11 percent) and negative in Morocco and Libya (–14 percent). In Tunisia, two positive and negative effects are expected in wheat productivity between 2071 and 2100. In Sahel, a reduction in rice, maize, and wheat (up to 10 percent) is forecast by the 2030s, with a positive response for millet productivity (+8 percent).

Impact on south Asia

South Asia comprises the countries of Afghanistan, Bangladesh, Bhutan, India, Iran, Maldives, Nepal, Pakistan, Sri Lanka, Burma, and Tibet. Agriculture is critical to its development. More than 75 percent of the region's poor live in rural areas and are dependent on rain-fed agriculture, livestock, and fragile forests for their livelihoods.[25] The Green Revolution increased food grain productivity and improved food security and rural wages, bringing a significant reduction in rural poverty, but further innovation is needed to increase food supply in the future; climate change will not make this process any easier. While impoverished sub-Saharan Africa is most at risk in the next 75 years, according to FAO analysts, the potential impact in Asia is varied. India may lose 125 million tonnes of current rain-fed cereal production, an 18 percent cut, while China could benefit from a 15 percent increase in its current potential of 360 million tonnes through climate change alone.

The impact of climate change on rice production in Asia is of particular policy interest, considering that rice is the most important component in millions of Asians' diet. Seventeen south, southeast, and east Asian countries produce 92 percent of the world's total rice supply, of which 90 percent is also consumed in these regions. Rice-growing countries in Asia are located at different latitudes, and the terrain conditions of the rice-growing areas vary as well. As such, climate change impact on rice production of the Asian countries is quite diversified and warrants a detailed assessment at regional level.

What must be described as the most at-risk region of south Asia—Bangladesh, Bhutan, India, Maldives, Nepal, Pakistan, and Sri Lanka—has 23 percent of the world's population, but is able to generate only little more than 2 percent of global income. These countries have 40 percent of the world's poorest people—those existing on less than US$1 a day. The region also has the greatest number of hungry people, with 35 percent of the world's populations calculated to be undernourished. Over 56 percent of the world's low-birth-weight babies are born in South Asia.[26] While the percentage of malnourished people in the South Asian region declined at the beginning of the millennium, to 22 percent from 26 percent in 1990–1992, the number of those suffering from hunger actually increased by more than 8 million people during the same period. Despite the Green Revolution, India still has one-quarter of the world's poor and hungry. While having achieved apparent food security in national terms, agricultural production and rural income growths have slowed and are being overtaken by the population growth rate.

It is therefore clear that this area of the world is the most vulnerable, in terms of the number of people likely to be affected, to any depressing effect of climate change on agricultural production, even more so than sub-Saharan Africa.

The Cranfield University studies on crop yield variation resulting from climate change show that in south Asia there is a general negative trend, especially on maize and sorghum in India. During the 2020s the most affected crop in this region is likely to be maize, especially monsoon maize (–21 percent) and winter maize (–25 percent). Sorghum, sugarcane, and rice are expected to decrease by up to 13 percent in India and rice productivity by 2 percent in Nepal. In Pakistan and Sri Lanka, on the other hand, the rice yield is expected to increase by 7 percent and 1 percent, respectively.

Estimates for the 2030s suggest negative variation (up to 12 percent) for maize, wheat, millet, rice, sugarcane, and sorghum with a range of uncertainties that include the possibility of productivity increasing up to 8 percent (wheat) or 4 percent (millet). In Sri Lanka the effects of climate change appear to be positive on rice productivity (+6.6 percent). Forecasts for the 2050s are negative for maize and wheat in aggregate for the whole region (–40 percent). In India the climate change impacts on sugarcane, rice, sorghum, and maize are negative, having the greatest impact on winter maize (–50 percent). However, in Sri Lanka and Pakistan, the rice productivity might be positively affected, rising by 6 and 7.5 percent, respectively. In the 2080s, the consequences of climate change would be similar to the ones predicted for the 2050s, but more extreme. Indian sorghum and rice crop productivity would be reduced by 32 and 42 percent, respectively, but the worst outlook would be for winter wheat (–60 percent). Rice in Nepal would also be reduced (up to 39 percent), but Pakistan (+7.5 percent) and Sri Lanka (+6 and +28 percent) are expected to benefit from the projected changes.

Some estimates suggest increases of up to 37 percent in wheat productivity in northwest India, depending on the variety, but there can be a reduction of about 40 percent if the CO_2 effect is ignored. Main season rice productivity might be positively affected (+27 percent) while second season is predicted to be reduced (–38 percent). Sorghum is forecast to decline by up to 13 percent under rain-fed and no-stress conditions. In Pakistan, the predictions for wheat are negative (as much as –31 percent and higher when CO_2 fertilization is ignored), but the uncertainty is high, with a potential positive (up to 30 percent) forecast also reported.

Southeast Asia

Southeast Asia includes Cambodia, Laos, Burma (Myanmar), Thailand, Vietnam, Malaysia, Brunei, East Malaysia, East Timor, Indonesia, the Philippines, Christmas Island, and Singapore.

Crop productivity predictions for the 2020s in Southeast Asia are slightly negative for rice in Bangladesh (up to –7 percent) and in Bhutan rice productivity could have some variation around current levels (±2 percent). General forecasts for the region predict a positive effect of global warming on sugarcane (up to +9 percent) and a small negative variation for cassava, wheat, rice, and maize, the last being the worst (–7 percent). The 2050s climate conditions will affect wheat productivity most, on average reducing yield in the region by –32 percent in Bangladesh. Rice production will also be reduced in Bangladesh (–8 percent) but increased in Bhutan.

Forecasted variations for the 2080s give general negative impacts on rice yield in Bangladesh (up to –14 percent) and in Bhutan (up to –12 percent) with some chances of an increase (+2 percent). Other studies predict positive effects on rice productivity in Bangladesh (up to +20 percent) and wheat variability but with a higher chance of it being negative (up to –15 percent) than positive (+5 percent).

summary and conclusions

These assessments of the effect of climate change would suggest that the implications for the most vulnerable areas of the world are both more immediate and the most serious. Without crop growing adjustments and mitigation action, indigenous supplies of the most important food staples will be seriously affected by the late 2030s and will have reached crisis levels by mid-century. Without radical improvements in crop varieties, in husbandry techniques, water conservation, and infrastructure improvement, the food import dependence of these regions will increase substantially.

A rise in the global temperature of an expected 2–3 percent over the next fifty years will harm Africa most seriously. While some analysts expect that climate change will not seriously affect agriculture globally until after 2050, it will affect and is affecting most vulnerable regions sooner. Carbon fertilization resulting from temperature rise will moderate the negative effects of warming on agricultural production, largely in temperate zones. European farmers are likely to gain from warming, but could suffer from increased pest incidence and water shortage. Although global warming will tend to increase agricultural production in the Northern Hemisphere, it is likely to be accompanied by irregular weather events with potentially disastrous effects on crop production. Overall, the food export capacity of Northern Hemisphere developed countries could rise, while food deficits in the south will increase. Africa has the highest population at risk of increased hunger and malnutrition as a result of global warming.

notes

1. S. Solomon, D. Qin, M. Manning, Z. Chen, M. Marquis, K. B. Averyt, M. Tignor, and H. L. Miller (eds.), *Contribution of Working Group I to the Fourth Assessment Report of the Intergovernmental Panel on Climate Change* (Cambridge: Cambridge University Press, 2007).

2. Nicholas Stern, *Stern Review on the Economics of Climate Change* (London: UK Government, 2006).

3. Food Chain Analysis Group, Department of Environment, Food, and Rural Affairs (DEFRA), *Food Security and the UK: An Evidence and Analysis Paper,* (London: UK Government, DEFRA, 2006).

4. National Oceanic and Atmospheric Administration (NOAA) Geophysical Fluid Dynamics Laboratory (GFDL), "Patterns of Greenhouse Warming," *GFDL Climate Modeling Research Highlights* 1, no. 6 (January 2007).

5. Gerald C. Nelson et al., *Food Security, Farming, and Climate Change to 2050: Scenarios, Results, Policy Options* (Washington, DC: IPFRI, 2010).

6. Lisa F. Schipper and Ian Burton, *The Earthscan Reader on Adaptation to Climate Change* (London: Earthscan, 2008).

7. Ibid., iv

8. Easterling, W.E., P.K. Aggarwal, P. Batima, K.M. Brander, L. Erda, S.M. Howden, A. Kirilenko, J. Morton, J.-F. Soussana, J. Schmidhuber and F.N. Tubiello (2007) Food, fibre and forest products. Climate Change 2007: Impacts, Adaptation and Vulnerability. Contribution of Working Group II to the Fourth Assessment Report of the Intergovernmental Panel on Climate Change, M.L. Parry, O.F. Canziani, J.P. Palutikof, P.J. van der Linden and C.E. Hanson, Eds., Cambridge University Press, Cambridge, UK, 273–313.

9. Solomon et al., *Contribution of Working Group I.*

10. J. Hansen et al., "Earth's Energy Imbalance: Confirmation and Implications," *Science* 308, no. 5727 (2005): 1431–1435. doi:10.1126/science.1110252.

11. Josef Schmidhuber and Francesco N. Tubiello, "Crop and Pasture Response to Climate Change," *PNAS: Proceedings of the National Academy of Sciences* 104, no. 50 (2007): 19703–8. doi:10.1073/pnas.0701976104.

12. M. L. Parry, T. R. Carter, and N. T. Konijn, eds., *The Impact of Climatic Variations*, vols. 1 and 2 (Boston: Kluwer Academic, 1988).

13. M. L. Parry, "Impacts of Climate Change on Agriculture in Europe," IPCC Meteorological Office presentation to informal meeting of EU Agriculture and Environment Ministers, London, September 11, 2005.

14. International Assessment of Agricultural Knowledge, Science, and Technology for Development (IAASTD), *Synthesis Report: A Synthesis of the Global and Sub-Global Reports* (Washington, DC: Island Press, 2009).

15. American Economic Association: Energy & Environment and Universidad de Politécnica de Madrid. "Adaptation to Climate Change in the Agricultural Sector," AGRI-2006-G4–05. Report to European Commission Directorate-General for Agriculture and Rural Development (ED05334), no. 1 (December 2007).

16. P. Ericksen, P. Thornton, A. Notenbaert, L. Cramer, P. Jones, and M. Herrero, *Mapping Hotspots of Climate Change and Food Insecurity in the Global Tropics.* CCAFS Report no. 5 (Copenhagen, Denmark: CGIAR Research Program on Climate Change, Agriculture, and Food Security, 2011).

17. World Bank, *Disasters, Climate Change, and Economic Development in Sub-Saharan Africa: Lessons and Future Directions* (Washington, DC: World Bank, 2007).

18. American Economic Association: Energy & Environment and Universidad de Politécnica de Madrid, "Adaptation to Climate Change in the Agricultural Sector."

19. World Bank, *Disasters, Climate Change, and Economic Development in Sub-Saharan Africa.*

20. David B. Lobell, Marianne Bänziger, Cosmos Magorokosho, and Bindiganavile Vivek, "Nonlinear Heat Effects on African Maize as Evidenced by Historical Yield Trials," *Nature Climate Change* 1 (2011): 42–45. doi:10.1038/nclimate1043.

21. Richard Joll, ed., *Human Development Report 1997* (New York: United Nations Development Programme, 1997).

22. FAO, *Climate Change and Food System Resilience in Sub-Saharan Africa* (Rome: FAO, 2011).

23. J. W. Knox, T. M. Hess, A. Daccache, and M. Perez Ortola, *What Are the Projected Impacts of Climate Change on Food Crop Productivity in Africa and S Asia?* Department for International Development Systematic Review Final Report (London: DFID, March 2011).

24. Ibid.

25. R. B. Singh, *Towards a Food Secure India and South Asia: Making Hunger History* (Bangkok: APAARI, 2009). Available at: http://www.apaari.org/wp-content/uploads/2009/08/towards-a-food-secure-india-making-hunger-history.pdf.

26. Ibid.

chapter 10

the world economy and the demand for food

Apart from population growth, the most important influence on the demand for food is the state of the world economy. World economic activity affects the demand for food in at least four ways. In times of increasing economic growth, the aggregate demand for food will increase. At the same time, growth will affect the pattern of demand for food, depending on the regional pattern. In developed countries, growth will stimulate a trend away from staples and toward more luxurious foods; in developing countries, by and large, it will increase the overall demand for food. It will also have the secondary effect of increasing consumption of the higher proteins and fats from meat and dairy products. But whether economic growth increases, stabilizes, or falters, the global demand for food will continue to increase due to other factors. The stage of economic growth and development of a country affects the rate of increase in demand for food.

main points

- Economic growth affects level of demand and change in dietary pattern.
- Price of energy and industrial exports most affects the purchasing ability of the least prosperous countries.
- Depressed demand in developed countries hits the income of less-developed countries.
- BRIC countries are driving development of the world food economy.
- Food price hikes are caused by several interconnected factors.
- Developing countries will provide the main long-term growth in food demand.
- Food price hikes are relatively rare but spectacular when they do occur.

The world economy may be divided into three main regions: the developed world, the least developed world, and, in between, the emerging once-undeveloped economies. In a subgroup of the latter are countries like Russia and Ukraine, recovering from the disruption of dismantling one-time command economies. Nonexistent or sluggish growth in the western economies has the important effect of reducing the demand for the food and other agricultural exports of less-developed countries. It is not without significance that despite the headline hype, food prices actually fell following the 2008 worldwide economic collapse. As some important areas of the developed economy recovered, demand for food rose at a higher rate, and prices also again increased as world agriculture was still responding to the food price hike of 2007–2008.

In addition to the price of food, the global food security situation is also heavily influenced by the prices of fuel and industrial export commodities. Fuel prices remain on a rising trend. In 2008, crude oil prices averaged nearly $100 per barrel (see Chapter 8). High energy prices are likely to amplify the rise in food prices by reducing further the amount of income poor households have to spend on food. In addition, higher transport costs within countries and continents, as well as trans-ocean shipping freight costs, intensify the financial burden on many countries by further increasing import and food distribution costs. Higher energy import bills are also likely to push out imports of necessities such as food and raw materials.

Financial pressures can be reduced, however, by compensating increases in the price of commodities exported by less-developed countries. Data for 2010 shows that this is likely to have been the case for several commodities. While the International Monetary Fund (IMF) food price index increased 11.5 percent between 2009 and 2010, the index increased at a faster rate for beverages, over 14 percent; agricultural raw materials (i.e., timber, cotton, wool, rubber, hides), nearly 34 percent; and metals, 40 percent. This was advantageous for countries such as Ghana, Ivory Coast, Ethiopia, Kenya, and Vietnam, which are major exporters of coffee, tea, and cocoa. Other beneficiaries of the commodities price rises were Mozambique, Tajikistan, and Ghana, which export aluminum, and Zambia, Peru, and Indonesia, major exporters of copper.

IMF estimates indicate that real gross domestic product (GDP) growth in almost all these raw material–exporting countries would have remained firm in 2011, in a range of 5 to 6 percent. Food and fuel price increases, however, would have been likely to stoke domestic inflation. GDP growth in developed country trading partners of the developing countries was estimated by the IMF to have remained modest in 2011, at an average of 2.2 percent. This would have been likely to depress demand from developed countries. China however, would have maintained its very strong 2010 GDP growth of 9.6 percent in 2011 as well.

economic factors that affect the demand for food

Systematic economic influences that affect all commodity markets include macroeconomic risks, such as labor market changes in developed economies, financial market risks, currency risks (including particularly the value of the U.S. dollar and to a lesser extent the euro), inflation in emerging countries (particularly in China), prospects for economic growth, and the income levels of developing countries on the demand side and climatic fluctuations on the supply side. Newer risks, such as uncertainties associated with increasing linkage of food production with the energy market through biofuel development, also have to be taken into account.

It remains to be seen how far the impact of the recession of 2011–2012 will affect LDC development, food prices, and world agricultural production. What is important and significant is that the emerging economies of Asia, most notably China and India, are continuing to grow and their propensity to import major agricultural commodities and second- and third-stage food products from the international market is a major factor in the world food market.

It is clearly essential that the economies and incomes of the developing countries should grow if there is to be any significant reduction of malnutrition. This income growth enables the population of these countries not only to meet their daily calorie needs, but also to diversify their diet to include more proteins. This development can be divided into three main phases.

In the first phase, extremely low-income countries spend nearly all of their income growth on additional food consumption, consisting principally of high-carbohydrate foods—rice, starchy roots such as potatoes or cassava, and pulses—with very little protein in the diet. Many countries in Africa are in this first phase of consumption.

In the second phase, while total daily calories needs may be met, people are showing signs of wanting to diversify their diets toward the more expensive proteins. Large parts of the populations of India and China are in this phase, consuming more proteins as their incomes grow.

In what might be described as the developed third phase, personal preferences and health concerns dominate the choice of dietary pattern. At this point demand for food becomes income inelastic, and increases in income do not result in any rise in consumption of food in general. Food expenditures represent a relatively small share of the household budget and consumers can afford to be selective. Consumers in Europe, Japan, South Korea, the United States, and Canada are generally in this category. Only those with very small incomes in these countries will consume more if their incomes rise.

While in the period to 2050 average per capita real income growth could grow by more than $10,000 per capita, this income growth is not likely to be evenly distributed.[1] Most important, it is expected that in the poorest region of the world, Africa, incomes will grow only by an inadequate $1,867 per capita, with much of that growth going to the African oil exporting countries and the relatively more developed South Africa. Most of Africa will continue to struggle to meet subsistence needs. Increased consumption of grains, including rice and starchy roots, is expected. Some small growth in vegetable oil and meat consumption is expected, but not yet at the levels experienced in Asia.

In contrast, incomes in Asia and Oceania are estimated by the United Nations to rise by $9,432 per capita, which is likely to allow significant diet improvement as well as significant dietary change. Latin America, particularly Central America and the northern countries of South America, are expected to achieve an increase of $8,858 per capita. In the developed world, while income growth is expected to be large, this will have little impact on food consumption other than some change in eating patterns.[2]

economic growth and food consumption in the emerging economies

World Bank analyses indicate that the five largest emerging market economies are Brazil, Russia, India, Indonesia, and China, the so-called BRIC group of countries. Their future role in global trade and growth potential remain uncertain, but what is certain is that growth in these countries will be greater than in the long developed countries.

As a group, the emerging countries have become a major power driving global agricultural markets. The combination of large populations and rapidly expanding economies make China and India the most significant expanding markets for food and agricultural commodities. Together these two countries have more than one third of the world's population. They are also areas of rapid dietary change, particularly toward increased animal protein consumption. As a consequence of limitations on arable land and other resource limitations—Brazil and Russia are exceptions—production increases have not been able to keep up with the growth in consumption; food imports have increased and are increasing. Russia and China are becoming major meat importers, but Russia has the resource potential to become a larger food exporter, particularly of grains. Others, such as Brazil, are major agricultural suppliers to the world markets.

Increasing urbanization is likely to play a major part in rising incomes and food consumption. The migration from rural areas to towns and megacities, growth in urban incomes, and widening wealth disparities are creating new economic issues.

Globally, according to the World Bank, the rate of increase in demand for food tends to be relatively stable, responding to slowly evolving factors (principally population and income growth), and this rate has not accelerated in the recent past.[3] Indeed, the rate of growth in global demand for major food groups has been slowing over the past half century. This trend is expected to continue as global population growth slows and the increment to per capita demand from rising incomes declines.

While per capita demand for food undoubtedly rises with incomes, after income reaches a certain threshold, the demand tends to level off. For grains (including indirect demand to produce meat), an important proportion of the world's population has already reached the point where per capita demand has plateaued. Demand for meat is still rising faster than the rise in population, but the differential is declining as meat consumption by large sections of the world's population approaches peak levels. Only demand for edible oils continues to rise much more rapidly than population and is expected to rise over the next twenty years or so, as poorer populations are increasingly able to afford the packaged and prepared foods that are heavy in edible oil content.

Expected higher growth rates for grains and edible oils reflect the diversion of some of these products to biofuels. Biofuel-related demand for food products—grain, sugar, and oilseeds—is expected to grow rapidly over the decade to 2020. It should be noted that not all of the food content of maize and sugar used in biofuel production is lost. About a third of maize used in biofuel production is returned to the food cycle as animal feed grain.

It is important to note that rising incomes in developed and emergent countries are the principal source of food price inflation in times of relative shortage.[4] Globally, price elasticity of demand as a result of increased income diminishes. In periods of relative shortage the more prosperous will maintain their consumption by paying higher prices. The richer consumers are, the less likely they are to reduce food consumption due to increasing prices. This is because the share of staple food in the total expenditure of relatively rich people is smaller relative to their income. As a result, an increase in prices does not necessarily lead to a decrease in demand. For the less prosperous, more of household income is spent on food, thus reducing demand for other nonfood goods and services.

This is true of richer and poorer consumers within countries as well. It also means that when supplies are short, the poorest consumers absorb the largest part of the quantitative adjustment necessary to restore equilibrium to the market. Government support for biofuel production tends to reinforce this uneven division of the food supply reduction because it makes the biofuel industry less sensitive to higher commodity input prices.

the food price crisis

The 2007–2008 international food price crisis caused hardship on a number of fronts. The steep rise in food prices led to economic difficulties for the poor and generated political turmoil in many countries. The crisis could also have resulted in long-term, irreversible nutritional damage, especially among children. The price crisis was triggered by a complex set of long-term and short-term factors, including policy failures and market overreactions. Rising energy prices until the middle of 2008, subsidized biofuel production, income and population growth, globalization, and urbanization were among the major forces contributing to surging demand. On the supply side, land and water constraints, underinvestment in rural infrastructure and agricultural innovation, and lack of access to inputs, as well as weather disruptions, impaired productivity growth and the needed production response.[5] And the world food economy was already finely balanced: between 2000 and 2007, cereal demand exceeded cereal production and cereal stocks consequently declined.

In addition to the supply and demand fundamentals, there is substantial evidence that the crisis was made worse by the malfunctioning of world grain markets and by the response of several countries to protect their own internal consumption. These reactions began as consequences, not causes, of the price crisis, but they exacerbated the crisis and increased the risks created by high prices. By creating a positive feedback loop with high food prices, they took on a life of their own, increasing the prices and their volatility even more, with adverse consequences for the poor and for long-term incentives for agricultural production. Because they impeded the free flow of food to where it was most needed and the free flow of price signals to farmers, these market failures imposed enormous efficiency losses on the global food system, hitting the poorest countries hardest.

the 2008 financial crisis and the world food economy

The financial crisis that struck the United States and the United Kingdom as well as other European economies in 2008 quickly affected all of the Western economy and subsequently spread to the rest of the world, leading to recession in many countries. The high world economic growth of the preceding decade put upward pressure on prices for energy and agricultural commodities, whose production cannot be quickly increased in the short run.[6] This is the major reason why world energy and agricultural commodity prices soared in 2007–2008.

The second feature of the crisis was that the growth involved major macroeconomic imbalances between two different groups of countries, mainly the United States and the United Kingdom on the one hand and various Asian countries, such as China, South Korea, and Taiwan, on the other.[7] Coinciding with the buildup of the macroeconomic imbalances were major developments in the United States and the Western financial system, such as the rise of new financial products and reduced regulation.

Given that the emerging and developing economies depend on the import demand of the developed economies for their nonfood exports, incomes in these economies in the medium term will be much lower than originally expected. Significantly, the volume of global trade in 2009 declined for the first time since 1982 according to the World Bank.[8] However, before the economic disruptions of the Eurozone after autumn 2011, it was expected that global economic growth would have been likely to boost incomes and demand for food imports in the less-developed regions, particularly in sub-Saharan Africa.

Growth in this region, the IMF's most recent report indicates, is led by the low-income countries (LICs), which are projected to have expanded by 6 percent in 2011.[9] Obviously, the oil-producing countries of sub-Saharan Africa are likely to benefit most from increasing global economic activity. For example, Ghana, now the third-largest LIC in the region, was projected to increase its economy by 13 percent in 2011 as oil production commenced in the Jubilee oilfield and growth in the non-oil sector remained robust. The recovery in other LICs, such as Kenya and Ethiopia, was also expected to stay strong, supported by infrastructure investment and improving agricultural production.

In its agriculturally oriented projections, the Food and Agriculture Policy Research Institute (FAPRI) expected that world population growth would slow from the current 1.2 percent to about 1 percent by 2020, with obviously significant differences across the main world regions. Such differences, it points out, coupled with income changes and demographic developments such as urbanization and aging societies, would have important influences on demand growth rates and distribution.

Inflation is a significant problem in many LDCs. While elevated in some developed countries, inflation is not assumed to be a major problem in countries where a relatively small share of budget is spent on food. However, many high-growth emerging economies have been battling inflationary pressures at least since commodity prices began to increase and are expected to continue doing so.

The U.S. dollar exchange rate is seen to be an important influence on world food prices. Many internationally traded commodities remain denominated in U.S. dollars, and depreciation of the dollar therefore has a significant impact on commodity prices denominated in local currencies. This affects the competitiveness of other exporting countries; Australia for example, with a strong currency compared with the US dollar, finds its wheat exports less competitive than US wheat on international markets. Both OECD-FAO and FAPRI assume a modest depreciation of the U.S. dollar in the short term and then a leveling off.

A late 2011 report from the World Bank confirmed the likely knock-on effect of economic recession in the developed economies on growth in the developing economies of east Asia, emphasizing that growth in these countries is likely to be less "because of weakening external demand."[10] Nonetheless, growth in the region was likely to have increased by a strong 8.2 percent in 2011 and possibly by 7.8 percent in 2012.

Prospects for growth in the region were likely to be further constrained by the natural disasters the region suffered in the late 2000s. Flooding in several countries, especially Thailand, which saw the worst floods in decades, has caused countries to revise growth downward. The World Bank warned that Asia must become less export-driven and boost domestic demand. The export-driven nature of the Asian economies makes them more vulnerable to economic downturns in U.S. and European economies. Significantly, the World Bank emphasizes that there must be more of a drive toward domestic and regional demand, if high growth is to be maintained.

In its 2010 outlook on agricultural production and consumption to 2019 the OECD foresaw a more positive growth in world economic outlook through the following decade.[11] The macroeconomic environment underlying the commodity projections is more positive than in its outlook of a year earlier. It assumed global economic recovery and a slow transition toward higher sustainable and noninflationary growth.

However, following the 2011 Eurozone crisis, the OECD stated: "A two-speed recovery appears to be underway, characterized by weak and hesitant growth with high unemployment in many OECD countries and by stronger growth and faster recovery in the large developing countries which is slowly spreading to the rest of the developing world and helping to fuel world income growth."[12]

The OECD also pointed out that high energy prices had returned and are assumed to dominate the immediate future economic development: "Further increases in oil prices could be expected to increase input and production costs, having an impact on crop supplies, prices and trade flows, and reinforce feedstock demand for biofuels."

The OECD confirmed that developing countries will, in the long term, provide the main source of growth for world agricultural production, consumption, and trade. Rising per capita incomes and urbanization, reinforced by population growth, will increase demand from developing countries. Growth rates in developing countries remain nearly twice that of the OECD area. With the rise in incomes, diets can be expected to continue to diversify away from staple foods toward increased consumption of meat and processed food. This can be expected to increase demand for livestock and dairy products. Also, with increasing affluence and an expanding middle class, food consumption in emerging economies—particularly the BRIC group of countries—is likely to become less responsive to price and income changes, as is currently the case in the developed countries. According to the OECD, "This implies that larger changes in price and incomes will be required for consumption to adjust to any unforeseen shocks."[13]

The OECD analysis emphasizes the importance of economic growth in the emerging economies in fueling world demand for industrial exports and for food commodities. While the developed OECD country economies are only expected to grow at an average of around 2 percent, those of the BRIC economies will rise 3–8 percent.

In summary, it can be expected that demand for food will be stimulated by the combination of economic growth, however modest, and the increase in world population. The growth in population is expected to average 1.1percent per annum to 2019, compared with 1.2percent in the 2000–2010 period. Population growth in the developed OECD countries is expected to average only 0.4 percent a year. Higher growth is likely in the developing countries, with Africa's population growing at over 2 percent per annum. Continuing urbanization and rising per capita incomes, emerging large middle classes, and underlying population demographics are likely to stimulate higher food demand in these countries.

What is clear from this analysis of the development of the world economy is that increased market integration, globalization, and rapid income growth in the developing countries will maintain pressure on food prices. Only increased production can moderate and stabilize global food prices. Key developing and emerging economies are now the major influence on world agricultural markets. This increasing influence of rising affluence and the need to feed expanding populations on international markets is being manifested in different ways.

"Initially the momentum arising from strong income growth boosts food demand and imports for a range of agricultural products and processed foods to feed large concentrations of people migrating from rural to mega urban centres," the OECD points out.[14] The report continues:

> Subsequently it provides the impetus for the development of domestic production capacity, financed from either domestic savings or from growing foreign direct investment flows to these developing and emerging economies. Investment in manufacturing, processing and domestic production capacity is expected to be particularly strong in the 'expanded' BRIIC countries of Brazil, Russia, India, Indonesia and China. It is also becoming a generally shared priority of other high growth emerging countries. One of the motivations behind such investments is to capture a growing share of the higher value added component of domestically consumed agricultural products.

The events of the later years of the first decade of the twenty-first century have contributed to the view that the global food system is becoming more vulnerable and susceptible to episodes of extreme price volatility. Greater integration of markets in the world economy certainly means that international shocks can emerge and strike domestic food markets much more quickly than before. Certainly, increased vulnerability is being triggered by an apparent increase in extreme weather events and a dependence on new exporting zones where harvests tend to be subject to weather variation.

The FAO highlights three factors that now play a significant part in increasing volatility:[15]

- a greater reliance on international trade to meet food needs at the expense of stock holding
- a growing demand for food commodities from other sectors, especially energy
- a faster transmission of macroeconomic factors onto commodity markets, including exchange rate volatility and monetary policy shifts, such as changing interest rate regimes

While it is conceded that the use of commodity derivatives as a portfolio hedge is not in itself a cause of greater volatility, evidence suggests that trading in futures markets may have amplified volatility in the short term.

What is an undoubted fact is that extreme price volatility creates an additional cost in securing food supplies, since market operators will have difficulty planning ahead and adjusting to fluctuating market signals. And it is the poor of developing countries who will bear this cost most seriously. Episodes of extreme volatility—especially large, unexpected price upswings—are a major threat to food security in these countries. The impact falls heavily on these people, who may spend as much as 70 percent of their income on food. Lack of dietary diversification aggravates their condition because price increases in one staple food cannot easily be compensated by switching to alternatives. Small farmers highly dependent on commodities for their livelihoods suffer large income fluctuations as a result of extreme volatility. They have little or no income buffer against such fluctuations, such as savings or insurance. Additional risks arise from the delay between production decisions and eventual production, as farmers base their investments and planning on expected future prices.

While sudden price rises undoubtedly pose a serious threat to food supply in the least prosperous countries, the evidence that greater volatility is likely to be a permanent feature of the world food system is hard to find. The OECD takes the view that "when looked at in the long term there is little or no evidence that volatility in international agricultural commodity prices, as measured using standard statistical measures is increasing and this finding applies to both nominal and real prices."[16]

Volatility has been higher since 2000 than during the previous two decades. This is also the case for wheat and rice prices in the most recent years (2006–2010) compared with the 1970s. The OECD points out however, that a major conclusion that emerges from the study of long-term trends in volatility is that periods of high and volatile prices are often followed by long periods of relatively low and stable prices. Finally, it is well established that agricultural markets are intrinsically subject to greater price variation than other markets, for reasons already made clear.

In early 2011 world food price levels as reflected in various measures, including the FAO world food price index, once again rose to the levels of 2007–2008, giving rise to expectations of a repeat of the earlier crisis. The same pattern of factors at the root of the 2007–2008 crisis reappeared: weather-related crop losses, export restrictions, high oil prices, and a depreciating U.S. dollar, against a background of a continuing closeness of supply to global demand. On the other hand, the 2010–2011 situation differed from the earlier episode in some important respects. One major difference was a good harvest in the previous crop year. The 2010 harvests in many food importing countries in Africa were above average or very good, so that prices tended to stabilize.[17] Stocks were also larger, which helped to hold down prices. Price increases were also differently spread among commodities. Meats, sugar, and dairy products were all affected, but these are commodities that are less important in the food bills of the most vulnerable. Moreover, while the index of prices for cereals came close to its 2008 level on average, and prices of vegetable oils were also very high, the price rises did not affect rice, contrary to the 2007–2008 situation. Because rice is the staple food of many millions of the world's most vulnerable consumers, the impact of price increases was different. Nevertheless, this knife-edge relationship between supply and demand illustrates the serious risks to food security from climatic and other events.

Growing population and income in emerging and developing countries will add significantly to the demand for food in the coming decades. Whatever the level of economic growth achieved by 2050, population growth (Chapter 6) and the consequent 50 to 70 percent increase in the demand for food will exert heavy pressure on commodity prices. According to OECD/FAO medium-term outlook projections, prices of crops and most livestock products will be higher in both real and nominal terms during the decade to 2019 than they were in the decade before the 2007–2008 price spikes. This trend can be expected to continue beyond 2020. If the rate of growth of agricultural production does not keep pace with demand, upward pressure on prices will result. A demand or supply shock in a situation where the supply-demand balance is already this tight, can, for the reasons explained above, result in increased volatility around the upward trend.

summary and conclusions

Development of the world economy, increased market integration, globalization, and rapid income growth in the developing countries will maintain pressure on food prices. The knock-on effect of the 2008 financial crisis heralded depressed demand for exports from emerging economies. Only increased production can moderate and stabilize global food prices. There is a four-way influence of world economic growth on demand for food: level of demand and change in dietary pattern; price of energy and industrial exports, which most affects the purchasing ability of the least prosperous countries; depressed demand in developed countries, which affects the income of LDCs; and BRIC countries driving development of world food economy both on demand and supply sides. Recent food price hikes were caused by several interconnected factors. Many factors combine to create greater food price volatility. Volatility has the most harmful effect on producers and consumers in less-developed countries. Developing countries, however, will provide the main long-term growth in food demand. Food production increases are vital to prevent further rises in food prices.

notes

1.   John Kruse, *Income Growth in LDCs: Estimating Demand for Agricultural Commodities to 2050* (Milwaukee, WI: American Agricultural Economic Association, 2010).
2.   Shida Henneberry, *Emerging Countries: Converging or Diverging Economies?* (Milwaukee, WI: American Agricultural Economics Association, 2010).
3.   World Bank, "Food Price Watch" (2011). Available at: http://siteresources.worldbank.org/EXTPOVERTY/Resources/336991-1311966520397/Food-Price-Watch-November-2011.htm.
4.   FAO Committee on World Food Security, *Price Volatility and Food Security: Report by the High Level Panel of Experts on Food Security and Nutrition* (Rome: FAO, July 2011).
5.   Organization for Economic Co-operation and Development–Food and Agricultural Organization of the United Nations (OECD-FAO), *Agricultural Outlook 2008–2017* (Paris: OECD, 2008).
6.   William M. Liefert and Mathew Shane, "The World Economic Crisis and U.S. Agriculture: From Boom to Gloom?" *Choices* (2010). Available at: www.choicesmagazine.org/magazine/print.php?article=59.

7. Mathew Shane, William Liefert, Mitch Morehart, May Peters, John Dillard, David Torgerson, and William Edmondson, *The 2008/2009 World Economic Crisis: What It Means for U.S. Agriculture*, WRS-09-02 (Washington, DC: USDA Economic Research Service, 2009).

8. World Bank, "Strong growth in developing East Asia faces risks from global uncertainty and natural disasters," Press Release No. 2012/160/EAP, November 22, 2011. Available at: http://web.worldbank.org/WBSITE/EXTERNAL/NEWS/0,,contentMDK:23052248˜pagePK:34370˜piPK:34424˜theSitePK:4607,00.html.

9. International Monetary Fund, *World Economic Outlook: Tensions from the Two-Speed Recovery* (Washington, DC: IMF, April 2011).

10. World Bank, "Strong Growth in Developing East Asia Faces Risks from Global Uncertainty and Natural Disasters."

11. OECD–FAO, *Agricultural Outlook 2010–2019* (Paris: OECD, 2010).

12. OECD, *The Economic Outlook and Policy Requirements for G20 Economies* (Paris: OECD, October 31, 2011).

13. Ibid.

14. Ibid., vii

15. FAO, *Price Volatility in Agricultural Markets: Evidence, Impact on Food Security and Policy Responses*, ES Policy Brief, note 12 (Rome: FAO, 2010).

16. OECD, *The Economic Outlook and Policy Requirements for G20 Economies.*

17. FAO, *Price Volatility in Agricultural Markets*, note 10.

chapter 11

the increasing demand for food

The average level of the world's food consumption is undoubtedly increasing, but not enough in the food-needy countries and too often too much in the more prosperous developed countries. The global average figures obscure the continuing need for the quantity and quality of food to increase in order to raise nutrition levels for the one-sixth of the world's population that still suffers from hunger or serious malnutrition. Undoubtedly, there have been significant improvements in average food consumption per person, and the increased availability of food in relation to population has dramatically reduced the prevalence of undernutrition in recent years. Unfortunately, due to a number of factors—most of them political—there are developing countries where food availability for each person has fallen—especially in sub-Saharan Africa.

main points

- Demand for basic food commodities has increased in the least developed countries.
- The pattern of world food demand is changing from static to declining in developed countries.
- Changes in dietary patterns are affecting food demand.
- A likely rising demand for meat and dairy products will put pressure on agricultural resources.
- Demand for rice is declining.

increasing demand for basic food commodities in the least developed countries

Food consumption per person rose by close to 400 kilocalories (kcal) per person per day in the last three decades of the twentieth century. The average rose from 2,411 to 2,789 kcal per person per day between 1969/ 1971 and 1999/2001.[1] But the average hides wide variations and serious shortfalls in the poorest countries. In Somalia, Burundi, Rwanda, and Kenya food availability has declined further from what was already a very low per capita food consumption level.[2]

What is obvious is that the overall world demand for food is going to increase by very significant amounts during the next four decades, almost exclusively in the developing countries. What is less obvious is where demand will increase most and what the pattern of demand for cereals, meat, dairy products, and other major foods will be. In developed countries consumption is most likely to remain static or increase by only very small amounts. In those countries with the greatest need to improve both the quantity and quality of their diets, it should increase by very large amounts; whether it does or not is another matter. The extent of the increase will be heavily influenced by economic growth in the most-hungry countries. The less-developed countries of sub-Saharan Africa, south Asia, Central America, and South America are likely to increase their consumption of cereals and meat particularly, but also of dairy products and more processed foods.

The extent to which the people of these countries will increase their consumption of food and how they will change the types of food they eat will depend principally on economic growth in these countries, but also in the developed world. A major factor in changing the scale and pattern of food consumption will be the urbanization of what are currently countries with the bulk of their population in rural areas.

Rising population and economic growth major factors

Increased food consumption is likely to be the product of a combination of population growth and increased economic growth. Reduction in the poverty level in countries with the major share of the world's undernourished population will be the major factor in the increase in world food consumption in the period up to 2050. In addition, emerging economies will be experiencing rapidly changing patterns of demand for basic staple food commodities such as rice and pulses.

The growth in gross domestic product (GDP) and the reduction in the numbers of people living below the poverty line (generally defined as an income of $1.25 per day or less) will be crucial to the rate of increase in food demand. Estimates made on the basis of the World Bank's ENVISAGE (Environmental Impact and Sustainability Applied General Equilibrium) model suggest that world income will nearly quadruple by 2050 compared with 2010.[3] Most of this growth will be in the developing countries. Though the rate of increase in economic growth in the LDCs in aggregate will tend to fall from its current level of around 6.5 percent per annum, it is still expected to be at more than 4 percent per annum in 2050. This increase will have an important influence on both the level of food consumption and the dietary pattern.

The largest area with the greatest need for increased food supply is likely to be sub-Saharan Africa (see also Chapter 10). Estimates of the likely increase in GDP in sub-Saharan Africa vary significantly among the leading international agencies. Of the three organizations that have devoted most attention to the issue, IFPRI, IIASA and FAO, the first is the most pessimistic, predicting a 1 percent per annum increase in GDP for the region, while IIASA and FAO estimates suggest an annual growth rate for sub-Saharan Africa of about 2.3 to 2.5 percent a year in the period up to 2050.

the changing pattern of world food demand

The most significant feature of increasing prosperity in the less-developed areas of the world is likely to be that meat and, to a lesser extent, dairy products will form a larger part of the diet. Increasing urbanization will play a major part in this change in the dietary pattern. According to the FAO there is increasing pressure on the livestock sector to meet the growing demand for high-value animal protein. The world's livestock sector is growing at an unprecedented rate and the driving force behind this enormous surge is a combination of population growth, rising incomes, and urbanization. Global annual meat production is projected by FAO to increase from 218 million tonnes in 1997–1999 to 376 million tonnes by 2030.

Until recently (i.e., the last decade of the twentieth century), the share of dietary energy supplied by cereals, about 50 percent, appears to have remained relatively stable. Recently, however, significant changes appear to be taking place. A closer analysis of dietary energy intake shows a decrease in the share of energy derived from cereals in developing countries, falling from 60 percent to 54 percent in a period of only ten years. This is because wheat and rice are becoming less-preferred foods in middle-income emerging economies such as Brazil and China, a pattern expected to continue over the next thirty years or so.

Improvements in food supply

In short, it would appear that the world has made significant progress in raising food consumption per person, but there is still a long way to go if hunger and malnutrition are to be eliminated. The increase in world average consumption would have been higher but for the declines in the transition economies in the 1990s. It is generally agreed, however, that consumption will increase in these countries in the near future. The growth in food consumption has been accompanied by significant structural changes and a shift in diet away from staples such as roots and tubers toward more livestock products and vegetable oils. Current food energy intakes on average range from 2,681 kcal per capita per day in developing countries to 2,906 kcal per capita per day in transition countries and 3,380 kcal per capita per day in industrialized countries. It is likely that that per capita energy supply has declined from both animal and vegetable sources in the countries in economic transition, while it has increased in the developing and industrialized countries.

It is likely that the average level of nutrition will improve, both globally and in key regions. According to estimates from the FAO and the World Health Organization, it is likely that the global average daily intake will rise from a current daily intake of around 2,940 kilocalories to 3,050 by 2030.While the intake of the industrialized countries will remain largely unchanged at 3,440–3,500 kcal/day, in the less-developed countries the average will increase from fewer than 2,850 kcal/day to 2,980 by 2030. Calorie intake in sub-Saharan Africa, however, will still remain inadequate, rising from fewer than 2,360 to only 2,540 kcal/day in 2030. Dietary intake in east Asia is likely to show the most marked improvement over the same period, rising from 2,872 to 3,190 kcal/day by 2030.

Similar trends are evident for protein availability, which has increased in both developing and industrialized countries but temporarily decreased in the transition countries. Although the global supply of protein has been increasing, the distribution is unequal. The per capita supply of vegetable protein is slightly higher in developing countries, while the supply of animal protein is three times higher in industrialized countries.

Growth in demand for animal proteins

All analysts recognize the strong positive relationship between income levels and the consumption of animal protein, with the consumption of meat, milk, and eggs increasing as consumption of cereals and other staple foods declines. Because of the falling real price of meat in the period up to 2006, developing countries are manifesting higher meat consumption at much lower levels of gross domestic product than the industrialized countries did some twenty to thirty years ago.

This trend has been reinforced and to a great extent stimulated by the increasing emigration of people from rural areas to towns and cities. There is little doubt that urbanization is a major stimulant of increased demand for meat and other livestock products. The more complex infrastructure of cities, including the development of supermarkets and their attendant cold storage facilities and improved transport, facilitates increased trade in perishable goods. Compared with the less-diversified diets of the rural communities, city dwellers have a varied diet rich in animal proteins and fats, with higher consumption of meat, poultry, milk, and other dairy products. There has, in particular, been a remarkable increase in the consumption of animal products in countries such as Brazil and China, although the levels are still well below the levels of consumption in North America and Europe.

While those anxious to limit greenhouse gas emissions may campaign against increased meat production, it is unlikely that consumers in less-developed countries will be seriously deterred from increasing their meat consumption by prescriptive sermons from those who already enjoy a more than adequate protein-rich diet. A higher protein diet is also necessary for people who are currently undernourished. As the World Health Organization points out: "As diets become richer and more diverse, the high-value protein that the livestock sector offers improves the nutrition of the vast majority of the world. Livestock products not only provide high-value protein, but are also important sources of a wide range of essential micronutrients, in particular minerals such as iron and zinc, and vitamins such as vitamin A."[4]

The reality is that diets in developing countries are changing and will continue to change as incomes rise. As the share of such food staples as cereals, roots, and tubers declines, that of meat, dairy products, and oil crops will continue to rise. FAO figures show that between 1964–1966 and 1997–1999 per capita meat consumption in developing countries rose by 150 percent and consumption of milk and dairy products by 60 percent. It is expected that by 2030, per capita consumption of livestock products will increase by a further 44 percent. Because of the relative ease with which its production can be increased, poultry meat consumption is predicted to grow the fastest. In the livestock sector generally, productivity improvements are likely to be a major means of meeting this increased demand. Milk yields are expected to improve, while breeding and improved management should increase average carcass weights and unit output rates.

The problem is that without technical and structural improvement demand in developing countries will grow faster than production, resulting in a growing and costly trade deficit for these countries. The FAO says that in meat products this deficit will rise steeply, from 1.2 million tonnes per year in 1997–1999 to 5.9 million tonnes per year in 2030 (despite growing meat exports from Latin America), while in the case of milk and dairy products, the rise will be less steep but still considerable, from 20 million tonnes per year in 1997–1999 to 39 million tonnes per year in 2030.

a model of the world food economy

The main underlying forces that form the demand side of the world food economy are likely to be population growth, income growth, government policies, including increases—or decreases—in protectionism, and changes in dietary patterns, including increased demand for meat and dairy products. On the supply side, the single most important factor is yield increase—or lack of it. Possible increase in farmed area is likely to be less important. But production increases will be seriously hampered by rising energy prices, shortages of water, and climate change, possibly linked to sporadic climate crises caused by such phenomena as La Niña and El Niño.

Population and income increases—keys to future demand

The calculation of food need has to be based, first, on expected population increases and then on the combination of factors that influence the ability of people in a given region to purchase food either from their own producers or by importing. Although the ability to purchase food increases with economic growth, the actual amount that individuals or communities will consume will depend on the income elasticity of demand. Therefore economic growth will have very little effect on demand for food in developed economies, whereas it will have a much more pronounced effect on demand in developing countries.

In developed economies the aggregate income elasticity of demand for food is very low—increases in income lead to only small rises in food consumption—and then more for luxury foods than for staple foods. In developing countries, in contrast, there are relatively large increases in food consumption when average incomes increase. The pattern of food purchase will also change with increasing prosperity, with an increasing preference for meat, dairy products, and other more desirable foods, while the consumption of rice and cereal-based staple foods will tend to decline.

Clearly, the levels of food consumption and the consumption of particular types of food will, in the aggregate and at any given time, be affected by the degree of economic growth that a country or region enjoys.

Climate change will affect both food supply and demand

Climate change is likely to affect both the supply and the demand sides of the world food equation. This is because, according to almost all impact assessments, it will tend to reduce both economic growth of developing countries and their ability to increase agricultural productivity and output. Climate change could also reduce the cereal output, and therefore the export capacity, of the major food-producing developed countries, although conclusions differ on this.

For example, according to the Commonwealth Scientific and Industrial Research Organisation (CSIRO) climate model[5] net cereal exports from developed countries will decline; the Model for Interdisciplinary Research on Climate (MIROC)[6] similarly shows a decline in developed countries' cereal production capacity, but it predicts a more serious outcome as developed countries become net cereal importers, mainly as a consequence of the negative effects of climate change on U.S. maize production. Both of these models indicate not only the uncertainty of projections, but also the importance of trade to increased global food security. There is also uncertainty about when climate change will most seriously affect world food production. Undoubtedly, some climate change effects have already been seen and are now developing, but most scientists agree that serious global warming is unlikely to affect world agriculture until the latter half of the twenty-first century.

Models of the global food system

The IMPACT model, a multimarket partial equilibrium model developed at the International Food Policy Research Institute (IFPRI), represents the agricultural sector in great detail combined with more simplified modeling of other parts of the economy. It simulates growth in crop production, determined by crop and input prices, externally determined rates of productivity growth and area expansion, investment in irrigation, and water availability. Demand is a function of prices, income, and population growth and contains four categories of commodity demand—food, feed, biofuels, and other uses.

Of all the data variations that have been applied to test the sensitivity of food security, the IMPACT model produces the most clearly advantageous outcomes for a postulated increase in productivity of 40 percent in the 2015–2050 period (a not unfeasible 1.1 percent per annum). World price increases for maize, rice, and wheat are reduced by 41 percent, 24 percent, and 34 percent, respectively, as compared with a scenario in which there is no increase in productivity. Such a rise in output would allow a large increase in the daily amount of kilocalories that is available to the average person in each country or region. In this model calculation, the number of malnourished children falls by an additional 12 percent from 2010 to 2050. According to this analysis, the most powerful improver of food security is likely to be yield growth.

World Bank quantitative scenarios, using their ENVISAGE model to 2030, confirm that that prices are particularly sensitive to assumptions of agricultural productivity growth.[7] In this modeling exercise an assumed global total factor productivity growth of 2.1 percent per annum results in a slight decrease in world agricultural prices in real terms. Most agriculturists would argue that this productivity figure is overly optimistic. If however the productivity factor in the calculation is halved, real prices would, in this model, rise by 35 percent. If only developing country agriculture is subjected to the lower productivity growth, the price increase result is 16 percent. The World Bank model expects sooner and more serious climate change effects than the IMPACT model. It indicates that climate change could substantially reduce real incomes in south Asia and sub-Saharan Africa by 2030, despite economic growth.

Other medium-term projections suggest very significant rises in real food prices if production does not increase adequately to meet growing demand from the rising population. And this is the most important conclusion from all models. Agricultural productivity has to increase if food supply is to be adequately increased. The most recent outlook projections for agriculture, published by the Organisation for Economic Co-operation and Development (OECD), projects average wheat and coarse grain prices to be 15–40 percent higher in 2020 relative to the period from 1997 to 2006.[8] Using the low-productivity and high-productivity scenarios in the Global Trade Analysis Project computable general equilibrium (CGE) model, OECD predicts world cereal prices rising on average by 32 percent (for low productivity) or declining by 16 percent (for high productivity) from 2000 to 2030. Prices for coarse grains under the low-productivity scenario rise on average by as much as 63 percent. It has to be admitted that some models produce some surprising and, frankly, nonsensical answers.

Summary of the key features of the likely development of the world food economy to 2050

- Economic development has a large positive impact on food-security outcomes for developing countries.
- World food prices over the period to 2050 are likely to increase in the main scenarios in a reversal of the trend in the twentieth century due to demand drivers such as population and income growth and supply-side assumptions on yield growth and possible reduced productivity because of climate change.
- Increase in productivity-enhancing research and applications of new techniques will be needed if significant price rises are to be prevented.
- Growth in total factor productivity (TFP) is important to attaining sustainable intensification.
- Prices appear particularly sensitive to assumptions about growth in agricultural productivity.
- Climate change will have negative effects on crop productivity, but there are large regional differences in impact. Moreover, results differ depending on the climate model used, demonstrating the uncertainty surrounding the impact of climate change on agriculture.
- International trade is important in ameliorating the impact of both the unequal distribution of climate change effects and idiosyncratic supply-side shocks such as droughts.
- Increases in protectionism amplify stresses on the food system by increasing prices and encouraging production in less-suitable areas.
- Changes in crop productivity have the greatest effects on food prices and food security outcomes.
- An increase in energy prices decreases food security outcomes indirectly by diverting household resources away from food consumption in countries that are dependent on fuel imports; this impact dominates any effects from higher input prices for agriculture.
- The impact of future biofuel production will depend on uncertainties such as energy prices, energy policies, and technological change; recent research has found that increased biofuel production results in food price rises, but this impact is reduced if second-generation technology is available or if international trade encourages production in more suitable regions.
- Rise in demand for livestock products in large countries such as China and India increases global demand for food and leads to increases in world food prices; global markets can lessen the impact if trade flows freely, otherwise the effects may be more severe.

a realistic assessment of the future development of the world food system

Most important in any estimation of the future food supply and demand pattern is to accept that it is not possible to achieve a realistic picture of the future pattern of world food supply and demand simply by multiplying current trends. Rather, we are dealing with a complex matrix of highly variable factors.

The two most obvious and most easy to assess are population increase and crop yield increases (or decreases). The really tricky variables in any assessment of the situation in 2050 are economic growth, changes in dietary pattern, changes in trade patterns, the availability and cost of energy, water resource availability, and climatic and environmental constraints. To obtain anything near an accurate picture, these factors have to be considered on a regional basis.

There is also the problem of unforeseen circumstances. The declines in food supply and stocks in the first decade of the twenty-first century, the Asian economic crisis of the late 1990s, and the failure of Soviet agriculture in the 1970s and its impact on world grain supplies are all examples of unpredicted, short-term events that disrupted predictions. But it is possible to project likely patterns of demand and supply, provided that it is accepted that the actual outcome is likely to be somewhere in the region of a reasonable set of possible scenarios. A major problem with existing econometric models of the development of the global food system is that they are relatively short term. For political, economic, social, and environment reasons, it is now necessary to make more long-term assessments. Limitations on natural resources, global climate change, and research priorities are vital issues that require long-term projections.

The difficulties of estimating the long-run pattern of food supply and demand have been summarized by one expert source: "Structural changes drive the long-term balance of world food supply and demand. The rate of growth of cereal yield per hectare in Asia, for example, has declined to nearly half the level of previous decades, while per capita consumption of livestock products in Asia has increased threefold in the past 20 years. Perhaps the production structure in many developing countries in the year 2020 will be quite different from the one prevailing now."[9]

While it is certain that the population will increase globally to the mid-twenty-first century, what is less certain is the pattern of increase. The population of sub-Saharan Africa is most likely to continue to have the greatest increase. In several key Asian countries, however, population growth is likely to taper off in the next forty years as the economic well-being of these countries increases. The scale of economic growth in these countries will also influence dietary change and therefore the level of demand for livestock products and for animal feed.

Demand for animal products to double

It is likely that the demand for meat and dairy products will at least double by 2030–2040 in east Asia and Southeast Asia, with a consequent rise in animal feed grain and oilseed imports to these countries. As the food-trade deficit in these countries increases, so will the grain and oilseed exports of the United States, Europe, and other developed and developing food-exporting countries. The price at which these cereal and other basic foodstuffs can be exported will depend on the exploitation of currently underutilized land and yield increases. Given environmental and political limitations on area expansion, failure to increase yields adequately would mean a significant rise in prices.

On the other hand, if yields increase, then prices could fall in real terms. This would not necessarily lead to greater consumption in the importing countries because increased demand is more dependent up GDP growth than on food prices.

To summarize the main elements of a simplified assessment of the long-term development of the supply and demand pattern, the variable factors on supply are:

1. Possible increase in farmed area, taking into account physical and political constraints.
2. Increase in yields, influenced heavily by the degree of effort put into research.
3. Climate change and energy availability limitations.
4. Changes in the pattern of trade.

The variable factors on demand are:

1. Population growth, analyzed on a regional basis.
2. Levels of GDP growth in east Asia and Southeast Asia and sub-Saharan Africa.
3. Changes in dietary pattern in emerging economies (closely linked to item 2 above).

Elements of a simplified model

The following calculations by the author are designed to give a reasonably clear picture of the future demand for and the supply of food, based on a realistic assessment of future population levels. As the examination of this issue in Chapter 6 clearly indicates, there are shortcomings in all calculations on future population levels. However, given current levels of increase and the likely impact of economic and other factors on population, the United Nations median population assessment would appear to provide a reasonable assumption on which to base a pragmatic assessment of future population growth.

In the UN median population increase estimate the global population rises from the current level of about 7 billion to more than 9 billion by 2050—an increase of more than 32 percent. It is generally agreed by most analysts that the world population is less likely to increase to the UN high population variant of more than 10.5 billion by 2050. It is also less likely that the global population will rise by as little as the low variant of more than 7 billion by 2050.

Food consumption is assumed to increase from the current global average of 2,855 kilocalories/per capita/per day to the current developed country average of 3,500 kcal/capita/day. This is possibly overly optimistic, but it is a possibility and it does provide a maximum marker for what is and is not possible. Obviously, if the developing country consumption does not catch up to this relatively high consumption level, then the global food demand will not be as high as assumed in these calculations. Total food requirement is calculated on the assumption that 4.12 kcal = 1 gram of grain. The gross figures are in terms of grain to include the feed requirement for a high degree of dietary change involving increased meat consumption in emerging and developing economies.

Nonfood demand for grain is assumed to increase at the rate of 1 percent per annum to take account mainly of increased use of grain for biofuels, as well as the increased use of cereals for industrial use in expanding economies of Asia.

The UN median population increase estimate indicates that the global population will increase by about 2.5 billion between 2011 and 2050—a rise of more than 32 percent. The demand for food could increase from the current global average of 2,855 kilocalories a day to 3,500—a rise of 22.6 percent. The latter figure represents the average current developed country level of consumption; the FAO estimate of the level necessary to properly maintain physical well-being is significantly less than this, probably around 2,800 kcal. If we were to recalculate the total world food demand on the basis of this lower figure, then it would be 20 percent less than shown in the various calculations in this chapter. In the case of the median population increase/trend level of production increase scenario (i.e., 0.9 percent per annum), then instead of a food deficit of 2.5 billion in 2050, there would be a surplus of 0.66 billion tonnes of grain. At this minimum level of desirable consumption, it would even be possible to tolerate a lower level of productivity increase than the current trend and still have a balanced world food supply and demand.

Uncertainty of Asian economic growth

The major problem is that calculations of world food demand have to take account of economic growth in Asia and the consequent increases in demand for meat and dairy products that will significantly increase the demand for grain. From these reasonably realistic assumptions it can be deduced that the actual demand for food will average out at a level somewhere between the FAO minimum requirement and the possible full industrial economy level of food consumption.

While it can be argued that the supply side of the food equation is relatively easy to estimate on the basis of possible and even likely technical changes, the demand side is a far more complex matrix. Population increase projections can be made on the basis of current trends, but levels of consumption of rice, other cereals, and animal products are dependent on levels of economic growth, varying regional economic and social changes, and levels of affluence or poverty.

To simplify, the alternative combinations can be slimmed down to fifteen probable and possible scenarios. These combine the most important likely developments in agricultural productivity, population increase, and food demand. Calculations have been made by the author on the basis of these reasonable alternative assumptions. They span possible outcomes from the least to the most likely.

Underlying conclusions

The important conclusion to be drawn from all of the fifteen possible scenarios is that if the technical fixes for increased food production fail and world food production actually declines in the next thirty years, then chronic food shortage will occur at not much more than current levels of average global food consumption.

To take the extreme example of high population increase, declining crop productivity, and reduced crop area, the world would be in serious chronic food supply deficit by 2015 at little more than the current global average per capita food consumption. It should be noted that in this scenario, in which population increases to the UN high estimate of 10.46 billion in 2050, the global food demand increase by 2050 would be between 80 and 90 percent.

It is reasonable to make estimates of likely global food consumption on the basis of the UN's three main population variations—medium, high, and low. These can be combined with the assumption that average food consumption, in terms of kilocalories per day, will reach the average of the industrial

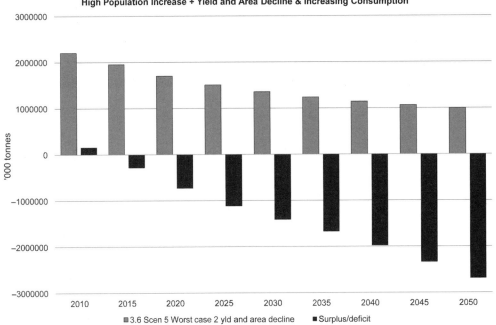

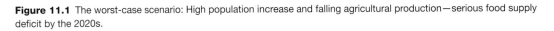

Figure 11.1 The worst-case scenario: High population increase and falling agricultural production—serious food supply deficit by the 2020s.

developed countries (3,500 kcal/day) by 2050. As already discussed, it is clear that a lower level of daily food consumption would put much less strain on the world's food production capacity. If, for example, the average were no more than the FAO's recommendation of a necessary minimum of 2,800 kcal/day, the total global demand would be considerably less—approximately 20 percent lower. In supply terms this would mean that the level of cereal production needed to feed the UN's median population increase figure of more than 9 billion by 2050 would be approximately 600 million tonnes less than the 3.28 billion tonnes indicated by calculating on the basis of 3,500 kcal/day.

The calculations show that if the parity with developed country diet basis is applied to a scenario where current levels of crop productivity (0.9 percent per annum) are projected through to 2050, and population increases at the UN median level (to between 9 and 9.54 billion by 2050), a mild gap between production and desired consumption would start to develop from 2025 onward and reach a deficit of approximately 250 million tonnes by 2050.

In the worst case, where yields decline by 0.5 percent and cropland area is reduced by 0.2 percent, the deficit would reach more than 2 billion tonnes by 2050—not far short of current global production. Fortunately, such a disaster scenario is unlikely unless the world is struck by some cataclysmic climate phenomena or a crop disease pandemic.

What is important and realistic to note is that crop productivity may not match the daily calorie intake ideal and that serious production shortfalls could persist, with the least prosperous parts of the population facing serious restrictions on their diet. With static crop area and a low productivity increase

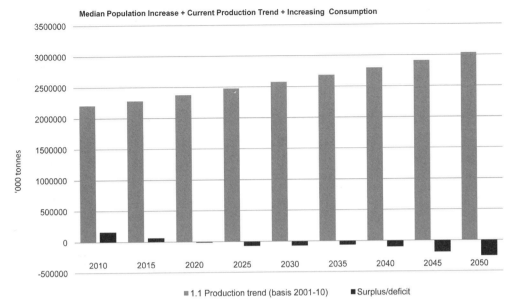

Figure 11.2 Current level of productivity increase is not enough to prevent a small but increasing deficit by 2050.

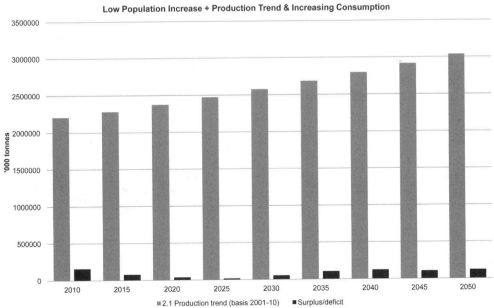

Figure 11.3 A possible most optimistic scenario: Low population increase and continuation of current agricultural productivity increase.

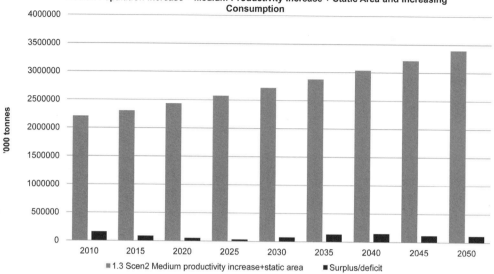

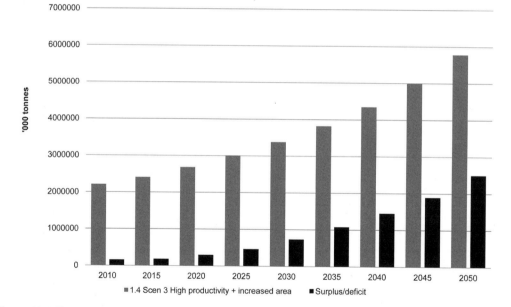

Figure 11.4 The most likely scenario based on the UN median population increase estimate: (a) a medium productivity increase results in a small surplus of production above consumption by 2050. A more optimistic, but technically feasible scenario (b) is that productivity increases by 1.5 percent per annum, and there is some increase in agricultural area.

average of 0.5 percent, for example, the grain supply deficit could reach 500 million tonnes by 2050 — about 20–25 percent of total current global production.

Only when productivity is maintained at what may be regarded as a minimum level of 1 percent per annum over the forty-year period does a safer margin between consumption and production begin to emerge (see Figure 11.3). Safer for world food security would be an annual increase in productivity of 1.5 percent per annum and a modest (0.2 percent) increase in cropland area. This combination would provide a comfortable margin of production of more than 2 billion tonnes over the consumption for a 9.3 billion world population.

What is in little doubt is that if the UN's high population increase variant were to eventuate, the strain on food supplies would be disastrous at almost any possible level of production increase, except the best possible level of productivity and cropland area increase (1.5 percent and 0.2 percent per annum, respectively). At both the current trend and modest productivity increase scenario levels of production increase there would be a grain supply deficit by 2050 of between 500 million and 900 million tonnes. A decline in yields would have the most devastating effect—at the extreme, a supply deficit of about 2.5 billion tonnes (see Figure 11.1).

Not surprising, a possible lower rise than the UN median variation in world population would put far less strain on the global food supply. If the population rose by the UN's low increase variant to just under 8 billion by 2050, only a fall in productivity increase from current levels would involve any gap between supply and demand. If productivity increase continued at the current level of 0.9 percent per annum, there would be a small margin of production over consumption by 2050. A modest increase in productivity to 1 percent a year would result in a surplus of grain production over consumption of about 500 million tonnes; a greater rise in productivity would be likely to result in a surplus output of between 2.5 and 3 billion tonnes. Reductions in productivity and cultivated area would mean deficits in the region of 1.5 to 2 billion tonnes.

The main conclusion to be drawn from these calculations is that whatever the increase in world population, the world cannot afford any reduction in crop production productivity if serious famine in the most vulnerable areas is to be avoided. More optimistically, it is likely that nutrition levels could still be improved even if the world's farmed area did not increase (a likely eventuality).

What is most likely is that population will increase by the numbers indicated in the UN's median estimate and that agricultural productivity will increase by a modest 1+ percent a year to 2050, with the farmed land area of the world remaining more or less static. This would result in a small margin of production over consumption. A more secure outcome—and one that is technically possible—is that agricultural productivity would increase by 1.5 percent a year and that there would be some small increase in the global farmed area. Despite the increase in consumption and the need for increased feed grains for livestock raising, there would still be a very comfortable margin of production above consumption that would allow a safe level of season-to-season stock to be maintained.

summary and conclusion

Contrary to the general impression created by press reports, the calculations in this book, based on realistic assessments of population and production probabilities, indicate that the world should be able to feed adequately a largely increased population in four decades' time. The FAO is also broadly optimistic on the ability of world agriculture to meet the challenge of increasing population and dietary change.[10] In its major assessment of the world food situation in forty years' time, "How to Feed the World in 2050," and subsequent updates, it sees production rising to meet the increased demand.[11] The FAO confirms that most of this increase will come from raising yields, although some area expansion is considered possible.

The FAO sees the possibility for farmland area expansion in the fact that in addition to the 1.6 billion hectares of land currently under cultivation in the world, there is a further 2.7 billion that could be cultivated. It points out, however, that while rising food prices will bring some of this currently marginal land into production, there are likely to be serious constraints arising from dangers of biodiversity loss, land degradation through erosion, and excessive carbon emission.

Climate change is seen as a serious handicap to increased food supply in key areas. It is likely to affect land suitability and yield levels, initially most seriously in sub-Saharan Africa and Asia, but eventually in all parts of the world. On yields, the FAO is most optimistic: "Yield increases have accounted for the majority of production growth in recent decades and will continue to do so in the future." It expects that the necessary increased production will come approximately half from improved crop varieties and the rest from increased inputs of fertilizer and irrigation water.

On future demand for food, the FAO, working on the basis of the UN median variation population increase, expects a total need for 3 billion tonnes of grain by 2050. This figure does not include probable increased use of grain for biofuels, which it sees as adding approximately 100 million tonnes (3.3 percent of this total need) to total demand by 2020. It estimates that almost all of the increased demand for grain will come from the less-developed countries, with total demand rising.

TABLE 11.1   FAO PROJECTIONS: WORLD CEREAL BALANCES (MILLION TONNES).

Year	Food	All uses	Production	Net trade	Self-sufficiency
		World			%
1999/2001	1334	2677	1884	3	101
2050	1439	3010	3012	3	100
		Developing countries			
1999/2001	784	1125	1026	-112	87
2050	1226	2096	1800	-297	86
		Industrial countries			
1999/2001	147	536	647	114	121
2050	159	678	926	248	137
		Transition countries			
1999/2001	69	205	211	2	103
2050	54	236	287	51	121

Source: Nikos Alexandratos and Jelle Bruinsma, *FAO World Agriculture Towards 2030/2050: The 2012 Revision* (Rome: FAO, 2012). Note that shortfall in the developing countries is compensated by the oversufficiency of the developed and transition countries.

In its analysis of the 2050 world food supply situation, the FAO makes clear that adequate supplies to the most-needy nations will only be maintained by trade and aid. Whereas its estimate of world production of grain in 2050 indicates 100 percent self-sufficiency (consumption = production), this does not mean that this desirable state of sufficiency is universal. In other words, it is likely to be global sufficiency rather than the self-sufficiency of any one country.

On the contrary, it is likely that there will be serious deficiencies of supply in the most vulnerable regions. In the developing countries as a whole it is estimated that there will be a shortfall of 297 million tonnes—14 percent short of the needed supply. In the industrial countries and the transition countries, on the other hand, there will be an oversupply of 37 and 21 percent, respectively—a total of 299 million tonnes. In theory, this surplus will provide the balance, hopefully through trade and aid, to fill the shortfall in the developing countries.

To summarize, the FAO is generally optimistic on global supply prospects, but

- Increased investment is needed to sustain productivity growth—in technology, infrastructure, and institutions as well as environmental services and sustainable resource management.
- There is an urgent need to increase access to food, not just supply—and not just in the aggregate, but for all people.
- There is a need to improve ability to adapt and respond to new pressures and uncertainties—not just on average, but at all times.
- Overall, there is a need to increase incomes not just in agriculture but in other sectors as well.

notes

1. Nikos Alexandratos, "Critical evaluation of selected projections," FAO Expert Meeting on How to Feed the World in 2050 (follow-up meeting), February 2010.

2. John Kearney, "Food Consumption Trends and Drivers," *Philosophical Transactions of the Royal Society* 365B (2010): 2793–2807.

3. Keith Wiebe, "*How to Feed the World in 2050*: Insights from an Expert Meeting at FAO, 24–26 June 2009." Paper presented at FAO–OECD Global Forum on Agriculture, Paris, June 30, 2009.

4. World Health Organization, *Global and Regional Food Consumption Patterns and Trends* (Geneva: WHO Press, 2009).

5. Commonwealth Scientific and Industrial Research Organization (CSIRO), *Climate Change: Science and Solutions for Australia* (Canberra: CSIRO, 2011).

6. Masahiro Watanabe, Hideo Shiogama, Tokuta Yokohata, Tomoo Ogura, Masakazu Yoshimori, James Annan, Julia Hargreaves, Seita Emori, and Masahide Kimoto, *Model for Interdisciplinary Research on Climate (MIROC)* (Tsukuba, Japan: MIROC Group for Climate Feedback and Sensitivity Studies, National Institute for Environmental Studies, 2012).

7. Dominique van der Mensbrugghe, *The Environmental Impact and Sustainability Applied General Equilibrium (ENVISAGE) Model* (Washington, DC: World Bank, October 2008).

8. OECD-FAO, *Agricultural Outlook 2010–2019* (Paris: OECD, 2010).

9. O. Koyama, *Projecting the World Food Supply and Demand Using a Long-term Dynamic Simulator* (Ibaraki, Japan: Japan International Research Center for Agricultural Sciences, 2010).

10. Ibid., iii.

11. "Feeding the World in 2050." Report presented at World Summit on Food Security, Rome, November 16–18, 2009.

chapter 12

access to food

The reason why too many people do not have enough food is not merely a matter of production; an equal or greater cause of hunger is the problem of access to food. Too many people do not have the means to buy the minimum amount of food they need to prevent hunger. While the world's food supply may be adequate to feed everyone, there will continue to be hungry people unless policymakers deal with the problem of access to food, improve income distribution, and fashion trade policies that ensure that what is now regarded as the human right to adequate food is realized in practice. A focus solely on increasing the production and supply of food is not enough to solve the undernutrition problem.

main points

- Global abundance of food does not ensure freedom from hunger.
- Richer emerging Asian economies have the most hungry people; China and India are the worst examples.
- Most needy countries are too dependent on grain imports.
- Most of those who depend on small farms for their living have plots that are too small.
- Hungry people are too often isolated from food markets by bad communications.
- In Asia there is a need for economic growth other than agriculture to improve access to food to overcome the problem of rural poor.

The International Assessment of Agricultural Knowledge, Science, and Technology for Development (IAASTD) has concluded: "The way the world grows its food will have to change radically to better serve the poor and hungry if the world is to cope with a growing population and climate change while avoiding social breakdown and environmental collapse."

According to the FAO statistics, of the 1 billion undernourished people in the world, 98 percent live in developing countries, including 543 million in Asia and the Pacific, 239 million in sub-Saharan Africa, 53 million in Latin America and the Caribbean, and 37 million in the Near East and North Africa. Significantly, from a development perspective, three-quarters of food-needy people live in rural areas.

Those who argue that providing the means to allow people to buy adequate quantities of food is more important than increasing production have a lot of empirical evidence on their side. In his illuminating 1981 book *Poverty and Famines,* Amartya Sen pointed out that hunger and malnutrition are not necessarily attributable to a lack of available food.[1] On the basis of a study of the worst famines of the twentieth century, Sen concluded that people may suffer from hunger despite rising yields and production because the incomes of the poorest groups remain too low while the incomes of others rise. Hunger arises largely from disempowerment, marginalization, and poverty. The poverty of governments must be included in this analysis because there are some regions of the world that are chronically short of food, where imports will be needed for a very long time because of a lack of resources and inadequate economic growth. Large parts of the Horn of Africa are a case in point. People there are too often not hungry because too little is produced; they are hungry because they cannot afford the food that is available on the markets or because they lack the necessary resources to produce food themselves.

Hunger and access to food remains a problem for millions of people in numerous countries and regions. Despite both underutilized agricultural production capacity and the annual production of food in excess of total world need, hunger and malnutrition persist. These facts emphasize the failure of governments and international development to deal with this chronic problem. It is an indisputable fact that enough food is produced to feed the world's 7 billion population. It is equally indisputable that one in seven people go hungry—and that this number has increased over the past decade.

definition of hunger

According to the FAO's definition, hunger is a reality when the individual diet does not meet the minimum target of 2,100 kilocalories a day for a sustained period. The World Food Programme (WFP) maintains that there are five main causes of hunger: natural causes, war, poverty, inadequate agricultural systems, and overexploitation of the environment.[2] Food has never before existed in such abundance, so why are more than a billion people in the world still hungry?[3]

The WFP says that natural disasters such as floods, tropical storms, and long periods of drought are on the increase—with calamitous consequences for food security in poor, developing countries. Drought is now the single most common cause of food shortages in the world. In 2006, recurrent drought caused crop failures and heavy livestock losses in parts of Ethiopia, Somalia, and Kenya. In many countries, climate change is exacerbating already adverse natural conditions. For example, poor farmers in Ethiopia or Guatemala traditionally deal with rain failure by selling off livestock to cover their losses and pay for food. But successive years of drought, increasingly common in the Horn of Africa and Central America, are exhausting their resources.

Africa's notorious internecine wars exacerbate already serious chronic food shortage situations. The WFP states that since 1992, the proportion of short-term and long-term food crises that can be attributed to human causes has more than doubled, rising from 15 percent to more than 35 percent. All too often, these emergencies are triggered by conflicts. From Asia to Africa to Latin America, fighting displaces millions of people from their homes, leading to some of the world's worst hunger emergencies.

Even when food production and supply conditions are potentially good, improving the food supply is made impossible by war. Since 2004, conflict in the Darfur region of Sudan has uprooted more than a million people, precipitating a major food crisis—in an area that had generally enjoyed good rains and crops. In many situations the food supply itself becomes a weapon. Soldiers will starve opponents into submission by seizing or destroying food and livestock and systematically wrecking local markets. Fields and water wells are often mined or contaminated, forcing farmers to abandon their land. Wars in central Africa in the 1990s increased the proportion of hungry people from 53 percent to 58 percent. In contrast, malnutrition is on the retreat in more peaceful parts of Africa such as Ghana and Malawi.

the 2008–2011 food crisis and hunger

The argument that such factors as poverty and lack of infrastructure, rather than the actual supply of food, are the major causes of hunger becomes clear in Asia. The brutal fact is that the two most vigor-ous emerging economies with the highest gross domestic product (GDP) growth in the world, China and India, have the largest number of starving and hungry people. The majority of the world's hungry, some 578 million, are in Asia, in particular in India and China. In sub-Saharan Africa, on the other hand, while the number of hungry people is lower, the proportion is much higher: almost one-third of the total population. Moreover, the number of hungry people there has risen more dramatically than in other re-gions, from 169 million in the early 1990s to an estimated 239 million in 2010. Asia's food security has been heavily affected by the 2006–2008 world food price crisis and the global economic crises. U.S. Department of Agriculture (USDA) estimates indicate that the number of hungry people on the continent has increased, despite recent progress in reducing food shortages.[4]

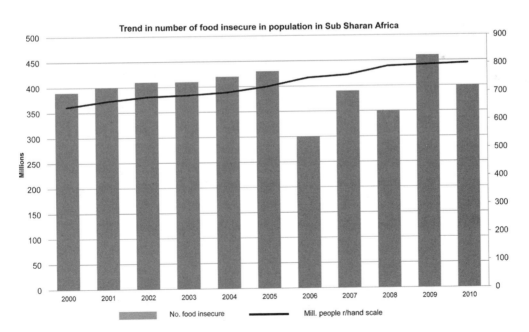

Figure12.1 Impact of food shortage in sub-Saharan Africa.
Source of data: USDA Economic Research Service Food Security Assessment (FSA), 2009–2010 Country Statistical Tables for sub-Saharan Africa.

The USDA estimates that the number of hungry people was between 11 and 13 percent higher in the period to 2010 than it would have been had the crisis not occurred. Integration of many of the Asian economies into the global economy has made the situation worse because they are more directly affected by the economic slowdown. Money transfers from migrant workers abroad make a significant contribution to the balance of payments in southern and central Asia, for example, and increase the funds available for food imports. In some regions, these remittances from overseas constitute an important proportion of the incomes of many poor households. Subsequently, there was a fall in the numbers of hungry as the global economy briefly recovered in 2010.

heavy import dependence of poorest countries

The increase in economic growth and rise in incomes in many less-developed countries has provided the means to increase the food supply. However, this has tended to lead to an increase in food imports rather than to significant increases in domestic agricultural production in these countries. This trend undoubtedly reflects the greater emphasis given to nonagricultural rather than agricultural development by the governments of these countries. With the increase in prosperity, however small, the dependency on imports has grown. The least prosperous of the less-developed countries have had to depend on an increasing supply of overseas aid to finance important parts of these imports.

Overall, food import dependency in many developing countries has increased during the past three decades; while this may have led to improved and more diversified diets, it does not improve the food security of these countries. Most important, a combination of lower income and increased import dependency makes these countries highly vulnerable to the impact of higher food prices. A larger import bill, particularly for countries with limited foreign exchange availability, too often leads to reduced imports and increased hunger.

The USDA Economic Research Service's ranking of the seventy lowest income countries by grain import dependence and daily calorie consumption highlights the seriousness of this problem.[5] Six of the low-income countries (Eritrea, Liberia, Haiti, Georgia, Burundi, and Zimbabwe) depend on grain imports for more than 40 percent of their diets and consume an average of fewer than 2,200 calories per day. Eritrea, for example, is highly dependent on food imports: 87 percent of grains, 51 percent of vegetable oils, and 100 percent of sugar. The degree of the country's vulnerability is starkly demonstrated by the fact that the bulk of its imports have to be financed by overseas aid. Eritrea's export earnings cover only 25 percent of Eritrea's import bill; the remainder is filled by external assistance. Eritrea's daily calorie availability of 1,465 in 2005 was among the lowest in the world. Any reduction in imports leads to a food crisis.

In the world's fifty least developed countries, thirty-two of which are in sub-Saharan Africa, the import share of supply for wheat increased from 93 percent in 1980 to 100 percent in 2005. For sugar, the share soared from only 4 percent in 1980 to more than 65 percent in 2005. A similar pattern is seen for vegetable oils, with the share rising from about 6 percent to 80 percent. Import dependency has continued to increase.

In 2002–2005, food aid accounted for about 9 percent of grain imports for the seventy low-income countries, according to the ERS assessment. The highest share—17 percent—was in sub-Saharan Africa, 10 percent in lower income Asian countries, 6 percent in the Confederation of Independent States, and 3 percent in the low-income Latin American countries. Some low-income countries—like Ethiopia, Sierra Leone, Malawi, and Niger—are so poor that they were financially unable to import grain even under historically lower prices and relied heavily on food aid to augment their food supplies. Higher prices inevitably creates problems for food aid delivery: food aid quantities fall as prices rise, because the United States and other major donors reduce food aid budgets. As a consequence, for the poorest countries, reductions in food aid are more of a problem than higher prices for food imports.

poverty and the supply of food

Poverty is the major obstacle to increasing the supply of food in developing countries, with farmers unable to buy seed to grow food and market crops that would provide for their families. Craftsmen lack the means to pay for the tools to ply their trade. Land or water is often not available to individual families in sufficient quantity to ensure even a subsistence level of food production. The poorest lack enough money to buy or produce enough food for themselves and their families.

Adequate agricultural infrastructure, including access to markets for inputs and for the sale of surplus, is essential to ensure food supplies. At present, too many developing countries are undergoing inappropriate urbanization; in the longer term, improved agricultural output offers the quickest fix for poverty and hunger, particularly in sub-Saharan Africa. According to the FAO, all the countries likely to achieve the first millennium development goal of adequate food supply have one thing in common— significantly better than average agricultural growth.[6] Still, too many developing countries lack the key features of agricultural infrastructure, such as enough roads, warehouses, and irrigation. This means they suffer the handicaps of too high transport costs, lack of storage facilities, and unreliable water supplies. All of these factors not only hold down agricultural yields and production but also limit access to food for those without land. Part of the problem is too often governments' obsession with urban development in their economic planning and consequent neglect of agriculture, despite the primary need to increase agricultural production.

The mismanagement of agricultural resources in too many developing countries, particularly in Africa, results in overexploitation of the environment. Poor farming practices, deforestation, overcropping, and overgrazing are too often allowed to exhaust fertility and productive capacity. Once fertile farmland has its productive capacity seriously reduced by erosion, salination, and desertification, it takes a heavy expenditure of resources—and time—to bring it back into production.

Table 12.1 PREVALENCE OF UNDERNOURISHMENT

	Total population (millions)	Numbers undernourished (millions)				Proportion of population undernourished (percent)			
	2009–2008	1990–1992	1995–1997	2000–2002	2006–2008	1990–1992	1995–1997	2000–2002	2006–2008
WORLD	6652.5	848.4	791.5	836.2	850	16	14	14	13
Developed regions	1231.3	15.3	17.5	15.4	10.6	–	–	–	–
Developing regions	5420.2	833.2	774	820.8	839.4	20	17	17	15
Least developed countries	796.7	211.2	249.4	244.7	263.8	39	41	35	33

Source of Data: FAO, WFP, and IFAD, The State of Food Insecurity in the World (Rome: FAO, 2012).

Table 12.2   THE INCIDENCE OF FOOD INSECURITY. ESTIMATES OF AND PROJECTIONS OF FOOD INSECURE PEOPLE (MILLIONS) IN 70 MOST-VULNERABLE LEAST-DEVELOPED COUNTRIES

	Total	Asia	LAC	NA	CIS	SSA
2009 estimate	953	445	61	0	5	442
2010 projection	882	433	58	0	2	390
2020 projection:						
Baseline	874	320	39	0	2	513
Scenario 1	777	275	27	0	2	473
Scenario 2	469	275	24	0	2	168

Source of Data: USDA Economic Research Service, *International Food Security Assessment, 2011–22* (Washington, DC: USDA Economic Research Service, 2011).

When a country is considered food secure

For the vast majority of the world's hungry access to land is a necessary condition to achieve an improved standard of living. Most of those who are hungry do not have access to enough land or the money to buy from those who do. The approximate 500 million people who depend on small-scale agriculture are too often hungry not only because the price they receive for their crops too low and less competitive than larger production units, but also because they cultivate plots that are often very small. They are too often trying to produce from soils that are arid, hilly, or without irrigation as they compete with larger farms for access to land and water. This means that the vast majority have to be net food buyers, but often lack the means to buy food.[7]

As the population increases and the productive capacity of land is degraded, the pressures on the remaining fertile land increases dramatically; plots cultivated are becoming smaller per capita and per household. In India, for example, the average landholding size fell from 2.6 hectares in 1960 to 1.4 hectares in 2000 and continues to decline. Similar patterns can be seen in Bangladesh, the Philippines, and Thailand, where the decline in the average farm size is combined with an increasing landless population. This trend can also be seen in sub-Saharan Africa particularly eastern and southern Africa, where the amount of cultivated land per capita has declined by half over the past thirty years. In a number of countries the average cultivated area now amounts to less than 0.3 hectares per capita. This diminution of individual productive resources is exacerbated by erosion and soil depletion. The FAO estimates that, worldwide, 5–10 million hectares of agricultural land are being lost annually to severe degradation.

These long-term trends have been exacerbated in recent years by government policies and commercial developments that have put further pressure on farmland. In many regions, under export-driven agricultural policies, large-scale plantations have developed for the production of food, energy, or cash crops. While this may improve the economic state of a country, it also creates problems by displacing small food producers from the land.

The fact remains that the major cause of food insecurity in developing countries is the inability of people to gain access to adequate food supply due to poverty. Africa, in particular sub-Saharan Africa, continues to lag behind the rest of the world in the struggle to reduce poverty. Factors contributing to this include the high incidence of AIDS, civil war, strife, poor governance, frequent drought, and famine. As a consequence, there is little doubt that food security on the African continent has worsened since 1970, while the proportion of the population that is malnourished has remained within the 33–35 percent range.

The prevalence of malnutrition in Africa varies by region; it is lowest in northern Africa (4 percent) and highest in central Africa (40 percent). Unsurprisingly, more than 70 percent of Africa's food-needy population live in rural areas. Fifty percent of these undernourished people are small-landholding farmers, even though they produce more than 90 percent of the continent's food supply. The rest of the food insecure population consists of the landless poor in rural areas (30 percent) and the urban poor.

Throughout the developing world, agriculture accounts for an average of about 9 percent of the GDP and more than half of total employment. In countries where more than 34 percent of the population is undernourished, agriculture represents 30 percent of GDP, and nearly 70 percent of the population relies on agriculture for their livelihood. This fact has in the past been used in support of the argument that such countries should moderate their dependence on agriculture and move into technology. Because more than 70 percent of the poor live in rural areas, where the largest proportion of the food insecure also live, it is evident that food insecurity cannot significantly be reduced without changing the living conditions of these people. There is a consensus view that agricultural development that increases the profitability of smallholder farmers while at the same time stimulating off-farm employment opportunities in rural areas is the only logical solution.[8]

The current pattern of rural poverty and hunger is caused by modes of production that have made small-scale farming generally nonviable and ensured that it remains no more than subsistence agriculture. Unable to compete with large plantations, small farmers working the poorest soils, principally the hilly, the arid, and the erosion-prone, have been pushed to the margins. The hopelessness of this situation has been the major factor behind migration to the cities. More than 1 billion people today—one in six people, and 43 percent of the population in developing countries—already live in slums, and by 2030, when the global population is likely to have reached more than 8 billion, that figure is likely to increase to one in three individuals. Those remaining in rural areas too often have been forced to subsist on inadequate agricultural resources, on which they barely manage to survive. These urban poor lack the purchasing power to buy the food available on the markets, with consequent increase in the numbers of those suffering from chronic hunger.[9]

barriers to market access

Small farmers in low-income countries are too often excluded from markets that would allow them to boost their incomes. There are many reasons for this. Poor infrastructure is probably the most important, with lack of adequate roads and transport barring access to markets. Lack of information, lack of or inadequate support organizations, and lack of supporting policies are also highly significant. Other barriers include market standards, limited information, requirements for large initial capital investments, and limited product differentiation. If access to local markets is difficult, delivery to international markets is even more of a problem, with high export costs limiting farmers' access. To overcome these obstacles, there is need for information, capital, technology, and expertise to which small farmers seldom have access.

political interference and access to food—the example of zimbabwe

An extreme example of a country where political interference is a major obstacle to access to food for a large part of the population is Zimbabwe. Despite being one of the most agriculturally rich countries in Africa, it is also one with the worst access to food problems This country has, to the extreme, all the elements that prevent people from being properly fed: inadequate food production, political interference with food distribution, and, despite once being Africa's major food exporter, heavy dependence on food imports and food aid. Too often, due to the crass mismanagement of the economy by a corrupt government, the funds to finance food imports are lacking. Zimbabwe is an outstanding example of a basically fertile country with substantial agricultural productive potential—sufficient to feed all of its population and bring in export revenue—where this potential cannot be achieved because of political obstruction.

The International Fund for Agricultural Development (IFAD) describes national food security as "the capacity of a nation to procure a stable and sustainable basket of adequate food." Zimbabwe fails this test on almost all counts.

Maize is Zimbabwe's staple food, with a 2008 annual national requirement of about 1.8 million tonnes: 1.5 million tonnes for human consumption and 0.3 million tonnes for livestock feeding. In terms of production capacity, recent maize yield ranges from 600 kilograms per hectare for communal farmers to 7 tonnes per hectare for large-scale commercial farmers. The government's so-called fast track land reform exercise has, however, been slow to achieve its major aim of increasing output; it has probably had the reverse effect by taking land out of the hands of the most efficient farmers and redistributing it among untrained would-be small farmers. Closely related economic difficulties have further exacerbated the reversal in food production. It remains to be seen whether a government wheat production program under contract schemes to promote food security by setting aside 150,000 hectares of land to produce the 2008 national requirement of 350,000–400,000 tonnes of wheat for national requirements, achieves any success.

Suffice it to say, food availability in Zimbabwe has been on the decline over the past decade. The performance of the country's food production and food supply policies are a continuing disaster. The 2006 maize harvest, for example, was at 1.1 million tonnes, well under the human consumption need of 1.4 million tonnes. Maize grain, while sold at subsidized prices, still remained out of reach for too many vulnerable households. Overall production of maize in 2008 was estimated at 575,000 tonnes—28 percent lower than 2007's already low levels.

Inevitably, aid agencies have had to step in to fill the gap left by government failure. The FAO/ World Food Programme (WFP) Crop and Food Supply Assessment Mission (CFSAM) estimated total domestic cereal availability for the April 2008–March 2009 marketing year at 840,000 tonnes, leaving a shortfall of about 1.2 million tonnes, including one million tonnes of maize, which had to be imported.

The ERS analysis states: "Current agricultural policy in Zimbabwe has adversely affected the production of maize and wheat due to market distortions."[10] It continues, "There seems to be little incentive for farmers to produce beyond their subsistence needs, given the lack of alternative marketing channels and price controls with static procurement prices in an environment of hyperinflation. The GMB, a government monopoly agency, buys and sells major cereals at controlled prices. The set prices discourage production, hence the negative effect on availability."

Table 12.3　ZIMBABWE FOOD SUPPLY AND AVAILABILITY (ACTUAL AND USDA/ERS ESTIMATES)

Year	Grain production*	Root production (grain equiv.)	Commercial imports (grains)	Food aid receipts (grain equiv.)		Aggregate availability of all food
			---1,000 tons ---			
2001	1,846	59	48	0		3,130
2002	909	60	482	298		3,143
2003	1,329	63	287	377		3,151
2004	2,168	65	381	267		3,192
2005	1,256	65	163	77		3,211
2006	1,947	64	442	148		3,564
2007	1,272	65	408	172		2,956
2008	689	65	726	366		2,922
2009(e)	1,446	67	494	229		3,324
Projections				Food gaps**		
				NG	DG	
2010	1,430	68	579	0	327	3,439
2015	1,549	73	767	0	310	3,924
2020	1,664	78	998	0	288	4,471

Source: USDA Economic Research Service, *International Food Security Assessment, 2011–22* (Washington, DC: USDA Economic Research Service, 2011).

(e) = estimate

*Grain production includes rice expressed in milled rice equivalent.

**NG stands for nutritional gap and describes the amount of grain equivalent needed to support nutritional standards on a national average level. DG stands for distributional gap and it describes that amount of grain equivalent needed to allow each income quintile to reach nutritional requirement.

For example, the maize purchase price during 2006/2007 marketing season was pegged at Z$52,000 per tonne (equivalent to about US$5 per tonne at the parallel market exchange rate at the time)—below the prices in the parallel markets. This rigging of the market has the dual harmful effect of discouraging farmers from maximizing production and denying food to the poorest; because there is no surplus, there is insufficient supply to feed the landless poor in rural areas. The parallel prices are often not affordable to the majority of the population. To make matters worse from the producer's point of view, purchase prices are announced at or after harvest, not at planting time.

The continuing decline in national food production clearly created the need for national food imports and aid. As a result of the failure of the food production system in the country, CFSAM estimated food assistance requirements in 2009 at around 395,000 tonnes—with the number of people requiring food assistance possibly rising to a peak of 5.1 million in the first quarter of 2009. The need for aid was necessitated by the Zimbabwe government's inability to import food because of the declining economy and consequent foreign exchange shortages. Zimbabwe's ability to import a variety of food to supplement local production has been further limited by soaring world food prices.

Zimbabwe's food imports have risen steadily through the past decade, with maize forming the bulk of the imports from the other southern African countries, particularly South Africa. The country operates a food distribution program called Operation Maguta, which is controlled by the Zimbabwe Defence Forces fulfilling their constitutional obligation to provide assistance to civil ministries and departments in times of crisis and need. The program is intended to be an augmentation of normal national agricultural activities. The Maguta program was initially successful when all government departments collaborated, until the Zimbabwe National Army began operating it without consulting the other ministries and government departments, with a consequent lack of impartiality in food distribution.

The scope for political control through the army can be seen from the method of food distribution. Selection of the recipients is first done at the village level by the kraal heads. The list of the beneficiaries from the village is taken to the ward level, where it is finalized by the village heads together with the ward councilors. The list is then passed on to members of the army, who approve the release of the inputs, which are usually kept at GMB depots. Access to the distributed food is dependent on the political party supported by the recipient.

improvement in food security

In general, the USDA/ERS assessment of global food security is more optimistic than that of the FAO. It estimates improvement between 2009 and 2010 for the seventy poorest countries most vulnerable to food shortage. According to the USDA/ERS, the number of food-insecure people is estimated to have decreased from about 953 million in 2009 to 882 million in 2010.[11] It is important to remember that most of the population in the least prosperous countries are likely to be close to—few above and most below—the nutritional target. This means that any economic downturn or food production shortfall is likely to mean millions of additional people being short of food.

Food supply conditions in the seventy at-risk developing countries is estimated to have improved between 2009 and 2010, principally because of economic recovery in many of these countries. However, it is unlikely that the number of food-insecure people in aggregate will significantly improve much over the next decade. The likely reduction is put at no more than 1 percent between 2010 and 2020. While there will be notable improvements in Asia and Latin America, the situation in sub-Saharan Africa is projected to deteriorate after 2010.

It is expected that by 2020, the number of food-insecure people in sub-Saharan Africa will be greater than 500 million in a total population of approximately 1 billion. Thus, without significant improvement in investment, agricultural development, or increased economic growth, more than half of the region's population will be receiving less than the nutritional target minimum. The region's food security position is likely to worsen compared with other LDC regions. In 2020, it is estimated that while the region will account for only 27 percent of the population of the seventy countries, it will have about a 59 percent share of the total number of food-insecure people.

In parts of Asia the access-to-food problem is even worse than in sub-Saharan Africa. In south Asia, the incidence of underweight, stunting, and wasting is much higher than anywhere else in the world, including sub-Saharan Africa.[12] The most recent data from the United Nations Children's Fund (UNICEF, 2006) indicate that underweight prevalence is 46 percent in south Asia compared with 29 percent in sub-Saharan Africa. In south Asia, females are also slightly more likely to be underweight (47 percent) than are males (44 percent). In addition to increased availability of food, both the education and status of women have been shown to make large contributions to the reduction of child malnutrition.

The type of development needed to deal with food poverty is likely to be different in Asia than in Africa, because of the different social and economic makeup of the two regions. In much of sub-Saharan Africa, agriculture is the strongest option for spurring growth, overcoming poverty, and enhancing food security, according to the World Bank.[13] In most of these countries agricultural productivity growth is vital for stimulating growth in other parts of the economy. To achieve accelerated growth will require significant productivity increases in smallholder farming combined with more effective support to subsistence farmers, many of them in remote areas.

In Asia, on the other hand, there has to be increased nonagricultural economic growth, to allow widening rural-urban income disparities to be checked, and more even distribution is needed to improve access to food in poverty-stricken rural areas. "Asia's fast-growing economies remain home to over 600 million rural people living in extreme poverty," says the World Bank and, it warns, "Despite massive rural-urban migration, rural poverty will remain dominant for several more decades." It is therefore necessary to generate rural employment and income by diversifying into labor-intensive, high-value agriculture linked to a dynamic rural, nonfarm sector.

Overall, it is expected that there will be a slight increase in food availability during the next decade, mainly because of improvements in Asia. But this is only likely to lead to a 5 percent drop in the number of people who will be seriously short of food in the seventy lowest income countries of the world. The surge in food prices during the first decade of the twenty-first century is likely to make an already bad situation worse. Projections of food availability indicate too low domestic production and, consequently, rising demand for food imports. Food import dependency has increased and continues to increase because of greater demand stemming from income and population growth and low investment in agricultural development, leading to minimal gains in domestic production. For highly import-dependent and food-insecure countries, any cut in import capacity as a result of rising food prices can only diminish food security.

summary and conclusion

The continuing ability of world agriculture to produce enough food for all does not ensure freedom from hunger in those countries without either adequate agriculture resources or income to import. Similarly, lack of infrastructure too often prevents the hungry from having access to food that is available. Hungry people are often isolated from food markets. Climatic shocks are likely to exacerbate food shortages in the most vulnerable regions. Wars and other political conflicts also obstruct food supply to the most needy. Zimbabwe is an outstanding example of political obstruction of access to food.

Ironically, the richer emerging Asian economies have the most hungry people, and China and India are the worst examples. In Asia generally there is a need for economic growth other than agriculture to improve access to food to overcome problems of rural poor. The 2008–2012 food crises made hunger worse by increasing the cost of food imports, illustrating that too many of the most needy countries are too dependent on grain imports. Greater self-sufficiency of the rural poor is made worse by the fact that most of those who depend on small farms for their living have landholdings that are too small to maintain a family. This situation is likely to worsen in the absence of imaginative new policies, because pressure from rising population means that farms get smaller. Any further surge in food prices will worsen conditions for the hungry.

notes

1. Amartya K. Sen, *Poverty and Famines* (New York: Oxford University Press, 1981).
2. World Food Programme, "What Causes Hunger?" Available at: http://www.wfp.org/hunger/causes, accessed December 2011.
3. FAO, *The State of Food Insecurity in the World 2011. How Does International Price Volatility Affect Domestic Economies and Food Security?* (Rome: FAO, 2011).
4. Shahla Shapouri, Stacey Rosen, May Peters, Felix Baquedano, and Summer Allen, *Food Security Assessment, 2010–20*, USDA Economic Research Service Outlook Report No. (GFA-21) 64, July 2010.
5. Ibid.
6. FAO, *The State of Food Insecurity in the World 2004: Monitoring Progress towards the World Food Summit and Millennium Development Goals* (Rome: FAO, 2003).
7. FAO, "Report of the Special Rapporteur on the Right to Food," United Nations A/65/281, General Assembly, August 11, 2010.

8. Angela Mwaniki, *Achieving Food Security in Africa: Challenges and Issues* (Ithaca, NY: U.S. Plant, Soil and Nutrition Laboratory, 2005).

9. Olivier De Schutter, Special UN rapporteur on the right to food, Twenty-sixth McDougall Memorial Lecture, Rome, November 18–23, 2009.

10. Ibid., iv.

11. Food-insecure people are de?ned as those consuming less than a nutritional target of 2,100 calories per day per person.

12. FAO, *The State of Food and Agriculture in Asia and the Pacific 2006* (Rome, FAO, 2006).

13. World Bank, *World Development Report 2008: Agriculture for Development* (Washington, DC: World Bank, 2008).

chapter 13

---

food supply policies

Governments throughout the ages have sought to direct, control, and regulate the production of food. Almost always the primary objective was to ensure security of supply. In the ancient world the pharaohs of Egypt famously imposed regulations on the quantities of food that should be held in storage in the years of fat harvests to cover the needs in the lean years. Governments have established policies not only to ensure adequate supplies of food to their populations but also to fulfill the strategic requirement of insulation from excessive dependence on imports. In the modern world, with the diversification of economic activity within nations and internationally, the once-accepted essentially autarchic approach to food supply policy has been tempered by the need to trade. In the nineteenth century, Great Britain, for example, saw the advantage of exchanging its highly competitive industrial goods for low-cost food imports from Russia and Ukraine and, later, the United States and Australasia. The repeal of the Corn Laws in the 1840s marked the end of British government protection of its own agriculture industry and abandonment of the implicit objective of food self-sufficiency. Countries with outright economic advantage in agricultural production and mastery of world agricultural commodity markets, such as the United States in the late nineteenth century, developed policies to sustain that predominance and to protect their own farm industries.

main points

- Governments have always sought food security.
- Security is often confused with self-sufficiency.
- European Union agriculture policy is a failed attempt at self-sufficiency.
- Both the EU and U.S. agriculture policy placed a heavy burden on taxpayers.
- New Zealand sets the example of competitive agriculture without subsidies.
- Food security can be achieved by a combination n of domestic production and imports.
- Developed country policies tend to harm agricultural development in less-prosperous nations.

At the 1974 World Food Summit, food security was defined as the "availability at all times of adequate world food supplies of basic foodstuffs to sustain a steady expansion of food consumption and to offset fluctuations in production and prices."

Discussion of food security can be confusing because food security for developed economies is multifaceted and complex with closely interlinked aspects. While definitions of national food security can be tempered to suit particular political objectives, there are common themes. These include availability of food; access of consumers to affordable, nutritional, and safe food; resilience of the food system to significant disruptions; and public confidence in that system.[1]

The most outstanding example of the desire of governments for absolute food security is the post–World War II development of the European agriculture policy, initially common to the six founder nations of the European Economic Community and now extended to almost the whole of Europe through the twenty-seven nations of the modern European Union (EU-27). The most important element of the original common agricultural policy (CAP) was the concept of community preference, the principle that no food should be allowed to be imported that could be grown by the farmers of the member states. If this principle could not always be abided by, then any imports carry heavy import taxes (levies), which raised prices higher than the target prices maintained for the domestic producers.

This self-sufficiency policy, combined with lavish market support subsidies, inevitably led to levels of production way beyond the capacity of European stomachs. The chronic surpluses that evolved had to be dumped on international markets.[2] Because these exports were produced at such high cost, they could only be exported competitively with large subventions from the European taxpayer. Subsidized European exports of wheat, butter, milk powder, beef, sugar, and even wine flooded world markets in the 1970s, 1980s, and 1990s and depressed the prices received by other, often unsubsidized, exporters. The EU's dumping of dairy product and sugar surpluses was particularly harmful to the agricultural exporters in developing countries.

The overriding preoccupation of politicians in the development of agriculture and food supply policies has been the quest for food security, seen very clearly in the development of the CAP. National attitudes have played an important part in the evolution of the mechanisms employed. Direct intervention in agricultural markets had been an important feature of German agricultural policy since the establishment of the first Reich in 1871 and the subsequent drift toward agricultural protectionism during the depression of the 1880s. Germany followed France in establishing substantial tariffs against food imports in the 1890s as the prairies and plains of North America began to pour their cheap and apparently endless bounty eastward into European markets. By the end of World War I, Germany had developed a system of state responsibility for food supplies through the establishment of state buying and storage of supplies direct from the farms or firsthand merchants.

German government control of food supplies was further developed under the National Socialists in the 1930s. France also developed a system of state regulation of grain supplies between the wars. To a great extent, the domestically and internationally damaging impact of the CAP has been substantially moderated by an evolving policy that is turning away from subsidizing agricultural production and commodity exports to subsidizing farm incomes and the provision of environmental services.

But despite the EU's modern role of a massive international trader in industrial products, services, and agriculture and food products, there are still influential European politicians who harbor continuing delusions of the merits of self-sufficiency in food supply that border on autarchy. This attitude continues to be well-represented in the European Parliament.

Despite its World War II preeminence in agricultural production and exports, the United States also began to suffer the financial and political penalties of oversupporting its farmers in the last decades of the twentieth century. As in Europe, high support prices negotiated in the late 1970s ran into difficulties by the early 1980s. Government costs began to escalate as government stocks accumulated in a declining world market. Three significant forces were at work. First, a major deficit problem tightened government purse strings. Second, Congress and most of the agriculture community became convinced that support prices were out of line to sustain growth in the export market. Third, technological efficiencies, especially in intensive livestock production, challenged the more traditional structure of the farm community.

Reacting to these pressures, the 1985 U.S. farm bill (the Food Security Act of 1985) resulted in a gradual step down in government support, maintaining the basic formula of supply control, but, with significant reduction in support for the production of major crops. All three pressures were addressed: less government, export competitiveness with lower support rates, and lower grain prices that began to fuel the expansion of intensive livestock production.

The farm bill in 1990 (the Food, Agriculture, Conservation, and Trade Act of 1990) addressed the same pressures with increasing emphasis on conservation and environment. The basic structure of supply control was maintained with considerably less government support. After the enactment of the 1990 farm bill, budget cuts continued each year at significant levels. As in Europe, subsequent U.S. farm support legislation has tempered the levels of subsidization of production and moved policy more toward farm income equalization and environmental and conservation measures.

Current development of U.S. agriculture policy could well prove a major challenge to President Barack Obama's declared intention to reduce America's protection of its trade. As in most developed countries, the reality is that the United States is continuing to liberalize all areas of trade—except agriculture. The most recent U.S. agriculture act, the Food, Conservation, and Energy Act of 2008, continued to perpetuate a panoply of measures designed to give the U.S. farmer formidable protection against the vicissitudes of the open market. It remains to be seen how well the 2008 legislation will stand up to inevitable assaults in continuing multilateral trade negotiations and what the U.S. response will be.

The 2008 farm act, in the words of the U.S. Department of Agriculture, "builds on previous policy and provides a new counter-cyclical revenue program and a permanent disaster fund for farmers." The new farm bill added further income stabilization provisions to already existing commodity market and income support policies. The Average Crop Revenue Election, with the amusing acronym ACRE, allows farmers to opt for an average income guarantee if they largely opt out of other commodity support programs. Production support policies are still present, but at much lower levels than in previous decades.

Seen from a trade policy point of view, there is little doubt that the ACRE program is a further addition to the armory of measures that might be classified by many economists as market distorting. The same can be said of the so-called green payments to farmers becoming the dominant farm subsidy in Europe. The payments from the U.S. budget to maintain farm incomes also maintain farm returns at higher levels than would be the case without them. They are therefore likely to maintain a higher level of production. This becomes obvious when the details of U.S. farm subsidy payments are examined. Subsidy handouts averaged $12,687 per farm on the 44 percent of U.S. farms growing crops eligible for subsidy in 2006. Payments accounted for about 8 percent of gross cash income and 39 percent of net cash income in 2006 for those farms. The picture is much the same in Europe, although the proportion of farm income coming from taxpayer subsidies rises to as much as 70 percent of total income in Scandinavia; the EU average is around 20 percent. The pattern of gain from government payments in the United States is very similar to that in the European Union, with the largest 10.6 percent of farms in terms of gross receipts receiving 55.9 percent of all government payments in 2006.

While the effect on production in the U.S. system may be the same as payments under the EU agriculture policy, the level of total government spending involved is considerably less. While the EU is committed to spending in excess of €50 (US$60) billion a year on market support and direct payments, as well as a further €30 billion from European national government coffers. U.S. government expenditures in the period to 2008 averaged about $16 billion per fiscal year. U.S. payments fluctuate with world prices; EU payments do not. U.S. government spending included peak expenditures of more than $20 billion in fiscal years 2005–2006 in response to low commodity prices and a rise in disaster and emergency assistance. Under current legislation it is expected that U.S. government expenditures on income support and commodity programs will average $11 billion over the period to 2013.

An important feature of U.S. food and agriculture policy—barely present in the EU system—is food aid to the domestic population that far exceeds expenditure on support of farmers. While this could be a means of stimulating domestic demand for agricultural products, it is clearly not market distorting in the usual way of agriculture policies. U.S. government expenditure on these schemes increased from $46.1 billion in 1995 to $71.8 billion in 2005 and the bulk of this was payments for food and nutrition assistance programs.

Both the United States and the EU maintain that their farmer support policies are increasingly not market distorting, in other words, they are not responsible for producing large quantities of major agricultural commodities and at a lower undercutting price than if the policies were not in place. The U.S. classification of what many regard as market-distorting subsidies as production neutral and therefore permissible under World Trade Organization rules (so-called green box subsidies) remains highly questionable. Subsidies in both the world's leading agricultural producing and exporting countries are major and contentious issues in international trade negotiations, particularly for less-developed agricultural exporting countries and nonsubsidizing developed country exporters who suffer the effects of subsided U.S. and EU exports.

The farm subsidy policies of both the United States and the EU are likely to come under increasing pressure in multilateral trade negotiations. The impact of exports from the subsidized farms of the developed countries have been made worse by the worldwide recession and will have particularly serious implications for primary-product exporting countries, leading to fresh pressure for the United States and EU not only to reduce their protection, but also to scale down subsidies to their own producers.

farmers without support—the example of new zealand

To demonstrate that governments do not need to excessively support and protect farmers in order to ensure food supplies and compete on world markets, there is the example of New Zealand. The country is the world's largest producer and exporter of lamb, as well as being a major exporter of dairy products; it dominates the world cheese market. Despite these achievements, it has the lowest level of government agricultural support in the developed world. Its degree of subsidization (producer subsidy equivalent, simply, the proportion of farmers' income coming from subsidy) is rated by the OECD at no more than 4 percent, against figures for the European Union, the United States, and most other developed countries of, historically, more than 30 percent, ranging up to more than 45 percent in years of low world prices (see Figure 13.1).

Current agricultural policy in New Zealand is heavily influenced by general economic reforms achieved in the 1980s. The critical feature of New Zealand's economic policy reforms, initiated in 1984, was minimizing government interference and subvention (both within the agricultural sector and across the economy) through the removal of subsidies, with the aim of allowing markets to be the primary factor in determining resource allocation. This approach has undoubtedly resulted in a more simplified agricultural policy framework.

The policy measures familiar in most developed country agriculture policies are largely absent from the New Zealand policy paradigm. New Zealand farmers and food processors have not received price or income support since before the 1990s. Since 2002 there has been no restriction on agricultural processing firms exporting from New Zealand. In the country's dairy industry, for example, there is no government manipulation of markets or subsidizing of exports. The almost unique feature of the New Zealand dairy industry is the domination of processing, marketing, and export of milk and milk products

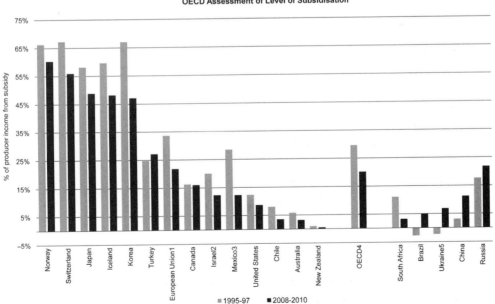

OECD Assessment of Level of Subsidisation

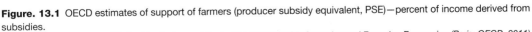

Figure. 13.1 OECD estimates of support of farmers (producer subsidy equivalent, PSE)—percent of income derived from subsidies.
Source: OECD, Agricultural Policy Monitoring and Evaluation 2011: OECD Countries and Emerging Economies *(Paris: OECD, 2011).*

by what is essentially a farmer-owned cooperative of which the marketing arm is Fonterra. This organization is responsible for handling almost all of the country's dairy output and has become a major operator in international markets.

No one would claim New Zealand's transition to an unprotected agriculture was without pain, least of all the farmers who were the most seriously affected. Many of the less-efficient farmers went out of business. Significantly, however, their land passed into the hands of more efficient operators; production increased and with lower resource cost. The structural change in New Zealand agriculture, and dairying in particular, since the 1980s was considerable and involved a long period of adjustment.

As the OECD commented in its 2011 report on OECD-country agriculture policies, "New Zealand's agriculture is a market- and export-oriented sector and domestic prices of agricultural products are aligned with world market prices. The level of support to agriculture in New Zealand is the lowest among OECD countries, at 1 percent of farm income, and most of its policy measures are sector-wide, representing general services to agriculture."[3]

Very few of New Zealand's policies before 1986–1988, which distorted agricultural production and trade, remain today. The level of producer support is currently the lowest across the OECD. Most domestic prices are aligned with the world prices, and payments are only provided for animal disease control and relief in the event of large-scale climate and natural disasters. Almost all sectors have been deregulated following statutory producer organization and marketing board reforms.

confusion of food security with food self-sufficiency

As is clearly demonstrated by the early development of European agriculture policy, there has always been a tendency for governments to confuse food security with food self-sufficiency, despite the clear difference between the two concepts:

- *Food security* means securing food supply from multiple sources, including imports—not necessarily complete dependence on national production. In other words, food security is meeting the various food needs of the population, in the economically, socially, and environmentally optimum way.
- *Food self-sufficiency*, on the other hand, introduces economic and political independence from other countries as primary aims in securing an adequate food supply.

A good example of a policy that achieved food security without food self-sufficiency was that operated by the United Kingdom between 1947 and 1973. While ensuring that its own farmers produced 40 to 50 percent of the national food supply, the government maintained preferential access to the other half of its massive food market for the cereal, dairy, and meat producers of Denmark, Ireland, Australia, New Zealand, Canada, Argentina, and the United States. It should be observed that these countries were the lowest cost producers of the products supplied to the UK. In this way the actual price of food in British shops was kept at what could fairly be described as the low world price. British farmers (deemed to be bearing higher production costs than their overseas competitors) were compensated for having to compete at the world price by direct payments. When Britain joined the European Economic Community's near-autarchic agricultural system in 1973–1974, prices for the major foods at the UK shop counter more than doubled. Over the subsequent five years, UK farmers' prices very nearly tripled, with consequent economic and environmental distortions. For example, more than 30,000 hectares of ancient grassland in the English Midlands were plowed up to grow high-cost wheat.

The UK's postwar and pre-European Community food and farm policy was one that, while not maintaining self-sufficiency, certainly achieved food sovereignty—control of the food supply to the benefit of consumers. Food sovereignty is another too often wooly concept due to its origins in the growth of the antiglobalization movement during the past three decades. Its use or misuse allows it to snarl legitimate arguments about self-sufficiency and food security.

The general interpretation of food sovereignty is the international right of populations, of their nations or unions, to define their agricultural and food policies without dumping towards third countries. It is therefore of a much more political nature than the other two concepts. Much as the antiglobalization movement may desire, food sovereignty has no international legal basis nor is it recognized as an objective by international institutions. It is generally interpreted as the right of a country or people to establish and operate food supply and agricultural policies best adapted to their populations, with the objective of guaranteeing supply through local production and frontier protection mechanisms (such as custom duties) while establishing priorities such as securing land availability for impoverished farmers. The goal is generally seen as encouraging local agricultural activities intended to supply local, regional, and national markets. It can be misinterpreted as an anti-intensive and protectionist agriculture movement.

developed country agriculture policies and the agricultural trade of developing countries

What is indisputable in any discussion of agriculture policy and politics is that the farm support policies of the developed countries have harmed both the domestic agricultural production and the potential exports of developing country food producers. Investigations by international organizations such as the International Food Policy Research Institute (IFPRI) demonstrate the impact of these policies on agricultural development in the poorest countries. According to estimates by researchers at IFPRI, developed country policies reduce agricultural exports from the developing world by in excess of $37 billion (more than 25 percent) annually by limiting access to the world's richest markets and diluting world prices for agricultural commodities through directly or indirectly subsidized exports.[4]

The direct impact on the agriculture of the developing countries is also significant. The agricultural gross domestic product (value-added) among developing countries is estimated by IFPRI to be reduced by about $25 billion annually. For specific countries producing particular commodities, the effects can be critical, as in the case of African cotton, sugar in Guatemala, or dairy exporters in the West Indies.

The impact—and hopefully benefit—of developed country farm policy reform will vary across developing countries, depending on, among other factors, their composition of production, dependence on food imports, trading costs, and national policies.[5] Almost all aspects of the EU's agriculture policy and other developed country policies are likely to disadvantage the agriculture and agricultural trade of LDCs, according to the Overseas Development Institute (ODI).Like the IFPRI, the ODI stresses that it is important to look at policy instruments in detail when looking at the impact of developed country farm policy reform on developing countries; they have different effects on different types of countries and products.

Import tariffs borne by exporting less-developed countries without preferential access remain high. For delivery into the EU for example, import tariffs average 54 percent for milk products, 34 percent for grains, and 32 percent for meat. So far, this protection wall has not been affected by the CAP reforms of the 1990s and 2000s, which have been principally concerned with reform of domestic policy mechanisms. The problem, as the ODI points out, is that while lower tariffs would help developing country exporters without preferential access, they would hurt those who already have tariff-free access. Lower import tariffs also would increase EU and world demand for specific commodities, thus raising their prices and damaging developing country consumers dependent on imports of food.

Whatever defenders of the CAP and U.S. agriculture policy may argue, direct payments to farmers, whether coupled to production or not, are bound to allow developed country farmers to sell at lower prices on world markets than they would if the subsidies were not paid. Payments directly connected to levels of production by definition must encourage increased output at lower prices; reducing them would result in reduced developed country output and lead to increased exports, and income, for many developing countries.

Direct decoupled payments that now form the main type of farm subsidy on both sides of the Atlantic, are a way of sweeping farm support under the carpet, but it is still there and still encouraging higher production at lower prices. Such subsidies are claimed to be non-market-distorting, but according to the ODI, "in practice there is growing evidence that by supporting non-competitive farmers they may induce farmers who would otherwise leave the industry to keep on producing. As payments are conditional on ensuring that the land to which they relate remains usable for farming, these payments help to retain more land in use for farming. Because direct payments increase EU supply, any reduction in such payments would allow an increase in developing country exports and higher world prices, although it would raise costs for developing country importers of CAP-affected products."[6]

Government payments for rural development schemes such as those made under the EU's CAP have economic effects on developing countries, depending on the extent to which they provide additional income based on measures the farmers would have taken in any case (with the same effect as direct payments), rather than compensating for extra spending on rural development or environmental measures. More obviously damaging is expenditure on export subsidies. The EU, for example, paid farmers indirectly via traders €1 billion in export subsidies in 2008 and €650 million in 2009. Most recently, these subsidies have been paid primarily on dairy products. Because export subsidies boost EU supply and therefore lower prices for exports, reducing these subsidies could hurt some developing country consumers as prices rise; retaining export subsidies, however, displaces developing country producers and exporters.

Despite reforms, the EU maintains market intervention at fixed prices, in principle, for cereals, beef and veal, and butter and skimmed milk powder, but only for quantities fixed in advance or at very low prices. Since 2009–2010, no cereals apart from soft wheat have been eligible for official buying-in (intervention). There are unlikely to be major effects in the future on the rest of the world. Of all the EU policy instruments, direct payments and rural development support now have the largest impact on developing countries.

The EU's agricultural policy is therefore in direct conflict with its overseas development policies. This is recognized in the EU's objective of policy coherence for development: "The EU seeks to take into account development cooperation objectives in non-development policies. The EU recognizes that some of its policies can have a significant impact outside of the EU and that either contributes to or undermines its development policy. The EU therefore seeks to minimise contradictions and to build synergies between policies other than development cooperation that have an impact on developing countries, for the benefit of overseas development."[7] How far is this being met in the evolution of its domestic agriculture policy?

The developing countries most likely to be affected by CAP reforms are those for which exports of any of the CAP-affected products are or likely to be important. They could gain increases in their real income because of moderation of EU export price or volume. Other food importing countries could lose because of more expensive imports. African and Latin American countries are particularly affected by CAP policy instruments.

Removal of direct payments to EU farmers could increase production in non-OECD countries. The impact is likely to be largest for cereals, but there are also likely to be increases for oilseeds, fruits and vegetables, rice, and plant-based fiber. Output would increase, especially in Latin America and, to a smaller extent, in Asian countries. Assessment of the impact of direct payments, border tariffs, and export subsidies on Africa, using the Global Trade Analysis Project (GTAP) model, suggests that these three measures together are likely to reduce Africa's gross national expenditures (a welfare measure including consumption, investments, public expenditures, and terms of trade effects) by 0.05 percent or $560 million.[8]

But probably the most important effect of further winding down of EU agriculture policy would be the effect on world prices. It has been suggested that the complete abolition of the CAP would lead to average increases in world prices of the order of 1–4 percent, but the size of the impact will vary across commodities and across countries.[9] The expected changes seem small compared to recent fluctuations in commodity prices of 50–100 percent in one to two years, but these are short-term variations around the trend, while reform would achieve a permanent shift.

For any change in EU policy, the effects on the prices faced by individual developing country exporters or importers depend on the structure of markets (the response of EU importers and exporters) and the structure of international trade. Countries with high transportation costs or other market imperfections are likely to see lower benefits.

policies in LDCs

But it is not only developed countries that create barriers to trade in agriculture and food products. For many reasons less-developed countries also seek to protect their farmers and agricultural industries from foreign competition. Often this can be justified on the grounds of fostering the growth of national production and therefore improving food security. Too often such policies fail to achieve this objective, succeeding only in raising the price of food for already hard-pressed populations.

They can also harm the trade and economies of other developing countries. This is because close to one-third of the agricultural trade of developing countries is with other developing countries, and this share is growing. Countries with expanding agricultural production and trade have substantial trade barriers on agricultural products. Brazil, China, India, and Mexico impose import tariffs on agricultural products averaging more than 25 percent—higher tariff levels than those imposed by many low-income countries.

It is significant that developing country governments that are united in seeking the benefits from re-duced agricultural subsidies and protection in the developed countries cannot agree on action to deal with their own agricultural trade barriers. Those countries with strong agricultural export potential press for more open markets, while those who fear negative impacts on their poor farmers, including coun-tries with potential for agricultural exporting, have not been keen on tariff reduction.

It is convincingly argued by development nongovernmental organizations (NGOs) that infant industry protection is justified to allow developing countries to develop their agricultural export industries. But LDCs have most to gain overall from liberalization of agricultural markets. Investigations by IFPRI indi-cate that reduction of agricultural protection among developing countries is different from the effects of developed country reforms. With joint developing country agricultural trade liberalization, research at IFPRI indicates that their overall GDP gains are likely to be nearly $40 billion annually, more than double the gain in developing country GDP (of $14.5 billion) when only the developed countries liberalize. The developing country trade policy reforms add an additional $15 billion annually to their aggregated agri-cultural exports.

Such additional gains come principally from consumer advantage of lower internal prices as import barriers are diminished. Consumers benefit most in more countries when both developing and devel-oped countries cut tariffs and nontariff barriers.

Unfortunately, the benefits of liberalization are not likely to be spread evenly between developing countries. There is inevitably an uneven spread between those developing countries best able to gain from protection reduction and those less able to do so. It is therefore inevitable that development poli-cies would be needed for some countries or regions and population groups, particularly among the very least developed, whose agricultural resources are limited and have other economic handicaps that would hamper their ability to benefit from liberalized agricultural trade.

Such policies would need to address such problems as price instability, malfunctioning markets, and the phasing out of food aid dependency in some countries. If and when trade barriers are reduced, the benefit to poor farmers and gains for food consumers in countries less able to compete in more open markets cannot come from multilateral trade liberalization by itself. Additional domestic investments and policy improvements will have to be applied.

land grabs—threat or boon?

Apart from the rich, agriculturally self-sufficient and exporting countries on the one hand and the poor, agriculturally deficient countries on the other, there is another group of countries that although materially rich in all other aspects are agriculturally poor. These include the oil-rich desert kingdoms of the Middle East and countries that have massive populations well out of proportion to their domestic food production capacity, such as China. In an uncertain world, these countries are like all countries, anxious to achieve food security. While trade may achieve this objective, they are seeking more solid forms of food security by using their wealth to buy food production resources in other land-rich but otherwise materially poor countries.

This development inevitably raises important questions: Does the takeover of land in poorer developing countries deprive those countries of potential food production capacity? Does it deny those countries income? Does the introduction of intensive farming methods into such countries harm the ecosystems and social systems? Does it displace people and more appropriate farming systems? Contrary arguments posed include, Does development of this nature introduce improved agricultural techniques? Does it bring in additional incomes and thus stimulate economic growth?

The desire to secure future food resources is led by food-importing countries short of land but rich in capital, such as the Persian Gulf states. Countries with large populations and the obvious lack of adequate agricultural production, such as China, South Korea, and India, are seeking to outsource a significant part of their food production. The hosts for such investments are likely to be developing countries with more abundant land and water and lower production costs. Other important factors are geographic proximity and climatic conditions favorable for stable production of the major food staples. Some countries are seeking land in other territory for the production of biofuel crops.

The scope and terms of contracts on these deals can differ widely. Some involve merely contract farming arrangements while others include such things as investment in rural and agricultural infrastructure, including irrigation systems and roads.

A World Bank assessment of the land acquisition issue, published in 2009, indicated that there were likely to have been more than 46 million hectares in large-scale farmland acquisitions or negotiations between October 2008 and August 2009.[10] The World Bank study was carried out by the International Institute for Environment and Development (IIED) at the request of the FAO and the International Fund for Agricultural Development (IFAD). Two-thirds of the deals were likely to have involved land concentrated in sub-Saharan Africa. It is important to note however, that fewer than half of the bank's 464 listed transactions detailed the land area involved, suggesting that the actual total land involved was likely to be more than double the bank's reported 46 million hectares. The most recent estimate of the scale of overseas purchases is that the area of land is probably more than 80 million hectares.

The World Bank stated that of these deals, the median size is 40,000 hectares, with one-quarter over 200,000 hectares and one-quarter under 10,000 hectares; 37 percent of projects deal with food crops, 21 percent with cash crops, and 21 percent with biofuels. This pattern suggests the vast diversity of investors and projects involved in these land acquisitions; the area of land, desired cropping, and the assortment of investors involved varies widely. Of the projects identified by the World Bank in 2010, 30 percent were still in an exploratory stage, with 70 percent approved, but in varying stages of development. While 18 percent had not started, 30 percent were in the initial development stage, and 21 percent had actually started farming.

The projects often involved investment in land through long-term leases, as opposed to outright purchases with such leases ranging between 25 and 99 years. Such leases have tended to be undertaken between national or district governments and investors. This is because the majority of land in Africa is owned by governments or is government controlled. Outright purchase by the land users are also much less common than leases due to several countries' constitutional bans on the sale of land to foreigners.

Some developed country governments are keen to prevent the land grab movement from disadvantaging developing countries. The European Commission, for example, is launching a joint initiative with the African Union to accelerate the implementation of the African land policy guidelines. The initiative will include a roadmap for the implementation of sustainable large-scale investments in farmland. The EC initiative particularly highlights the need to protect land rights and secure access to natural resources for smallholder farmers and pastoral communities. The FAO is also currently developing guidelines for land acquisition. It has already outlined a number of general recommendations for investors, host governments, civil society organizations, and international development agencies on the matter.

The World Bank has pointed out, in its 2009 study, that with land acquisitions on the increase in Africa and other continents, there is a risk that if agreements are not made properly, poor people will be evicted or lose access to land, water, and other resources. It warns that such deals "can bring many opportunities (guaranteed outlets, employment, investment in infrastructures, increases in agricultural productivity) but can also cause great harm if local people are excluded from decisions about allocating land and if their land rights are not protected."

The World Bank's examination of the issue found that as land-based investment has risen over the past five years, domestic investors are playing a more major role in land acquisitions than is generally recognized. Nonetheless, foreign investment still dominates. Private sector deals are more common than government-to-government arrangements, though governments of host countries are using a range of tools to indirectly support private deals.

Concerns about food and energy security are key motivations for land acquisition deals, but other factors such as investment opportunities and demand for agricultural commodities for industry are also involved. Although large-scale land claims remain a small proportion of suitable land in any one country, the World Bank points out that, contrary to widespread perceptions, there is very little empty land, because most remaining suitable land is already under use or claim, often by local people.

Significantly, the report found that many countries do not have adequate mechanisms to protect local rights and to guard local interests, livelihoods, and welfare. It says, "A lack of transparency and of checks and balances in contract negotiations can promote deals that do not maximize the public interest. Insecure local land rights, inaccessible registration procedures, vaguely defined productive use requirements, legislative gaps and other factors too often undermine the position of local people."

It calls for the careful assessment of local contexts, including existing land uses and claims, securing land rights for rural communities, the involvement of local people in negotiations, and proceeding with land acquisition only after their free, prior, and informed consent is obtained. Lorenzo Cotula and his colleagues at IIED, coauthors of the 2009 World Bank assessment, caution that land acquisitions vary greatly and that blanket statements about land-grabbing are highly misleading. "Ultimately, whether international land deals seize opportunities and mitigate risks depends on their terms and conditions — what business models are used, how costs and benefits are shared, and who decides on these issues and how," say Cotula and his colleagues. "This calls for proper regulation, skilful negotiation and public oversight."

Alexander Mueller, head of the Environment and Natural Resources Department at FAO, stresses the need to see foreign investment and large-scale land acquisitions in the context of global food security challenges. He said: "This new trend is a result of the recent food crisis and volatility of food prices, among other factors. The new challenges of global food insecurity and global investment should be addressed through appropriate regulations, and well-informed agricultural and food policies. The study should help to link decisions on investment with an awareness of all implications, including social and environmental ones. Developing guidelines for land governance, or a code to regulate international investments might be useful to improve decision-making and negotiations. FAO and its partners are currently working together to develop such guidelines, and this study is a first step in this process."[11]

Foreign development of land in developing countries can bring benefits to the local population. "I would avoid the blanket term 'land-grabbing,'" says Rodney Cooke, IFAD director, Technical Advisory Division. "Done the right way, these deals can bring benefits for all parties and be a tool for development. The poor women and men that IFAD works with every day must not be side-lined. Their input and their interests must be central, and we must ensure that any benefits promised, such as employment, infrastructure, agricultural know-how, do materialize."[12]

summary and conclusions

In developed countries, attempts at food self-sufficiency have usually meant subsidies for farmers and heavy costs for taxpayers and consumers. Such policies have always been and remain a threat to developing country food producers and exporters. In contrast, among developed countries New Zealand sets the example of development of an internationally competitive agriculture without subsidies. Food security does not inevitably mean food self-sufficiency; security can be achieved by a combination of domestic production and imports. Clearly there is a tendency for developed country food and farm policies to harm agricultural development of less-prosperous nations with developed countries' agricultural policies often in conflict with their development policies.

Too often developing countries also operate discriminatory agricultural and food trading policies against each other. Recent growth in land-grab activity by economically rich but land-poor countries is a symptom mainly of a search for food security following the food crises of the first decade of the twenty-first century. Such land acquisition deals can be of advantage to host countries, but rights and food production capacity of inhabitants has to be protected.

notes

1. Food Chain Analysis Group, Department of Environment, Food, and Rural Affairs (DEFRA), *Food Security and the UK: An Evidence and Analysis Paper,* (London: UK Government, DEFRA, 2006).

2. Dumping is defined as selling on world markets at less than the domestic production cost.

3. OECD, *Agricultural Policy Monitoring and Evaluation 2011: OECD Countries and Emerging Economies* (Paris: OECD Publishing, 2011).

4. Joachim von Braun, Ashok Gulati, and David Orden, *Making Agricultural Trade Liberalization Work for the Poor* (Washington, DC: IFPRI, 2004).

5. Overseas Development Institute, "Making the EU's Common Agricultural Policy Coherent with Development Goals," Briefing Paper 69, September 2011.

6. Nicola Cantore, Jane Kennan, and Sheila Page, *CAP Reform and Development: Introduction, Reform Options and Suggestions for Further Research* (London: Overseas Development Institute, 2011).

7. European Commission, "EU Report on Policy Coherence for Development," Commission Working Paper (Brussels: European Commission, 2007).

8. C. Costa, M. Osborne, X. Zhang, P. Boulanger, and P. Jomini, *Modelling the Effects of the EU Agricultural Policy* (Melbourne: Australian Government Productivity Commission, 2009).

9. P. Boulanger, P. Jomini, X. Zhang, C. Costa, and M. Osborne, *An Economic Assessment of Removing the Most Distortive Instruments of the Common Agricultural Policy* (Copenhagen: European Trade Study Group, 2010). Available at: www.etsg.org/ETSG2010/papers/Boulanger_Jomini_Zhang_Costa_Osborne.pdf.

10. L. Cotula, S. Vermeulen, R. Leonard, and J. Keeley, *Agricultural Investment and International Land Deals in Africa* (London and Rome: IIED/FAO/IFAD, 2009).

11. Quoted in Cotula et al., *Land Grab or Development Opportunity?*

12. Quoted in Cotula et al., *Land Grab or Development Opportunity?*

chapter 14

sustainability of the world food production system

Definitions of sustainability can be so loose and compendious as to be meaningless. The concept of sustainability has even been described as a "dialogue of values that defies consensual definition."[1] In agriculture, the concept, if not the term, has been known to farmers since the beginning of settled agriculture—not taking more out of the land than can be put back. Modern agriculture is regularly accused, with and without justification, of not abiding by this fundamental rule. The most important question to be answered is, Can the level of global food production needed to feed 9–10 billion people be sustained into the twenty-second century and beyond? In addition, in maintaining this level of food supply, will modern agriculture have side effects that are not sustainable—such as high greenhouse gas emissions, other forms of air pollution, contamination of rivers and oceans, strained water supplies—and threaten biodiversity or destroy flora, fauna, and priceless landscapes? Will genetically engineered crops and livestock be needed to sustain the necessary level of production, and is such genetic modification a threat to the world ecosystem?

main points

- Sustainability is difficult to define.
- Maintaining a high level of output without damaging the ecosystem is problematic.
- Levels of agriculture's greenhouse emissions are heavily disputed.
- Greenhouse gas emission reduction is only possible through massive change in diets away from ruminant animal products.
- Organic approach to agriculture is unlikely to alleviate potential world food supply problems.
- Food miles–based objections to food trade are too often based on incomplete analysis.
- GM crops are not a panacea for increased global food production.
- Water resources available to agriculture are under serious strain; areas with the greatest food need have the most strain.

The current situation was succinctly put by a recent OECD report: "Globally, the area of agricultural land is projected to expand in the next decade to match the increase in food demand from a growing population, intensifying competition for land. Agricultural land is expected to peak before 2030 and decline thereafter, as population growth slows down and yield improvements continue. Deforestation rates are already declining, and this trend is projected to continue, especially after 2030 when demand for more agricultural land eases."[2]

What is meant by sustainability in an agricultural context? The most concise modern definition of sustainability is that evolved by the Brundlandt Commission in 1987: "development that meets the needs of the present without compromising the ability of future generations to meet their own needs."[3] This definition has been subsequently extended beyond the obvious environmental condition to include social and economic conditions as well. It is obvious that ensuring that agriculture sustains the productive capacity of the soil of the planet is essential to the survival of the human race and most other fauna and flora.

What is also obvious is that because food is essential to life, human communities will seek the easiest way of maximizing the food supply; in terms of the long-run productive capacity of the soil, this may not be the optimum. Without doubt, feeding more than 7 billion human bodies currently involves a large part of Earth's resources. It is estimated that about 38 percent of Earth's land surface and about 20 percent of its net primary production resources are involved in the production of food.[4] Also to be taken into account is the impact of the production of the resources needed to produce agricultural inputs: irrigation water, fertilizers and pesticides, machinery, and energy. The resource costs of delivery to consumers—packaging, transport and retailing facilities—also have to be taken into account.

In determining the level of food production, farmers are responsible for influencing the state of a large part of the global environment. Agriculture is therefore in a position to cause the loss of natural ecosystems and add globally significant and environmentally detrimental amounts of nitrogen and phosphorus to terrestrial ecosystems. It has been estimated that the quantities involved could triple if past practices are used to achieve another doubling in food production.[5]

While there is a general consensus that world agriculture has the capability to feed between 8 and 10 billion people and to feed the most needy better, there is little agreement on how this can be done without damaging the global ecosystem. The objective of sustainability means maintaining a high level of output through high yields but with agricultural practices that have acceptable environmental impacts. The main environmental impacts of agriculture have and will come from conversion of natural habitats to agricultural uses and from the overuse of fertilizers and pesticides that pollute watercourses, oceans, and terrestrial habitats. Surplus agricultural nutrients—both from arable farming and livestock—enter the environment via leaching, volatilization, and effluents of livestock and humans. But continuation of these trends is not inevitable.

How can such costs be minimized while at the same time food production is increased? In one sense, the answer is simple: increased technical productivity. Crop and livestock production must increase without an increase in the negative environmental impacts. That is not so easy in practice, since this means large increases in the efficiency of nitrogen, phosphorus, and water use, combined with what is described as integrated pest management, which minimizes the need for toxic pesticides.

agriculture's role in greenhouse gas generation

World agriculture is believed to be responsible for generating between 20 and 30 percent of total anthropogenic greenhouse gas emissions—depending on which set of figures are to be believed. Most of this emission is calculated to come from the production of livestock-based food products. In addition, substantial amounts of GHGs are emitted from the production of artificial fertilizers, feed manufacture, and the construction of farm machinery.

That the agriculture industry's greenhouse gas emissions are significant is obvious. What is not obvious is the scale of those emissions or what measures would be effective in reducing them. Extreme analyses suggest that the livestock sector could be responsible for more than half of total world GHG emissions; more moderate estimates put the share at less than 20 percent. Clearly, such basic questions as how emissions are calculated and what emissions should be included in the calculation are crucial to understanding the problem and prescribing the right solutions. In calculating the industry's total GHG output, the relationship between livestock production and crop growing is also highly important.

The main direct climate impact of the meat and dairy industry comes from methane (CH_4) produced by enteric fermentation from cattle and sheep digestion (rumination); nitrous oxide (N_2O) is also important. Methane is reckoned to be to be more than 20 times more powerful a greenhouse gas than carbon dioxide (but persists in the atmosphere for only 8 years compared with the 100 years of CO_2). Although methane and nitrous oxide are released in smaller quantities than carbon dioxide, they are said to have a far higher global warming potential (GWP)—296 and 23 times higher, respectively—than CO_2.

The assumption that meat production is a major GHG emitter is based mainly on two reports from international organizations, the UN Food and Agriculture Organization (FAO) in 2006[6] and a predictably more extreme case made by the Worldwatch Institute in 2009.[7] The FAO calculated that the world's livestock and meat production and delivery industries produce approximately 18 percent of total anthropogenic greenhouse gases (AGHGs), while the Worldwatch Institute argues that this is a massive underestimate and puts the total contribution at over 50 percent.

According to FAO calculations, while livestock contributes only about 9 percent of total carbon dioxide emissions, it is responsible for 37 percent of methane and 65 percent of nitrous oxide. Methane and nitrous oxide are emitted from rumen fermentation and livestock waste, while it is argued that carbon dioxide is released when previously forested areas are converted into grazing land or arable land for feed. By displacing forests, this expansion of pasture and cropland releases significant amounts of carbon dioxide into the atmosphere. Intensification of livestock production results in alleged pasture and arable-land degradation and a net loss of organic matter.

The livestock industry's emissions could increase. Although developed country livestock emissions will decline, the demand for meat will rise and the GHG output from livestock industries in developing countries will increase as developing country economies expand, according to the FAO. A Worldwatch paper, written by World Bank environmental specialists, argues that the levels of GHG emissions linked to livestock production have been seriously underestimated.[8] The Worldwatch Institute's recalculation and its achievement of an amazingly massive 51 percent total AGHG share arise principally from two major assumptions: first, that the FAO has not counted the CO_2 emission arising from livestock respiration, and second, that all increases in livestock feed production are automatically achieved through cutting down forest or ploughing up pasture with consequent loss of GHG sequestration capacity. Both of these contentions are highly questionable, but this does not deter the Worldwatch analysts from using these arguments to add close to 12 million tonnes and 15 percentage points to the livestock GHG bill.

The FAO, with considerable justification, argues that plant matter consumed by livestock is itself created through the conversion of atmospheric CO_2 into organic compounds. Since the emitted and absorbed quantities are likely to be equal, livestock respiration is not considered to be a net source of emissions. Equally, the production of monogastric (nonruminant) animal feed is likely to come more from the increased productivity of existing arable land than from the clearing of new land, while much of the ruminant livestock production—particularly in Europe—comes from permanent pasture and reseeded redundant arable land, both of which add to carbon sequestration capacity.

Where the other additional 15-plus percentage points of GHG output conjured up by Worldwatch comes from is obscure. It is also likely that Worldwatch has not counted significant parts of the non-agricultural GHG emissions, which obviously increases the apparent proportion coming from livestock industry. A large part of the Worldwatch report is devoted to promoting plant-based substitutes for meat, principally soya. The irony that increased soya production to replace meat, which they suggest should be eliminated, can only come from expansion of crop production into forest and grazing land in South America seems to have escaped their attention.

Reducing the analysis to a more comprehensible European level, an assessment by the European Commission's Joint Research Centre indicates that meat and dairy products contribute on average 24 percent to the environmental impact of total final consumption in the EU-27.[9] What is obvious about these diverse and often conflicting analyses of the role of livestock production in GHG emissions is that different questions inevitably lead to different answers. In particular, there are questions on the GHG element in imported foods (sometimes characterized as independent land-use change, [ILUC]). Swedish studies have found that while total GHG emissions from domestic animal production in Sweden decreased by 14 percent between 1990 and 2005, mainly due to improved efficiency and reduced production volumes, consumption of animal products increased. Since more animal products were imported to compensate for declining national animal production, Sweden's total per capita GHG emissions from the consumption of animal products increased by 16 percent between 1990 and 2005.

What about possible action that might achieve a reduction in GHG emissions on a global scale? Calculations by Tara Garnett of the UK Food Climate Research Network indicate that a massive reduction in meat eating that would be needed in the developed and the more prosperous developing nations to reduce significantly the GHG output from livestock.[10]

Garnett made calculations on the basis of the suggestion that one target for reduction would be consumption in developed countries so that it matches levels projected for those living in developing countries by 2050. This is anticipated to be 44 kg of meat and 78 kg of milk per person per year. Globally, this would cut meat consumption by 15 percent and milk consumption by 22 percent. This would mean halving the average per capita meat consumption in developed countries (current average 80 kg); in some EU countries such as Belgium and Germany, consumption would need to be reduced by 60 percent, while reducing U.S. consumption by 80 percent. However, even these cuts would not be sufficient, as global demand is expected to be 70 percent higher for meat and 45 percent higher for milk by 2050 compared to 2000 levels as demand from developing and transitional economy countries increases.

Even stabilizing consumption at current average levels would mean that by 2050, world average per capita consumption would have to be held at 25 kg of meat and 53 kg of milk a year, or the equivalent of current developing world consumption. However, even this extreme scenario would not reduce GHG emissions unless there was greater emission-reducing technical and managerial improvements.

While consumption of less meat and more vegetable foods might reduce GHG emissions, it would certainly change dramatically the pattern of land use. It would reduce overall the amount of land required to provide what would still be a nutritionally adequate food supply. It would, it is argued, have additional environmental advantages and free production resources to produce other products, ranging from biofuels to increased amenity facilities, carbon sequestration, and other non-food environmental goods.

This at least is the view of analysts at the UK's Cranfield University Business School who looked at the impact of a change away from a diet dominated by meat and dairy products on GHG emissions and land use.[11] In a study examining the land-use and greenhouse gas implications of changing UK food consumption away from meat and dairy consumption and associated production toward more crop-based foods, they concluded that the UK agricultural land base could support increased consumption of plant-based products arising from the reduced consumption of livestock products and still free land for other nonfood production purposes.

Examination of the effects of a 50 percent reduction in livestock product consumption indicated that a nutritionally adequate diet would still be maintained. Under what is regarded as the most radical scenario, meat consumption would be cut by 36 percent of current consumption and consumption of milk and eggs by 60 percent. The reduction in meat and dairy product consumption would be balanced by increasing plant-based food consumption to maintain constant food energy supplied. This would involve a 50 percent increase in fruit and vegetable consumption and an increase in basic carbohydrate foods such as cereals and potatoes plus oil-rich commodities (except palm oil).

The most important conclusion is that all the posed consumption change alternatives reduce the estimated total agricultural land required to support the UK food system. Not surprisingly, however, a switch from red to white meat consumption increases the need for overseas arable land for feed grain production, although a larger area of UK arable land is released for cultivation. Most significantly, on the basis of a direct reduction of meat consumption and its replacement with vegetable-based foods, the total amount of extra land required for the increased direct consumption of plant-based food products is less than the amount of arable land freed from reduced livestock feed production.

A shift in emphasis from beef and sheep meat to pig and poultry meat by any country would inevitably mean an increase in imported feeds, although it would release considerably more arable land in the

UK. An additional 55,000 hectares of UK land would be needed—compared with the reduction of all meat consumption scenario—while the additional third-country land use would be 466,000 hectares, principally for the production of additional soya. The area of arable quality grassland freed in the UK would be greater than the extra overseas land needed for producing this feed. Impact on UK land use would be a net release of between 1.6 and 2.9 million hectares of potentially arable land in the UK, plus the release of 1.3 to 6.6 million hectares of land suitable only for grassland.

What conservationists might regard as the ideal of a substantial reduction in all meat consumption, involving a 50 percent reduction in white meat consumption replaced by an increase in vegetable foods, would involve no changes in grassland requirements. Increases in demand for arable land for direct human consumption in the UK would amount to about 154,000 and 172,000 hectares (domestic and overseas, respectively), but these are more than compensated for by the release of arable land from feed production (341,000 and 668,000 hectares domestic and overseas, respectively).

As for GHG emission reduction, all of the consumption scenarios tested reduce greenhouse gas emissions from primary production. The largest reduction would be achieved from reducing the consumption of all meat, from 81 million to 66 million tonnes carbon dioxide equivalent (CO_2e; the CO_2 equivalent emission is a standard measurement for comparing emissions of different GHGs)—a reduction of 19 percent. The switch from red to white meat reduces emissions by 9 percent, while a 50 percent reduction in white meat consumption would achieve a reduction of only 3 percent. The researchers stress that the net effect on emissions would depend substantially on the alternative use of the grassland released from food production. Were all tillable grassland released to be converted to arable cropping, about 160 million tonnes of CO_2e per year would be released over twenty years through the effects of this land-use change.

Were all released land with the potential to support good tree growth converted to woodland, it is estimated that this would result in a net carbon uptake equivalent to about 220 million tonnes of CO_2e per year in soil and wood per year over twenty years.

The analysis of land-use statistics in this study emphasizes the large proportion of UK land currently used for cattle and sheep husbandry. Far from a decline into dereliction, as the meat production interest would argue, without livestock this grassland would "revert to natural vegetation—deciduous woodland in many cases," it is claimed. "The use of livestock to retain semi-natural grasslands is not dependent on the current high level of livestock product consumption. A 50 percent reduction in demand still leaves a market which is large enough to support this activity."[12]

It is admitted that such a scaling down of meat production would have serious knock-on economic, social, and environmental effects. "Livestock systems provide a wide range of services that are currently used by society. In a reduction scenario, rural areas lose skills and employment in the livestock sector and there would be ramifications for linked industries such as the meat processing or veterinary sectors. Culturally important features, for example, hedgerows and stone walls, and much of the fauna and flora associated with grassland would be no longer needed."[13]

There would however be countervailing advantages. Pointing out that the land most likely to be taken out of production is in areas that are the most difficult to farm, it is argued for example, that upland moorland and common land already in a seminatural state could change to fully natural vegetation cover. "In upland areas, various natural communities including scrub, bracken, bramble, and woodland with their own assemblage of flora and fauna are likely to develop, with potential increases in wild herbivores such as deer, hares, and rabbits."[14]

According to the OECD's *Environmental Outlook to 2050* (2012), Europe, parts of Asia, and southern Africa are likely to suffer the biggest reduction in species (due mainly to urbanization and agriculture?): "The main pressures driving biodiversity loss include land-use change and management (agriculture), the expansion of commercial forestry, infrastructure development, human encroachment and fragmentation of natural habitats, as well as pollution and climate change."[15]

While highly theoretical, this study would indicate that considerable changes in food consumption, deemed by some politicians and activists to be desirable, could be achieved without increasing land use, as opponents of any policy aimed at persuading people to eat less meat would argue. It also suggests that diet changes could result in production changes that would reduce overall greenhouse gas emissions from the food system, including those from overseas feed producers. The Cranfield researchers claim that an analysis on the same basis would yield similar results for the European Union as a whole.

However, given the importance of livestock production to rural communities in both developing and developed countries—firmly acknowledged by the FAO—the unwillingness of the increasingly prosperous people of developing countries to forgo the pleasures of increased meat and dairy consumption, and the unlikelihood of developed country consumers significantly reducing consumption, political choices will have to be made.

Even more contentious would be a change in the supply of milk and other dairy products. The dairy sector accounts for about 4 percent of all global AGHG according to the FAO.[16] This figure includes emissions associated with the production, processing, and transportation of milk products as well as emissions related to meat produced from animals originating from the dairy system. Considering just global milk production, processing, and transportation and excluding meat production from dairy animals, the sector is estimated to contribute 2.7 percent of global AGHG emissions. In 2007, it is estimated, the dairy sector emitted 1,969 million tonnes of CO_2e, of which 1,328 million tonnes are attributed to milk, 151 million tonnes to meat from culled dairy animals, and 490 million tonnes from calves from the dairy sector that were raised for meat. The global average of GHG emissions per kilogram of milk and related products works out at 2.4 kg CO_2e.

Given the massive ruminant activity of the average dairy cow, methane contributes most to the global warming impact of milk production, accounting for about 52 percent of the agricultural GHG emissions in both developing and developed countries. Nitrous oxide emissions account for 27 percent of GHG emissions in developed countries and 38 percent in developing countries. Carbon dioxide accounts for a higher share of emissions in developed countries (21 percent) than in developing countries (10 percent). The FAO's analysis covers all major milk production systems from nomadic herds to intensified dairy operations. It focuses on the entire dairy food chain, including the production and transport of inputs (fertilizer, pesticide, and feed) used for dairy farming, on-farm emissions, and emissions associated with milk processing and packaging, as well as the transportation of milk products to retailers. It is admitted that the margin of error of the estimates could be as much as ±26 percent.

A report from the UK Committee on Climate Change (CCC) argues that greenhouse gas emissions from agriculture can be significantly reduced without significant changes in consumption of the major foods.[17] While reductions in livestock numbers resulting from recent EU agriculture policy changes will automatically reduce emissions, farmers need to be offered financial inducement to further reduce the industry's emission levels. Although the report concentrates on the UK situation, inferences can be drawn for other west European countries, as European leaders continue to struggle with agreement on the renewable energy issue. The current EU compromise calls for the EU to reduce greenhouse gas emissions by 20 percent from 1990 levels by 2020. The agreement also calls for a substitution of 10 percent of renewable energy sources for fossil fuels by the same time.

The CCC has outlined the potential scope for CO_2 mitigation in agriculture, land use, land-use change, and forestry. It points out that agricultural origin non-CO_2 emissions have decreased by 18 percent over the period 1990–2006, from 54 million tonnes CO_2e to 44 million tons CO^2e. This is a more modest decrease than most other non-CO_2 sectors, but it is more than has been achieved in CO_2 emission reduction over the same period (6 percent). The reduction of emissions in agriculture is largely attributable to decreasing livestock numbers as a result of common agricultural policy reform and reduced use of fertilizer.

The CCC report also says that there is scope for reducing emissions through dietary change, but warns that there are a number of complexities that make measurement difficult and obstruct implementation. Food and animal feed ingredients are both imported and exported; this would mean that changes in national food consumption would not necessarily affect UK food production and therefore the farm industry's emissions.

The level of ruminant animal numbers is to a great extent fixed by land type. Large numbers of animals are kept on land that is unsuitable for arable cropping. Food products with different nutritional characteristics are not necessarily substitutable. Probably most important of all, consumers are unlikely to be willing to be dictated to on what they should and should not eat.

Clearly, one major obstacle to emission reduction in the agriculture sector is the diverse nature of the industry, both geographically and economically. This, combined with the large number of small production units, will make the achievement of any targets far more difficult than in other sectors where production units are much larger and each holds significant percentages of the industry's output.

is organic farming the answer?

Organic farming, according to its proponents, will solve most of the environmental problems created by modern agriculture. If widely adopted in developed countries and, more important, in developing countries, can it meet the challenge of the need to nearly double food production over the next forty years? This is the question that proponents of the organic way cannot answer satisfactorily; their claims that it can are based essentially on recalculating the world's potential pattern of future food consumption to fit their own green agenda.

First, what is meant by *organic farming*? Most definitions are pretty woolly and do not stand up well to critical scientific analysis. Take this one from an organic farming promotion website: "Organic farming is the process of producing food naturally. This method avoids the use of synthetic chemical fertilizers and genetically modified organisms to influence the growth of crops. The main idea behind organic farming is 'zero impact' on the environment. The motto of the organic farmer is to protect the earth's resources and produce safe, healthy food."[18] The Soil Association states: "Our definition of organic food is food that is produced using environmentally and animal friendly farming methods on organic farms." The really cynical critic of these claims could pose the counterquestion: Is not all farming by scientific definition organic?

The hard truth is that no one has yet found any scientific evidence that food produced by Soil Association–approved organic standards is any more nutritious, free of chemical contamination, or in any other way better than food produced by normal husbandry techniques. This fact at least has been scientifically established by the UK's Food Standards Agency, which has stated, "Consumers may choose to buy organic fruit, vegetables and meat because they believe them to be more nutritious than other food. However, the balance of current scientific evidence does not support this view."[19]

Nutrient levels in food vary depending on many different factors, as does the level of contamination with alien substances. These include freshness, storage conditions, crop variety, soil conditions, weather conditions, and how food animals are fed. All crops and animals therefore vary in nutrient level to some extent. The available evidence shows that the nutrient levels and the degree of variation are similar in food produced by both organic and conventional agriculture. The nutrient content of all processed food, including organic, depends on the ingredients, recipe, and cooking methods. The impact of processing on nutrient levels will be the same for products made from organically and conventionally produced ingredients.

Increasing the food choices of the affluent middle class in developed countries, which is essentially the function performed by the organic food movement, is peripheral to the question of the long-run sustainability of the food-producing resources of the planet. The important question is, could the widespread adoption of organic methods improve and increase the food production capacity of those areas where increased production is most needed? Would universal adoption of organic methods reduce the global hunger bill by one starving child? The answer has to be a resounding no.

The question has to a great extent been answered by the FAO's Director-General Jacques Diouf, who has pointed out that organic farming could not on its own solve the world food problem: "You cannot feed six billion people today and nine billion in 2050 without judicious use of chemical fertilizers." This raises important questions on the strategies that poor, developing countries with large numbers of undernourished people should adopt to improve their food supplies.

To this end, greater self-sufficiency in the most-hungry countries is the primary objective. In many situations, if not most, what developed country agricultural experts might define as organic methods do have a major role to play. This is because what are regarded as organic principles properly applied in countries with an obvious surplus of labor, but little else, will conserve soil fertility, reduce the need for external inputs, and preserve the long-term fertility of the soil and therefore its productive capacity—good husbandry, in other words, rather than necessarily organic husbandry.

What is wrong with much of the research on the possible advantages of organic farming—much of it computer-generated and therefore highly suspect from the outset—is that it transposes the obvious advantages of applying such good practices to the most needy countries to the whole world food production system and then draws the wrong conclusions. An outstanding example of this type of solipsism is a study by the Danish Research Centre for Food and Farming.[20] This report claimed to confirm "the potential of a new organic farming paradigm to secure more than enough food to feed the world, and with reduced environmental impacts." The problem is that the environmental assumptions of the organic enthusiasts get bolted on to the vitally important struggle to eliminate hunger and in the process mightily confuse the issue.

Using a computer model developed by the International Food Policy Research Institute (IFPRI), the Danish research claims to prove that conversion of global agriculture to organic farming, without increasing the world farmed area or the use of synthetic nitrogen fertilizers, would result in a global agricultural supply sufficient to provide the entire world population with 2,640 to 4,380 kcal/day/person.

Much more important and relevant is the report's conclusion that a 50 percent conversion to organic farming in sub-Saharan Africa would help feed the hungry by reducing the need to import subsidized food, and produce a diverse range of certified organic surpluses to be exported at premium profit. The key statement in this report is that "sustainable intensification of organic agriculture could increase production by up to 56 percent" in sub-Saharan Africa. Given the human and other resources of much of Africa, any intensification of small-scale agriculture would have a massive impact on the local supply of food. This region currently produces less food per person than it did thirty years ago, and the number of chronically malnourished people has doubled since 1970, from 96 million to over 200 million in 1996.

The FAO has compiled evidence that what has been called organic management systems have undoubtedly doubled yields in arid and degraded soils in critical areas of Africa such as Tigray in Ethiopia.[21] What is likely is that what has been applied there are husbandry methods that are relevant to dealing with the specific problems posed by these particular soil and climatic conditions; they are not necessarily organic methods as understood in Europe. The importance of these more relevant husbandry methods to the problems of the least agriculturally advantaged developing countries is well summarized in the FAO's report. It emphasizes the fundamental point that productivity in organic production systems is management specific. It points out that while switching to organic management commonly results in yield reductions of up to 50 percent and, during the conversion period for high external input systems in areas with favorable crop growth conditions, up to 40 percent. In regions with medium growth conditions and moderate use of synthetic inputs, organic productivity is comparable to conventional systems. Most important, in subsistence agricultural systems, these new, more relevant methods result in increased yields of up to 180 percent.

The FAO also emphasizes that food shortages suffered by the most needy are the result of structural as much as agricultural failures.[22] Too often apparent national food security resulting from increases in production or increased external supply does not result in the equitable distribution of food to the hungry and poor living in remote areas; production inputs, when available, are not affordable to the poor and appropriate extension assistance systems are often inadequate or nonexistent. The importance of the application of organic methods in these circumstances is that it increases local food self-sufficiency without needing often nonexistent external inputs of fertilizer or crop protection chemicals.

The essence of the problem and its solution is summed up in the following statement: "The strongest feature of organic agriculture is its reliance on locally available production assets and, thus, its relative independence from crude oil availability and increasing input prices. Working with natural processes increases cost effectiveness and resilience of food production."[23] Through crop rotation and mixed cropping, farmers utilizing an organic approach use their labor, the most readily available input they have (in abundance), and naturally available resources such as predation, pollination, and soil nutrient recycling not only to intensify production, but also to ensure its sustainability. These low-cost good farming practices reduce cash needs and credit dependence. It is pointed out, however, that although organic enterprises increase returns to labor inputs and offer rural employment opportunities, such methods will be constrained if there is a shortage of manpower.

This improved husbandry gives local food systems much greater resilience against crop failure or severe reduction of harvests due to climatic and other uncontrolled incidents. "Due to its agro-ecological approach, organic agriculture is an effective means to restore environmental services. This factor is much more important than individual practices (e.g., use of drought-resistant crops) in preventing system imbalances such as new pest and disease outbreaks. It is organic management's self-correcting process that gives a climate-related value to the agro-ecosystem."[24]

As the FAO analysis notes, organic agriculture is not a universal panacea and has its own limits in addressing challenges posed by the spread of modern lifestyles—most obviously urbanization. Its external environmental costs, however, are much lower than those of conventional agriculture and, in some areas, it can reverse problems of natural environmental degradation. Moreover, what the FAO designates as non-certified organic systems, "increase food availability and access exactly in those locations where poverty and hunger are most severe."

That said, it is relevant to speculate that what is being discussed here is in fact not the artificial, Western idea of organic farming, but the wider application of good husbandry principles that have been applied in India, Indochina, other parts of Asia, and South America for centuries. This is admitted by the FAO when it points out that analysis of several case studies on organic agriculture in Asia, Africa, and Latin America indicates strongly that the economic effects of converting to organic agriculture depend on the previous method of farming. When converting from some types of traditional low external input dependent farming to organic agriculture, input costs decrease, while yields and income tend to rise. Conversely, when converting from intensive farming, yields and incomes tend to fall, although there may be exceptions depending on the intensiveness of the new organic production system.

What has to be accepted is that there is a world of difference between the minuscule percentage of the world's farmed area that is devoted to production of high-value organic cash crops for the benefit of affluent Western consumers and the vitally needed improvement in basic food supply and quality for the desperately needy of the poorest countries of the world. Confusing the two, as some enthusiasts appear to, will do nothing to solve the basic food supply problem.

Widespread adoption of the European version of organic farming methods is unlikely to meet the world's inevitably increasing food needs and is likely to form an obstacle rather than an aid to increased food supplies. The adoption of such methods may achieve reduced GHG emission, habitat conservation, and claimed better food, but it does not face up to the prime issue of feeding a population of more than 9 billion.

This would certainly appear to be the position of the European Commission's Environment Directorate. It sees EU farm policy as having an increased focus on protecting biodiversity, promoting sustainable farming, and achieving GHG reduction.[25] A key commission staff working document on policy fostering organic farming endorsed the view that the main benefits of organic farming include the protection of soil, nature, biodiversity, and habitats, as well as reducing the use of pesticides and thus improving water quality. It is conceded that organic farming would be unlikely to achieve the yield levels of conventional husbandry.

Currently, only 2 percent of the EU's farmers are certified organic and about the same percentage of the EU's food supplies come from organic sources. The official European Commission view tends to be that the percentage needs to be increased if agriculture is to play an important role in reducing GHG emission and improving the natural environment. While the current 20 percent yield drop that can be expected in Europe from adoption of organic methods is something that the EU and other rich developed countries might be able to afford, it is doubtful whether developing countries can.

For the FAO the need for increased output is indisputable. Director-General Diouf has observed: "Agriculture will have no choice but to be more productive. Our analysis shows that future production increases would mostly come from yield growth and improved cropping intensity. . . . And this will require substantial increases in investment . . . better access to modern inputs, more irrigation systems, machinery and implements, more roads and better rural infrastructures, as well as more skilled and better trained farmers."[26]

is food trade sustainable?

It is strongly argued by environmental groups that trade in food products is highly detrimental to the environment and therefore not sustainable, principally because transporting food long distances adds unnecessarily to the emission of GHGs. This unnecessary addition to climate change pressure should be avoided, it is argued, by greater national and even local self-sufficiency in food production. So-called food miles should be reduced to the absolute minimum, it is contended, to minimize the GHG output of the food delivery system. Unfortunately, this simplistic argument does not stand up when all the costs and benefits of trade are accounted for.

A complete life-cycle examination of all aspects of food production, distribution, and trade shows that a crude calculation of food miles traveled from production to delivery does not necessarily give a correct assessment of a food's carbon footprint. Buying local can often result in much higher carbon emissions than opting for the imported product. But much more important, as Oxfam and other aid charities have emphasized, is the effect of this misguided perception on the food export trade and incomes of poor developing countries. Produce grown under the African sun and flown to Europe can have a total emissions bill lower than produce grown in Europe in heated glasshouses and transported relatively short distances by train, boat, or road.

Importing basic agricultural commodities often involves lower environmental cost than domestic production does. New Zealand butter and lamb and Spanish tomatoes are two good examples of products that are produced at such low cost—in fuel, fertilizer, labor input, and carbon emission—that they can be delivered to the UK market at lower environmental cost than the local product. There is also a wider economic and social issue involved in the food miles argument: the responsibility of developed countries to aid economic growth in less-developed countries. Development experts argue that if European consumers want out-of-season vegetables, fruits, and flowers, less-prosperous African and Asian countries should not be denied the economic benefit of supplying them. According to James MacGregor and Bill Vorley of the International Institute for Environment and Development (IIED), "From a development and poverty reduction angle, the inclusion of sub-Saharan Africa in these high value markets has been a success story. Food miles as a concept is blind to these social and economic benefits associated with trade in food, especially from developing countries."[27]

Just as a British consumer buying tomatoes grown under glass in Lancashire will incur more GHG emission than if he or she bought its Spanish-grown equivalent, so green beans air freighted from Kenya are likely to have a lower total carbon footprint than a heated polytunnel-grown equivalent in Kent. Both Oxfam and liberal free trade economists now agree that the buy local obsession is often yet another form of protectionism in disguise.

Recent research at Lincoln University in New Zealand has shown that producing milk in New Zealand and shipping dairy products to Britain was less than half as costly—in terms of energy and emissions—than producing and marketing it in the UK.[28] The total energy required to produce and ship a tonne of milk solids from New Zealand to the UK was calculated to be only slightly over one-half the cost to produce and deliver it in the UK, while the CO_2 emissions involved were less than one-half for the New Zealand product than for UK-produced product. Total production and transport energy requirement for the New Zealand dairy product was 24,368 megajoules per tonne of milk solid compared to 48,368 megajoules per tonne for the UK product. For CO_2 emissions, the respective figures were 1,422.5 kg/tonne of product and 2,920.7 kg/tonne respectively.

Similarly, a study for the UK food and farming ministry DEFRA showed the environmental advantage of UK consumers buying tomatoes from Spain rather than from local growers.[29] The optimum temperature for tomato growth is 16 to 21°C. As a consequence, glasshouses in the UK are heated to this level mainly by natural gas–fueled systems at the rate of 11 kilowatt hours of energy per kilogram of tomatoes. Tomatoes in Spain, in contrast, are grown outdoors, generally under plastic sheeting, with no heating required. The energy used in transport, processing, and packaging of the tomatoes is likely to be identical between the two countries, except for the transport from Spain to the UK, which is mainly by road. Despite this greater transport cost, the CO_2 emission involved in production and delivery of the British tomatoes is calculated to be 2,394 kg/tonne compared with only 630 kg/tonne for the Spanish product.

The DEFRA study also demonstrated that in the modern food delivery system, the logistical systems of major retail chains is a much greater generator of GHG emissions than transcontinental sea transport. The DEFRA analysis concluded that the major increase in the environmental footprint of the food industry arises not from increases in domestic production inputs (which have actually declined) or the burden of transport of imported produce, but almost entirely from the change in the domestic food distribution pattern. A good example is new potatoes grown in western Cornwall transported to a supermarket's central distribution portal in Bristol then shipped back to its store in Truro—a pointless round trip of over 250 miles.

A major source of the rise in the economic and environmental costs of domestic transport is undoubtedly the concentration of the European food supply base into fewer, larger suppliers. This has led to major changes in delivery patterns with most goods now routed through supermarket regional distribution centers using larger heavy goods vehicles (HGVs). The annual amount of food moved by HGVs in the UK has since 1978 increased by 23 percent, with the average distance for each trip also increasing by 50 percent. Moreover, as a result of the centralization and concentration of retail food sales in supermarkets, a weekly shopping trip by car has replaced frequent pedestrian shop visits.

The DEFRA report says, "The rise in food miles has led to increases in the environmental, social and economic burdens associated with transport. These include carbon dioxide emissions, air pollution, congestion, accidents and noise. There is a clear cause and effect relationship for food miles for these burdens—and in general higher levels of vehicle activity lead to larger impacts." A synthesis of comparative data on emissions from locally produced and imported foods produced by Oxfam in collaboration with the International Institute for Environment and Development (IIED) demonstrates that even when food is transported long distances by plane it often produces lower overall emissions than food that travels shorter distances, because of other sources of emissions in the chain of production and delivery, principally those incurred in the production process. It points to studies by the UK farm ministry DEFRA and other bodies that show that transport accounts for only 10 percent of the total emissions in the food chain in the United Kingdom and the United States. The bulk of GHG output comes from food production, processing, distribution, and storage

The establishment of trade in high-value food products between, particularly, African developing countries and Europe is essential to the economic growth of those countries, Oxfam argues.[30] Such trade provides comparative advantage not only in economic but also environmental terms. "Climate change will hit poorer rural people in developing nations first, fastest and hardest," says Jodie Keane and colleagues of IIED. "High-value trade with such nations is critical to build rural economies that are resilient to climate change. The trade in fresh produce is one part of a global solution to this challenge."[31]

Keane and colleagues believe that when focusing on food miles consumers are too often ignoring other social and environmental issues embedded in their shopping decisions. Pointing out that more than one million livelihoods in rural Africa are supported in part by UK consumption of imported fresh produce, they say, "We urge consumers to avoid knee-jerk reactions and think instead of 'fair miles' and recognise that there are also social and ethical aspects to choices about where food comes from."[32]

There is no doubt that air transport has the highest level of GHG emission but what is important in this argument—essentially about free and fair trade—is that food's air freight contribution to overall UK and indeed European greenhouse gas emissions is small compared with road transportation. It is even smaller when produce travels in the holds of passenger aircraft that would be making the journey anyway. It is likely that air freighting of food products into the UK contributes less than 0.1 percent of the total food sector GHG transport emissions. What is important, both in terms of producer income and consumer choice, is that such imports had been increasing by an average 6 percent a year through the 2000s. These air-freighted imports support a large number of farmers and workers in regions outside the UK. More than £105 million worth of vegetables and £89 million in fruit are exported to the UK from sub-Saharan Africa each year and in the process support 1–1.5 million livelihoods, according to Oxfam estimates.

A UK Labour government's food policy strategy document contained a reasoned reendorsement of the need for liberal globalized trade in food as an important part of any future food security policy. "We live in an inter-connected world with globalised food systems," it acknowledges. "Global trade offers a way to manage volatility by spreading risk, encourages productivity growth, keeps prices competitive and increases diversity of supply—it is critical to global economic prosperity and food security."[33]

New Labour's *Food 2030* document endorsed the view that international trade has been a major driver of global growth and prosperity, especially important for many developing countries: "As trade has expanded, global incomes have grown and open economies have been able to harness the power of trade to boost competitiveness and productivity, helping to improve living standards and sustain economic growth."[34] Despite recent progress on trade liberalization, protectionism continues to damage economies, most significantly those of developing countries. To promote such policies on the grounds of environmental protection is not only perverse but irrational.

reducing the intensity of farming—an environmental improvement?

However great the productivity increase is that can be achieved through genetic improvement—the only major means of boosting production if inputs are reduced—sustainable production on a national or European scale can only mean lower production levels. This essential dichotomy in agricultural policy development is honestly recognized in a plea for a new sustainable European agriculture policy by five major, mainly wildlife protection, nongovernmental organizations (NGOs).[35]

"Trade-offs and choices over appropriate land use are inevitable, depending on the specific needs and objectives in any given locality," says their report.

For example, high input farming maximises production per unit of land, with the potential to free land for ecological purposes, but it often has serious environmental impacts, including a long term deterioration of soil fertility.

Conversely, less intensive systems have a lower environmental impact and greater ecological stability, but often have lower productivity and require more land. Appropriate approaches are likely to vary from region to region.

The authors admit that the full extent of the environmental and social costs and benefits of different technologies and management systems are not always known.

So-called high nature value (HNV) farming systems are a prime example.[36] These are typically low-intensity farming systems that have a lower impact on the environment compared to more resource-intensive forms of production and are characterized by a high proportion of seminatural vegetation and farmland features. These include extensive livestock systems, low-intensity permanent and arable crops, and small-scale mixed farming systems with a high density of seminatural features. The NGOs say such farming patterns play a key role in maintaining biodiversity, provide Europe's most distinctive landscapes, and represent the backbone of rural societies in many remote and marginal regions.

"These systems are under threat in many parts of Europe because of low farm incomes, due in part to the failure of the historic system of CAP payments. They struggle to compete on a free market due to lower yields, difficult market access and higher labour requirements, and can fall victim to land abandonment or agricultural intensification, both of which can have detrimental environmental and social effects."[37] An inevitable conclusion is that the nonproduction services that these farms and regions provide have to be supported by specific subvention from the public purse. But to a great extent dealing with this less-advantaged area problem is a side issue to the mainstream question of how adequate food supplies are to be maintained if lower output sustainable farming methods are applied throughout the food production system. If society decides that it wants such inevitably low-output agriculture then it will just as inevitably need to import more of its food supply. Exclusion of the imported product in order to buy local will not result in either long-term sustainability or adequate and varied food supplies.

a role for genetically modified crops

Most of the scientific effort to raise crop yields by genetic engineering has been directed toward creating arable crops, vegetables, and fruit that combine desirable genes from various species to create new genetically altered crosses with enhanced nutritional, productive, and ecological value. The difference from traditional plant breeding is that while historically plant breeders have sought improvement from crosses of different strains within a species, GM involves genetic transference between unrelated species not occurring biologically in nature.

Opponents of GM argue that the process of combining interspecies genes, through recombinant DNA technology, does not have the checks and balances imposed by nature in normal reproduction. Without these, it is said, there is a risk of genetic instability. For this reason opponents argue that no one can make any accurate predictions about the long-term effects of GM foodstuffs on human beings and the environment. Extensive testing in this regard is either very expensive or impractical.

Claimed advantages of gm crops:

- GM crops are productive and have a larger yield.
- Such crops can be more nutritious and have better flavor.
- It is possible to build in resistance to pests, weeds, and disease.
- These crops are capable of thriving better in regions with poor soil or adverse climates.
- They can be more environment-friendly because they require fewer herbicides and pesticides.
- They can be resistant to bacterial breakdown and therefore able to stay ripe for longer periods, allowing long distance shipping or keeping on shop shelves for longer periods.
- GM crops may be one answer to feeding growing world populations.

Arguments against gm crops and foods:

- Scientists do not yet know where in the DNA to precisely insert genes and have no way of controlling gene expression. It is argued that changing selected genes could change the whole structure, with possible unpredictable and different effects under different circumstances.
- Proponents of GM promote genetically modified food without sufficient risk evaluation.
- There is a danger of overstandardization of taste and flavor—GM crops could end food diversity.
- Herbicide-resistant and pesticide-resistant crops could give rise to superweeds and superpests that would subsequently need new stronger chemicals to destroy them.
- GM crops could cross-pollinate with non-GM plants and create ecological problems. If this happened with GM foods containing vaccines, antibiotics, or contraceptives, for example, it could pose a threat to human health.
- GM technology companies patent their crops and engineer crops so that harvested grain will not germinate if used as seed. Third World farmers have to buy new seeds from the originating company every time.

It has never been justifiably argued that the widespread use of genetically modified crops or livestock would be a general panacea to solve the world food problem. More rationally, it is argued by respected scientific sources that it is one development that could boost agricultural productivity in both developed and less-developed countries.

A review of the possible benefits of genetically engineered crops for developing countries by the UN Food and Agriculture Organization concludes that while genetically modified crops are not likely to be the major means of increasing food supplies, they do offer the possibility to improve diets and to raise agricultural productivity and the living standards of small and poor farmers in the less-prosperous countries. The FAO concludes that potential environmental problems and health risks from the production and consumption of GM crops are likely to be small.

The FAO contrasts the development and potential of what might be characterized as the current agricultural biotechnology revolution with the Green Revolution of the recent past. Whereas the development of the maize and wheat varieties that were the major elements of the Green Revolution of the second half of the twentieth century was publicly funded and its benefits disseminated without hindrance, the development of genetically engineered food crops has been largely by private companies and their distribution strictly controlled by both the companies themselves and by governments. While government regulation may be necessary, the distribution of GM seeds and animal and plant genetic material will have to be much less restricted than at present if they are to benefit the poorest of the world's farmers, the FAO argues.

The FAO's 2004 report, *Agricultural Biotechnology: Meeting the Needs of the Poor?*, made clear that whatever misgivings there may be in Europe and other developed countries, there are definite benefits to be gained from the use of GM crops in the developing world.[38] Such characteristics as built-in insect resistance and the incorporation of enhanced protein content and vitamin characteristics are of particular advantage to developing countries. Claims of dangers to human health remain unfounded.

The assistant director-general of FAO's economic and social department, Dr. Harwig de Haen, argues that GM technology can improve agricultural production in three major ways: by raising farmers' production and incomes, by increasing food supplies and thus reducing prices, and by contributing to the nutritional quality of crops. While greater regulation may be needed, governments, as well as private corporations, must be more involved in the research and development of new seeds to ensure benefits to less-developed countries. "FAO believes that biotechnology, including genetic engineering, can benefit the poor, but that the gains are not guaranteed."[39]

The FAO recognizes the potential of transgenic crops to improve world nutrition but insists that case-by-case studies are needed to assess the risks. Currently commercially available transgenic crops, it says, pose no threat to human health.

The question of environmental risk is still open. The report points out that scientific opinion differs on the environmental impact, since it is clear that that genes from GM crops can be transferred to wild species. It emphasizes that more research is needed to assess the environmental consequences of this so-called gene flow. The report also highlights environmental and health benefits from using transgenic crops. These include reduction in pesticides and toxic herbicides that have "demonstrable health benefits" for farmers and workers. Some GM crops, such as insect-resistant cotton, "are yielding significant economic gains to small farmers."

The FAO challenges the charge made by the anti-GM lobby that engineered crops only benefit the companies that develop them. It points out that while private companies have been largely responsible for marketing transgenic seeds, "it is the producers and consumers who are reaping the largest share of the economic benefits of transgenic crops. This suggests that the monopoly position engendered by intellectual property protection does not automatically lead to excessive industry profits."

The FAO, however, is critical of the private sector in focusing too much on technology for crops that benefit big commercial interests, such as maize, soya beans, canola (oilseed rape), and cotton. Basic food crops for the poor, such as cassava, potatoes, rice, and wheat, have received little attention from scientists. The report illustrates that 99 percent of land planted with transgenic crops in 2003 was in only six countries—all practicing large-scale agriculture: Argentina, Brazil, Canada, China, South Africa, and the United States. Currently there are only four main transgenic crops—maize, soybean, canola, and cotton—and they are engineered for only two traits, insect resistance and herbicide tolerance.

agriculture's water needs—sustainable or not?

On a global scale, it is calculated that 40 percent of crop output is produced on the 16 percent of agricultural land that is irrigated. Irrigated agriculture is the main source of agriculture's water withdrawals, accounting for around 70 percent of all the world's freshwater withdrawals. Irrigation played an important part in the increased yields achieved during the Green Revolution of the second half of the twentieth century. A major challenge of the twenty-first century is likely to be how to increase food production without increased use of irrigation. Areas where the need for production increase is greatest and where irrigation need is highest are also regions of incipient water shortage.

Unless water-use efficiency is increased, greater agricultural production will require increased irrigation. Fortunately, there are indications that the rate of increase in use of irrigation water in agriculture is declining. Globally, per capita irrigated area has declined by 5 percent since 1978, and new dam construction may allow only a 10 percent increase in water for irrigation over the next thirty years.

Many countries, in a band from China through India and Pakistan and the Middle East to North Africa, either currently or will soon fail to have adequate water to maintain per capita food production from irrigated land.[40] It is also estimated that about 20 percent of the irrigated area of the United States is supplied by groundwater pumped in excess of the precipitation capacity to replace it; overpumping is also a serious concern in China, India, and Bangladesh.

The OECD in its 2012 Environmental Outlook report does not expect the global area of irrigated land to increase in the period to 2050 for at least three reasons: it does not expect any significant extension of irrigable land; with increasing urbanization, domestic use will take precedence over crop irrigation; and there are likely to be governmental controls on any extension of irrigated land.[41]

There is, of course, important competition for water for nonagricultural uses, and this demand is increasing. Urban water use, the use of streams and lakes for recreational use, freshwater fisheries, and protection of natural ecosystems are all providing competition for water resources previously used mainly for agriculture. There is also the danger of increasing contamination of water supplies as irrigation water returned into the system inevitably carries more salt, nutrients, minerals, and pesticides into surface and ground waters than in source water. This is likely to be an increasing threat to downstream agricultural, natural systems, and drinking water.

In developing countries, 15 million hectares are now estimated to have experienced reduced yields owing to salt accumulation and waterlogging. Whether or not this trend can be diminished by increasing the water-holding capacity of soil by adding manure, reducing tillage, and or other approaches that maintain or increase soil organic matter remains to be seen. The cultivation of crops with higher water-use efficiency and the development of crops with greater drought tolerance can also contribute to yield increases in regions where there are serious constraints on irrigation water supplies.

Asia has the largest share of the world's total irrigated area, followed by Latin America. In sub-Saharan Africa, only 6 percent of cultivated area is currently irrigated. Despite a projected doubling of irrigated area in sub-Saharan Africa, the region will still account for a very minor share—about 2 percent—of global harvested irrigated area by 2050. The growing scarcities of water and land could increasingly constrain food production growth, causing adverse impacts on food security and human well-being goals, if mitigating plant breeding and husbandry changes are not made.

Clearly, the major conflict with irrigation water is likely to come from intensifying urbanization. Sharp increases in nonirrigation water demands are expected over the next fifty years, with increases concentrated in the LDCs. Nonirrigation water consumption is expected to more than double by 2050, approaching more than 700 cubic km per year. Developing countries are projected to contribute most of the increase in demand, whereas total nonirrigation water consumption in developed countries is expected to increase only moderately.

The predicted substantial growth in livestock production to meet emerging economy demand is expected to be a significant factor in increasing water demand, particularly owing to the demand for water to grow fodder crops such as maize, other coarse grains, and soya beans.

Even in developed countries there are regions already experiencing serious water supply stress; there will have to be limitations on future expansion of use. There is a growing body of opinion that believes that the use of water by the European agricultural industry, for example, is already too high, will have to be controlled, and ultimately will have to be reduced. Agriculture in the European Union, it is estimated, currently uses about one-quarter of the area's water supply. It is clear, however, that quantities of water used and the degree of competition with other water users varies from region to region.

Any potential conflict with other users is likely to be greater in the drier southern Mediterranean regions of Europe than in the north and west where rainfall levels are much greater. Therefore, any accurate assessment of agriculture's share of water use in any region should be based on the actual extraction rate. This is very much larger than the overall share of water use: agriculture is estimated to use more than 80 percent of the water taken out of reservoirs, wells, and other storage sources. According to some expert sources, such a level of water use by agriculture is not sustainable.

Such experts believe that measures to improve water-use efficiency should be incorporated into the EU's common agricultural policy.[42] The CAP needs to be reconciled with the EU's Water Framework Directive, they argue. Abstraction of water for agricultural irrigation puts the greatest stress on water supplies, and until such use is costed and charged, much water will be wasted. "No one really meters abstraction of water for agriculture," says Daniel Villesot, former president of Eureau, the EU's water and wastewater industry lobby. "We need first to put a meter to measure the quantity of water used and then manage the quantity. As long as we are not paying the right price for water, we don't care about the quantity."[43]

For most of northwestern Europe, precipitation levels are high in relation to overall usage; water supply is therefore not a critical issue. The European Environment Agency indicates that agricultural water use is only a serious issue in the dry south of the EU. In northern member states, agriculture's contribution to total water use varies from almost zero in a few countries to more than 30 percent in others. While water for irrigation is important in northern regions, the largest proportion of water use in northern countries goes to livestock consumption and cleaning livestock housing and facilities.

In the United Kingdom, for example, irrigation and livestock use each account for around 50 percent of the estimated 300 million cubic meters of water abstracted for agriculture each year. The European Environment Agency says the use of water for livestock in the north occurs in areas with sufficient rainfall, where water stress is rare.[44] The challenge to sustainability comes from crop irrigation in southern Europe where irrigated crops predominate and its adverse impacts are most marked. But this pattern may change with global warming. As warmer weather patterns move northward, farmers will be encouraged to grow crops that will need irrigation. Overall, the EU requirement for irrigation water is expected to increase.

For southern European countries, irrigation is vital to profitable agricultural production. In Italy and Spain, for example, OECD figures indicate that irrigated agriculture contributes more than 50 percent to total agricultural production and more than 60 percent to the total value of agricultural products. Despite this, the total irrigated land area is proportionately small: only 21 percent and 14 percent of total agricultural land in Italy and Spain, respectively. This pattern is repeated at the regional level. In the Castilla–La Mancha region of Spain, for example, the irrigated area represents about 11 percent of the region's agricultural land while providing more than 40 percent of total agricultural production. The production gains from irrigation in the more arid regions of the EU are substantial, compared with rain-fed conditions. In northeastern Portugal for example, full irrigation has been shown to increase the yield of potatoes by up to 360 percent.

Both national and EU subsidies have given substantial support to irrigated crops. These subsidies have encouraged increased water use and a shift of traditional rain-fed crops to irrigated cultivation. In Spain, for example, traditional rain-fed olive production is now irrigated with the result that olive production is now the main water consumer. In the Guadalquivir River basin, 300,000 hectares of land devoted to olive production are now irrigated.

CAP subsidies have also stimulated the cultivation of water-intensive crops such as cotton and rice that are too often grown using inefficient irrigation techniques. In Greece, for example, a significant proportion of cotton is grown using flood irrigation, which requires 20,000 liters of floodwater to produce a kilogram of harvested crop. This is due to high levels of surface runoff and evaporation. The European Environmental Agency (EEA) points out that the use of drip irrigation of cotton would use substantially less water: 7,000 liters per kilogram of output of crop. Even at this level, however, the water requirement is still seven times higher than the volume of water needed for the production of a kilogram of wheat.

Climate change could make a significant difference to the pattern of water use in crop production, according to the EEA. Rises in average temperature are expected to lead to a longer European crop-growing season, resulting in increased crop yields and a general northward shift of cropping pattern. Such change is already showing. Winter wheat, for example, now flowers two to three weeks earlier compared to thirty years ago. The extent to which these potential future increases in crop yield are achieved will be strongly dependent on the availability of water—either from rainfall or irrigation.

While global warming may have the effect of increasing annual average rainfall, there is the countering factor that it will tend to fall at the wrong time of year, thus placing greater strain on stored water facilities. Climatologists expect that rainfall in the more northerly areas may be lacking in the key summer months when crop growth is at its height. In the south, increased temperatures and decreased precipitation will result in a general decrease in water availability, increasingly exacerbated by an increase in the frequency and severity of droughts. Overall, this is likely to mean an increase in irrigation water demand. "Without appropriate management the competition for water between agriculture and other sectors is likely to increase," the EEA warns, "with a progressive worsening of water scarcity. In some southern locations, lack of water in the future may limit agricultural output."

There will have to be an improvement in the efficiency of irrigation methods. The EEA says that pressurized pipe networks should replace gravity-fed open channels, and drip and sprinkler systems should be used in place of furrows. Such improvements in technique, however, could create greater overall irrigation water demand, driving an expansion of the area irrigated and resulting in either no reduction or even an increase in total water use.

The EEA concludes: "The overall abstraction and consumption of water resources is currently sustainable in the long-term. However, some areas may face unsustainable trends, especially in southern Europe where much improved efficiency of water use, especially in agriculture, is needed to prevent seasonal water shortages. In addition, climate change may affect water resources and water demand."[45]

In these areas traditional approaches that aim to secure a sufficient supply of water for agriculture by, for example, building reservoirs, establishing interbasin transfers, and exploiting new abstraction points from both surface and groundwater will not be enough. Generally, such practices are not sustainable in the longer term and simply exacerbate the adverse impacts of agricultural water use. Potentially more sustainable supply approaches would include reusing treated wastewater, improving irrigation systems, modifying agricultural practices, implementing policy measures such as water pricing, and establishing farmer advisory schemes

The EEA emphasizes that in the future agriculture will have to pay for more water: "Introducing water pricing across all sectors will be critical to achieving sustainable water use. The EU Water Framework Directive recognises this, by establishing that pricing provide adequate incentives to use water resources efficiently, plus covering the full cost of water services. Full cost recovery not only encompasses the cost of water supply, maintenance and new infrastructure but also environmental and resource costs. As such it reflects the 'water user pays' principle."[46]

summary and conclusions

In conclusion, it should be said that while much of modern agriculture places too great a strain on resources and on the environment, with important modification in many regions 'food production is likely to be sustainable. Most developed countries are now evolving agricultural systems and matching policies that will conserve the soils' productive capacity. Policies are also being pursued that seek to conserve native flora and fauna. Potential contamination by agricultural activities of the immediate environment and water supplies is being reduced. Increasingly, husbandry practices are being adopted that reduce soil degradation, fossil fuel dependency, and GHG emissions. The major global challenge is the establishment of more productive sustainable agricultural production systems in the less-prosperous developing countries. National governments and development agencies need to foster the growth of agricultural systems that will not only increase food production and availability but also reduce the risk of loss of future productive capacity.

The important question is, can the level of production needed to feed 9.5 billion people be sustained? It has to be accepted that intensified production has undesirable side effects. The central problem for the future is how to maintain a high level of output without damaging the ecosystem. While agriculture's greenhouse gas output is substantial, its actual GHG emission level is heavily disputed. The reality is that reduction of agriculture's GHG emission would only be possible through massive change in diets away from ruminant animal products. While an organic approach to agriculture is unlikely to alleviate potential world food supply problems, good husbandry based on organically sound principles are vital to solving the LDC's food supply problems.

More fluid food trade is and increasingly will be vital to global food security. While GM crops are not a panacea for increased global food production, they can provide solutions to serious production problems in less-developed countries. It is unquestionable that water resources available to agriculture are under serious strain, with the areas with greatest food need suffering the greatest strain. More water conservation measures, physical and political, will be needed in the future to sustain food production in the most vulnerable regions.

notes

1. B. D. Ratner, "Sustainability as a Dialogue of Values: Challenges to the Sociology of Development," *Sociological Inquiry* 74, no. 1 (2004): 50–69.

2. OECD, *OECD Environmental Outlook to 2050* (Paris: OECD Publishing, 2012).

3. World Commission on Environment and Development, *Our Common Future* (New York: Oxford University Press, 1987).

4. FAO, *Food and Agriculture Statistics Global Outlook,* (Rome: FAO Statistics Division, 2006).

5. David Tilman et al., "Agricultural Sustainability and Intensive Production Practices," *Nature* 418 (August 8, 2002): 671–677.

6. FAO, *Livestock's Long Shadow—Environmental Issues and Options* (Rome: FAO, 2006).

7. Robert Goodland and Jeff Anhang, *Livestock and Climate Change: What if the Key Actors in Climate Change Are Cows, Pigs, and Chickens?* (Washington, DC: Worldwatch Institute, 2009).

8. Ibid.

9. European Commission, Joint Research Centre Institute for Prospective Technological Studies, *Environmental Improvement Potentials of Meat and Dairy Products* (Brussels: European Commission, 2008).

10. Tara Garnett, "Animal Feed, Livestock and Greenhouse Gas Emissions: What Are the Issues?" Food Climate Research Network, Centre for Environmental Strategy, University of Surrey. Paper presented to the Society of Animal Feed Technologists, Coventry, January 25, 2007.

11. E. Audsley et al., *Food, Land and Greenhouse Gases The Effect of Changes in UK Food Consumption on Land Requirements and Greenhouse Gas Emissions*. Report for the Committee on Climate Change (Bedford, UK: Cranfield University, 2010).

12. Ibid.

13. Ibid.

14. Ibid.

15. OECD, *OECD Environmental Outlook to 2050.*

16. FAO, *Greenhouse Gas Emissions from the Dairy Sector: A Life Cycle Assessment* (Rome: FAO, 2010).

17. Committee on Climate Change, *Building a Low-carbon Economy—the UK's Contribution to Tackling Climate Change* (London: Committee on Climate Change, 2008). Available at: http://www.theccc.org.uk/reports/building-a-low-carbon-economy, accessed July 2011.

18. http://www.living-organic.net/

19. *Comparison of composition (nutrients and other substances) of organically and conventionally produced foodstuffs, a systematic review of the available literature*. Report for the Food Standards Agency Nutrition and Public Health Intervention Research Unit at London School of Hygiene & Tropical Medicine. www.food.gov.uk/foodindustry/farmingfood/organicfood/

20. Danish Research Centre for Food and Farming Statens Jordbrugs- og Fiskeriøkonomiske Institut Rapport nr. 99 Organic Agriculture in Denmark Economic Impacts of a Widespread Adoption of Organic Management Els Wynen Copenhagen 1998.

21. Nadia El-Hage Scialabba and Caroline Hattam, *Organic Agriculture, Environment and Food Security* (Rome: FAO, Environment and Natural Resources Service Sustainable Development Department, 2002).

22. Jelle Bruinsma, *The Resource Outlook to 2050: By How Much Do Land, Water, and Crop Yields Need to Increase by 2050?* Report to Expert Meeting on How to Feed the World in 2050 (Rome: FAO, 2009).

23. Ibid.

24. Ibid.

25. European Commission, "European Action Plan for Organic Food and Farming" [policy statement] (Brussels: European Commission, 2004).

26. Jacques Diouf, FAO Director-General, "Opening Statement to High-Level Expert Forum on How to Feed the World in 2050," Rome, October 12, 2009.

27. Kelly Rae Chi, James MacGregor, and Richard King, *Fair Miles: Recharting the Food Miles Map* (London: Oxfam International, 2009).

28. Caroline Saunders, Andrew Barber, and Greg Taylor, *Food Miles—Comparative Energy/Emissions Performance of New Zealand's Agriculture Industry.* Research Report No. 285 (Canterbury, NZ: Lincoln University, July 2006).

29. Alison Smith et al., *The Validity of Food Miles as an Indicator of Sustainable Development,* Final report produced for DEFRA (Oxon: AEA Technology, 2005).

30.   Ibid., xxi

31.   Jodie Keane, James MacGregor, Sheila Page, Leo Peskett, and Vera Thorstensen, "Development, Trade and Carbon Reduction: Designing Coexistence to Promote Development," Working Paper no. 315 (London: Overseas Development Institute, 2010).

32.   Ibid.

33.   UK Government, Cabinet Office, The Strategy Unit, "Executive Summary," in *Food Matters: Towards a Strategy for the 21st Century* (London: Cabinet Office, 2008).

34.   UK Government, *Food 2030* (London: DEFRA, 2010).

35.   BirdLife International, *Proposal for a New EU Common Agricultural Policy.* Report prepared by European Environmental Bureau, European Forum on Nature Conservation and Pastoralism, International Federation of Organic Agriculture Movements-EU Group, WWF—World Wide Fund for Nature (Cambridge: BirdLife International, 2010).

36.   The concept of high nature value farming developed from a growing recognition that the conservation of biodiversity in Europe depends on the continuation of low-intensity farming systems.

37.   BirdLife International, *Proposal for a new EU Common Agricultural Policy.*

38.   FAO, *Agricultural Biotechnology—Meeting the Needs of the Poor?* (Rome: FAO, 2004).

39.   Ibid.

40.   David Tilman, Kenneth G. Cassman, Pamela A. Matson, Rosamond Naylor, and Stephen Polasky, "Agricultural Sustainability and Intensive Production Practices," *Nature* 418 (August 8, 2002): 671–677.

41.   Ibid.

42.   Directive 2000/60/EC of the European Parliament and of the Council establishing a framework for the community action in the field of water policy.

43.   Ibid.

44.   European Environment Agency, *Water Resources across Europe—Confronting Water Scarcity and Drought,* EEA Report No. 2, March 17, 2009.

45.   Ibid.

46.   Ibid.

chapter 15

conclusion

> The most recent U.N. demographic projections show world population growing to 9.3 billion by 2050, an addition of 2.3 billion people. Most people think these demographic projections, like most of those made over the last half century, will in fact materialise. But this is unlikely, given the difficulties in expanding the food supply, such as those posed by spreading water shortages and global warming. We are fast outgrowing the earth's capacity to sustain our increasing numbers.[1]

This quotation from Lester R. Brown, a leading luminary of the cult of neo-Malthusianism, succinctly sums up what could be described as the worst-case scenario in the future outlook for the world's food supply. Just like Malthus himself argued two hundred years or so ago, Brown suggests that the expected increases in population over the next four decades will be cut off by famine. People will starve and die until the population matches the amount of food available to sustain it. More important, it assumes that the human race will take no steps to produce new crop varieties, to moderate the strain of agriculture on resources, or to ameliorate the impact of climate change.

The main conclusion of this book is that it will take such action. The scientific evidence would suggest an optimistic outlook on the world's future food supply prospects. The world has the material means and the knowledge to banish famine.

Despite this, hunger and premature death continue to rampage through the still famine-stricken lands of sub-Saharan Africa and south Asia. In these areas the supply of food is not only inadequate but maldistributed. In too many places the day's wages are too little to buy enough grain to feed a family. Those who are rich are able to buy enough food—usually more than enough—to feed themselves, no matter how bad the world's harvests. Shortages and high prices, resulting sometimes from inadequate production but more often from inefficient distribution, raise prices and reduce the food supply of those who are already starving or suffering near-starvation.

When harvests fail it is still the landless and the poor who suffer. The Philippines, for example, with a rapidly growing population and shortage of suitable land for crops, is the world's largest importer of rice. Its people are therefore the most vulnerable to rising prices. In the world food commodity price crisis of 2008, rice prices soared to record highs. Food consumption for people already malnourished declined even further. It should be noted, however, that the major cause of the escalation of prices was not an incipient lack of supply, but export restrictions imposed by traditional rice exporters. This privation could have been prevented by increased imports—subsidized or not.

Thus, unlike the fearful people of previous ages, we do know how to prevent apocalyptic famines, how to grow more food, how to do so without destroying the means of production, how to insure against weather and disease, and how to move food from areas of plenty to those of shortage. To apply a well-worn but apt phrase: the conquest of famine and malnutrition is no longer beyond the wit of man. We have the means and the methods to banish famine forever. The fact that we have not done so is too often a matter of willful stupidity and, in the extreme, mendacity—not a lack of means.

The challenge to the twenty-first century global food production complex comes not only from the likely massive increase in population but from the way that population is likely to increase. First, it will occur almost exclusively in those countries least well equipped to increase their own food supply. Second, almost all of the increase will take place in towns and cities. This second factor is likely to make the problem of better access to adequate food for the hungriest people more difficult. This is because urbanization absorbs large areas of land—usually the best land—which is inevitably taken out of agricultural production. At the same time, the land that is left has to produce more and its product has to be transported to urban markets. Too often, the infrastructure to facilitate the transfer from producer to consumer is inadequate or, in the extreme, does not exist.

The demand for food most likely will be complicated by increasing prosperity. Economies of the developing and emerging economy countries will continue to grow. As people in those countries prosper, their demand for a more varied diet will result in increased demand for those foods that are more costly to produce—meat and dairy products.

Much as the overfed Western middle class may preach against the perceived evils of meat eating, the new rich of the East will undoubtedly want more of it. This is a reality that has to be built into any model of the future food production system. This changing consumption pattern will put increased pressure on the world's agricultural resources. Depending on how the increased production is achieved, it will also involve additional environmental strain. At the same time, production in the most food supply vulnerable countries will be hampered by climate change.

Allowance for climate change has to be built into any assessment of the future food supply and demand balance. The consensus among climatologists is that we can expect a rise in the global temperature of 2–3 percent over the next fifty years. While such a level of increase will harm Africa most seriously, such a level of change will not seriously affect agriculture globally until after 2050. Indeed, some important food producing regions will actually benefit from this change. Agricultural production in the Northern Hemisphere is likely to rise because carbon fertilization resulting from any temperature rise would moderate the negative effects of warming on agricultural production. Unfortunately, production in the Southern Hemisphere, where increase is most needed, is likely to be adversely affected. Africa, already one of the two most vulnerable regions, has the highest population at risk of increased hunger and malnutrition as a result of global warming.

There would, however, be some general beneficial impact from this expected level of warming for global food security because the food export capacity of Northern Hemisphere developed countries could rise, while the food deficit in the south increases. The most important overall effect of global temperature increase would be that almost all of the world's 1 billion food insecure people will be negatively affected—either through increased food shortages or higher food prices. Even in

Europe, farmers could suffer additional crop loss and costs due to increased pest incidence and water shortages.

Food production will become more costly. Whatever new productivity-increasing methods are adopted, agriculture's major production factor, apart from the soil itself, is energy. The additional oil for motive power and gas needed for fertilizer production will cost more. While food production is calculated to be responsible for 4 percent of world energy use, energy accounts for a very large proportion of total food production cost, on average 45 to 50 percent of the cost of producing the major food and feed grains. This is why oil and grain prices are so closely linked. While new agricultural techniques have cut fuel usage by developed country farmers by nearly 50 percent in the last half century, rising energy prices threaten food production in many disadvantaged areas.

While oil is essential to tillage and harvesting operations, the cost of the other major input, fertilizer, has been pumped up by the steadily increasing cost of natural gas used to synthesize nitrogen for fertilizer. On the plus side, natural gas prices are less likely to rise further than those of oil; the supply is likely to increase with new exploitation. At the end of the first decade of the twenty-first century, there are signs of an increasing world surplus of nitrogen fertilizer.

Similarly, while conventional oil production may have peaked, higher prices are stimulating new exploitation. Nevertheless, the agriculture industry has to face the prospect of a projected likely rise in the real price of oil by 35 percent or more by 2035. This is likely to lead to a long-term rise in the real price of food.

The perceived threat of modern agriculture to the physical environment will also lead to increased cost of producing food. A watershed has now been reached in the political approach to future methods of food production. The extreme green view is that the only way to avoid future food safety and quality crises and to lessen environmental pressure is by abandoning modern methods of production involving the use of artificial fertilizers, pesticides, intensive breeding of plants and animals—with or without genetic manipulation—and intensive rearing and reverting instead to low-technology, small-scale organic production. At the other end of the spectrum is the view that production and standards can only be maintained by the application of modern scientific agricultural practices. In its extreme form this view maintains that the world will only be able to feed itself on a shrinking cultivated land area by the widespread application and further development of biotechnology. The solution lies between these two extremes.

What is clear is that food production has to be increased. Most important, production has to be increased in the least developed countries that cannot afford to be dependent on their present scale of food imports. Output also has to rise in the developed countries to ensure food security on a planet inhabited by 9 billion or more people. To achieve this, it is necessary to maintain at least current levels of annual productivity increase, which will require the application of both conventional and new plant breeding technology.

The United Nations Development Programme (UNDP) Report on Human Development, published in 2001, emphasized that developing countries need biotechnology and genetically modified crops to improve yields and the nutritional quality of staple food crops such as rice, millet, sorghum, and cassava. While the UNDP said that modern biotech methods are needed to develop new varieties of these crops to increase and improve the staple diet of millions in the poorer countries, it certainly did not suggest that biotech is the single answer to the productivity challenge.

This potential application of agricultural biotechnology provides serious challenges to the current conventional wisdom on the future of the rural environment. It certainly should have a part to play in compensating for the effects of climate change, the pollution and overextraction of water, soil salination, and urbanization on world food production capacity.

Currently, development of agricultural biotechnology in Europe particularly but also in the less-developed countries is severely hampered by a political atmosphere too often hostile to science, which has led to the erection of a battery of regulatory barriers. The development of potential productivity-enhancing biotechnology is seriously hampered by overregulation, political hostility, and a poor business environment for the start-up of innovative companies.

Despite the fact that more than 10 percent of the world's cropland, more than 30 million hectares, is now successfully growing genetically modified crops, with no evidence of any harm to man, beast, or the surrounding environment, the use and development of such productivity boosting innovation is banned from large areas of the world. Biotech crops are excluded from all but three African countries, despite the fact that this is the area that could benefit enormously from genetically engineered crop varieties to give protection against pests and disease and obviate the use of pesticides—chemicals that poor farmers cannot afford to buy.

But it is not only the development and application of biotech methods that is obstructed by legislation originating in the misplaced environmental obsessions of voters who appear to have little concern for the food supply problems of the world's poorest. Even conventional productivity-raising agricultural techniques are increasingly hamstrung by restrictive legislation. It has, for example, been calculated that European Union legislation to ban a wide range of crop protection chemicals—most of them posing no serious threat to humans, animals, or the environment—will cut European crop yields by as much as 20 percent.[2] Can the world afford the luxury of this latter-day Puritanism?

What the world cannot afford is the widespread adoption of so-called organic farming methods that come highly recommended by influential sections of the Western intelligentsia. Leaving aside the important point that there is no scientific evidence that organic food is any better than food produced under nonorganic conditions, there is clear evidence that adoption of what are deemed to be organic methods results in substantial reductions in yields. This is most evident in the context of developed country agriculture.

A study in Denmark indicated that mandatory adoption of organic farming would cut Danish cereal production by 62 percent, reduce pork and poultry output by 70 percent, and reduce potato production by 80 percent. Denmark, currently a major food exporting country, would be unable to feed itself.[3]

While adoption of low-yield organic methods by developing and major food exporting developed countries is something that the world's hungry can do without, there is an argument for the adoption of low-input agriculture in the least prosperous and hungriest countries. In many such situations, what developed country agricultural experts might define as organic methods have a significant role to play;

organic principles properly applied in countries with an obvious surplus of labor and a shortage of imported inputs will reduce the need for external inputs and preserve the long-term fertility of the soil and therefore its productive capacity. Good husbandry, in other words, rather than necessarily organic husbandry.

But given the increasing political constraints, and accepting that global food production has to be increased, where is the increased food production to come from? There are four possible main ways in which global output can be increased: by bringing more land into production, by investing more in research and agricultural development, by improving infrastructure in the most food needy countries, and by increasing investment in agriculture in those same countries.

The OECD and most international agencies suggest there are significant areas of land still available for agriculture. Fortunately, most of it is where it is most needed: in sub-Saharan Africa and South America. There is little unused or underutilized land in the other key food needy region—south Asia. In Europe and North America there is little unfarmed land, but there is, particularly on parts of the European land mass, a great deal of underutilized land. According to the OECD there are 1.56 billion hectares of land available for crop expansion[4]—at first glance, more than enough to provide the extra 2.5 billion tonnes of grain needed to feed a 9.5 billion world population. However, the pressure of urbanization means that the practically realistic figure for additional available land is likely to be significantly less.

Much of this additional available land is likely to be increasingly difficult to exploit, particularly in Africa. Land that can only be farmed with increased use of scarce irrigation water or is subject to severe fertility problems would probably involve unacceptable environmental and social costs. Consistently higher commodity prices would be needed to bring much of this marginal land into production. However, in countries where there are no technical barriers to increased output, such as Ukraine, Russia, and parts of eastern Europe, food production is likely to rise. In land-scarce regions such as south Asia, increased output can be achieved by more multiple cropping and other methods of intensifying production.

Despite portents of increasing famine seen by the pessimists, realistic assessments of the prospects for improvement are hopeful. A recent World Bank assessment, for example, expects real food commodity prices to decline in the period to 2030 as a result of production response to rising food prices.[5] This increased output is likely to come from productivity improvements and the cultivation of unused and underutilized land. Significantly, the World Bank has factored temperature rise and water challenges into its calculations: "Over the next 20 years, assuming sufficient investment is forthcoming in developing and high-income countries," says the World Bank, "the spread of more-intensive production techniques coupled with improved varieties emerging from recent advances in biotechnology, should allow global productivity gains on par with historical trends despite some productivity losses caused by climate change."[6]

This assessment emphasizes that most of the increased food production has to come from greater output from the existing global farmed area and more research and development on a worldwide scale. Since there is generally a ten-year time lag between research project initiation and its impact on production, new investment in research needs to be stepped up now and through to 2030, if production is to meet the requirements of the increased population of 2050. If current research efforts do not at least match those of the last three decades of the twentieth century, then it is unlikely that such a food production target will be met.

While the emerging economies of South America, China, and India are investing heavily and will continue to invest in agricultural research and improved infrastructure, the same cannot be said of the countries of sub-Saharan Africa. Even current European agricultural research is considered to be well short of the level needed to maintain and increase sustainable productivity growth. In the developing countries, where it is most needed, the research and infrastructure investment will have to come from outside. In many of these countries, agricultural investment and rural infrastructure improvement has been neglected while governments concentrate on often inappropriate nonagricultural industries and urban development. This has had and is having a negative impact on food production while increasing the pressure on food supplies.

Use of cereals for the production of biofuels is unlikely to have a long-term, or even medium-term, effect on food supplies or prices. Biofuel production may have possibly contributed to higher short-term food crop price rises in the recent past, but the agricultural production capacity of both Europe and North America is easily able to cope with the level of production of cereals required both to meet current renewable energy mandates and to maintain food supplies. Though many critics argue that neither the economic nor the environmental sums add up on biofuels, they could represent an opportunity for profitable production in developing countries.[7]

In these countries additional ethanol and biodiesel production need not imply reducing food crops production. So-called second generation biomass fuel crops can be grown on land that is marginal to food production. Brazil, for example, is a low-cost producer of ethanol from sugarcane and has an estimated 180 million hectares of pasture that could be used to produce additional sugarcane for ethanol—without reducing the food sugar crop. Many sub-Saharan African countries, including Angola, Mozambique, and Tanzania, also have the potential to produce ethanol profitably from sugarcane on land that is not used for food crop production. In addition, nonfood crops such as jatropha can be used to produce biodiesel in many developing countries.

To feed the expected 9–9.5 billion world population of 2050 at a minimum level will require a global grain harvest of more than 3 billion tonnes, or approximately 40 percent more than 2011 production. This is only sufficient to provide everyone on the planet with the dietary minimum; because this is an average figure; those who have money will consume more and those without will consume less. The production figure needed to maintain a safe level of supply therefore needs to be much higher. A much more desirable target would be to aim to increase the average diet to 3,500 kilocalories a day. On this basis, a minimum of a 50 percent increase in production to 3.5 billion tonnes would be needed.

The main calculations of necessary production in Chapter 11 are made on this basis. To achieve such an average, larger production would be needed to allow for higher than average consumption in some developed countries, switches in dietary patterns leading to greater consumption of livestock products in developing countries, and wastage at all stages in the food chain. A production level closer to 4 billion tonnes a year would therefore appear to be necessary.

Is such an increase in production possible? At present levels of average crop productivity, production and supplies could by the mid-twenty-first century be on a knife edge, with stocks able to be maintained on little more than a hand-to-mouth basis and frequent price hikes. On the basis of achieving average consumption on parity with developed country diets, current levels of crop production productivity (0.9 percent per annum) projected through to 2050 would show a mild gap between production and desired consumption starting to develop from 2025 onward, reaching a deficit of approximately 250 million tonnes a year by 2050.

In the worst-case scenario, it is possible, but not probable, that yields could decline by 0.5 percent and cropland be reduced by 0.2 percent. In that case, the cereals deficit would reach more than 2 billion tonnes, not far short of being equal to current global production. Fortunately, such a disaster scenario is unlikely, unless the world is struck by some cataclysmic climate phenomena, a crop disease pandemic, massive political disruption, or a combination of all three.

More likely and most probable are a modest increase in productivity and some increase in farmed area. World food security would be ensured by an annual increase in productivity of 1.5 percent a year and a modest (0.2 percent) increase in cropland area. This combination would provide a comfortable margin of production of more than 2 billion tonnes over the consumption by a 9.3 billion world population with an adequate average intake of 3,500 kilocalories a day.

Truly apocalyptic would be the combination of higher than expected population increase and declining agricultural production. If the UN's high population estimate increase variant of 10.5 billion by 2050 were to occur, the strain on food supplies would be disastrous at almost any possible level of production increase. At both the current trend of increase and modest productivity increase, there would be a grain supply deficit by 2050 of between 500 million and 900 million tonnes. A decline in yields would have the most devastating effect: at the extreme, a supply deficit of about 2.5 billion tonnes.

The main conclusion to be drawn from these figures is that if it is assumed that the UN's medium population increase estimate is the most likely, and all the available evidence would suggest that it is, then with reasonable assumptions about productivity and land utilization there will be more than enough food to feed a 2050 population of 9.5 billion. The crucial element of this calculation is however an increase in productivity by 2035–2050 of at least 1 percent a year, although 1.5 percent a year would be safer.

In addition, if food security is to be improved on a global scale the world food system needs to be bolstered against potentially apocalyptic food supply events, such as sudden climatic disasters or disease outbreaks. A fluid food trading system, unobstructed by panic imposition of protectionist measures, is essential to maintaining and improving world food security. An important part of this would be the availability of improved information on world food production, supplies, stocks, and demand, which would allow governments to make rational rather than panic-stricken responses to any supply shocks. A major lesson of the food crisis of the early twenty-first century is that it was made much worse by export bans in countries that could have significantly increased the globally available grain supply.

Unchecked, such policies could have an even greater impact in the future. If, for example, a particularly vulnerable region of the world were to be affected by the most likely climatic shock to production—drought—the effect on that region would be much worse if export restrictions were placed on potential supplying countries than if trade were to function without restriction. The UK government's 2008 Future of Food and Farming project postulated the likely effect of a drought in south Asia on food supplies and prices, calculating the impact with and without export restrictions in potentially exporting countries.[8]

Such a drought would likely cut crop yields in Bangladesh, India, and Pakistan by 2 percent a year for a period of six years. Computer modeling of the impact indicated that, as a consequence, the region would change from being a net exporter of rice to being a heavy importer and its imports of maize would increase substantially. There would be price increases for the staple food grains in all countries of the surrounding east Asian region. It is estimated that this weather shock on a large food-consuming region would result in the price on the world market of rice rising by 16 percent, of wheat by 32 percent, and of maize by 67 percent. Food supplies to the most impoverished and hungry would be severely reduced. It is calculated that the numbers of hungry children would increase by three-quarters of a million.

The impact, both immediate and longer term, would be considerably worse without free movement of exports and imports. Any such drought on its own is estimated to increase food crop prices generally by around 39 percent; imposition of export controls by other countries in the region would likely raise the price increase to 45 percent or more.

The vulnerability of the hungriest people, illustrated in this theoretical example, highlights that improved access to food is equally as important as increased production. Global abundance of food, even if it were to be achieved, does not ensure freedom from hunger. War and other political conflicts continually obstruct food supply to the most needy in many countries of sub-Saharan Africa and Asia. That too many governments are not ensuring supply to the neediest sections of their populations is evidenced in the richer emerging Asian economies, which have the most hungry people—China and India being the worst examples.

The most-needy countries remain too dependent on grain imports. Rural populations of these countries cannot adequately feed themselves because most of those who depend on small farms for their existence have plots that are too small. Pressure from rising population will make this worse; farms will get smaller. In such regions hungry people are too often isolated from food markets by bad communications. Not only does this obstruct supply, but it also prevents small farmers from selling what surpluses they may have.

Increasing agricultural productivity remains the major challenge in maintaining future food supply. This can only be achieved by stepping up research, large-scale agricultural investment, and knowledge creation and dissemination through improved agricultural extension services. Without these essentials, food production in the most impoverished countries will not keep pace with demand. The World Bank has warned that if this is not done, "These countries will become increasingly dependent on imported food." If productivity growth in developing countries is not massively increased, "global food prices will be higher, and many developing countries—especially those with rapidly growing populations—will be forced to import more-expensive food from high income countries."[9]

More has to be spent on agricultural development in the poorest developing countries. But rather than increasing, as it should have done, investment in agriculture and overseas development generally fell in the latter decades of the twentieth century. Such expenditure fell from 17 percent in 1980 to

3 percent in 2006. More specifically, agriculture spending declined by 58 percent in real terms in this period. Spending on agriculture also needs to be increased and redirected by the governments of the LDCs. In Africa generally, governments spend only an average of 4.5 percent of their budgets on agriculture.

In conclusion, the message is clear. The answer to the world food problem is increased production. To ensure the food security of 9.5 billion people, there is no scintilla of doubt, no argument, that the world's food supply has to be increased. While all of the present 7 billion population could be adequately fed by current levels of production, to feed an additional 2.5 billion will require substantial increases in output, however well or badly that future food supply is distributed.

The hard fact is that production must be most significantly increased in the less-developed countries of sub-Saharan Africa and south Asia. This is where the population will increase the most; ensuring greater food security in these most needy areas is a priority. But, in addition, because of the climatic and other risks that food production is and will be subject to, the safety net of production from the developed countries also has to be increased in order to fill inevitable gaps in the production of the most food-needy regions. Without increased production, food shortages will be apocalyptic. If agricultural productivity and production does not increase, the numbers of underfed and starving could easily triple. Food prices for those who could still afford to buy could rise by and remain more than 50 percent greater than in the second decade of the twenty-first century. In this dire situation, Thomas Malthus's terrible prophecy could well come to pass.

notes

1. Lester R. Brown, *Full Planet, Empty Plates: The New Geopolitics of Food Scarcity* (Washington, DC: Earth Policy Institute, 2012).

2. DEFRA, *UK Food Security Assessment: Detailed Analysis* (London: DEFRA, 2009; updated January 2010).

3. Bichel Committee, *Organic Scenarios for Denmark* (Denmark: Bichel Committee, 2000).

4. OECD–FAO, *Agricultural Outlook 2009–2018* (Paris: OECD, 2009).

5. World Bank, *Global Economic Prospects 2009: Commodities at the Crossroads* (Washington, DC: World Bank, 2008).

6. Ibid.

7. OECD-FAO, *Agricultural Outlook 2011–2020* (Paris: OECD, 2011).

8. UK Government Office for Science, *The Future of Food and Farming: Challenges and Choices for Global Sustainability Foresight* (London: UK Government, 2011).

9. World Bank, *Global Economic Prospects 2009*.

bibliography

Alexandratos, N., ed. *World Agriculture: Towards 2030/50, Interim Report. An FAO Perspective*. Rome: FAO, 2006.

Alexandratos, N., and J. Bruinsma. *World Agriculture: Towards 2030/2050: The 2012 Revision*. Rome: FAO Agricultural Development Economics Division, 2012.

American Economic Association: Energy & Environment and Universidad de Politécnica de Madrid. "Adaptation to Climate Change in the Agricultural Sector," AGRI-2006-G4–05. Report to European Commission Directorate-General for Agriculture and Rural Development (ED05334), no. 1, December 2007.

Asian Development Bank. *Food Prices and Inflation in Developing Asia: Is Poverty Reduction Coming to an End?* Special Report. Manila, Philippines: Asian Development Bank, 2008.

Audsley E. et al. *Food, Land and Greenhouse Gases The Effect of Changes in UK Food Consumption on Land Requirements and Greenhouse Gas Emissions*. Report for the Committee on Climate Change. Bedford, UK: Cranfield University, 2010.

Bailey, R. *Growing a Better Future: Food Justice in a Resource-constrained World*. Oxford: Oxfam International, 2011.

Bichel Committee. *Organic Scenarios for Denmark*. Denmark: Bichel Committee, 2000.

BirdLife International. *Proposal for a New EU Common Agricultural Policy*. Cambridge: BirdLife International, 2010.

British Petroleum. *Statistical Review of World Energy*. June 2011. Available at: bp.com/statistical review.

Brown, L. R. *Full Planet, Empty Plates: The New Geopolitics of Food Scarcity*. Washington, DC: Earth Policy Institute, 2012.

Brown, L. R. "The Great Food Crisis of 2011," *Foreign Policy Magazine,* January 2011.

Brown, L. R. *Outgrowing the Earth: The Food Security Challenge in an Age of Falling Water Tables and Rising Temperatures*. New York: W. W. Norton, 2004.

Brown, L. R. *Plan B 2.0: Rescuing a Planet Under Stress and a Civilization in Trouble*. New York: W.W. Norton, 2006; Washington, DC: Earth Policy Institute, 2006.

Bruinsma, J. *The Resource Outlook to 2050: By How Much Do Land, Water and Crop Yields Need to Increase by 2050?* Jelle, Expert Meeting on How to Feed the World in 2050. Rome: FAO, 2009.

Bruinsma, J. *World Agriculture: Towards 2015/2030*. Rome: FAO, 2003.

Canning, P., A. Charles, S. Huang, K. R. Polenske, and A. Waters. *Report: Energy Use in the U.S. Food System*, ERR-94. Washington, DC: USDA Economic Research Service, 2010.

Cantore, N., J. Kennan, and S. Page. *CAP Reform and Development: Introduction, Reform Options and Suggestions for Further Research*. London: Overseas Development Institute, 2011.

Chi, K. R., J. MacGregor, and R. King. *Fair Miles: Recharting the Food Miles Map*. London: Oxfam International, 2009.

Committee on Climate Change. *Building a Low-Carbon Economy—the UK's Contribution to Tackling Climate Change*. December 2008. Available at: www.theccc.org.uk/reports/.

Costa C., M. Osborne, X. Zhang, P. Boulanger, and P. Jomini. *Modelling the Effects of the EU Agricultural Policy.* Australian Government Productivity Commission, 2009. Available at: www.pc.gov.au/_data/assets/pdf_file/0005/92777/european-agricultural-policy.pdf

Cotula, L., S. Vermeulen, R. Leonard, and J. Keeley. *Land Grab or Development Opportunity? Agricultural Investment and International Land Deals in Africa.* London and Rome: IIED/FAO/IFAD, 2009.

Commonwealth Scientific and Industrial Research Organization (CSIRO). *Climate Change: Science and Solutions for Australia.* Canberra: 2011.

De Schutter, O. "Food Commodities Speculation and Food Price Crises," Briefing Note 2 by the UN special rapporteur on the right to food (September 23, 2010). Available at: http://www.srfood.org/index.php/en/component/content/article/894-food-commodities-speculation-and-food-price-crises.

Department for Environment, Food, and Rural Affairs (DEFRA). "Ensuring the UK's Food Security in a Changing World: A DEFRA Discussion Paper." London: DEFRA, July 2008.

Department for Environment, Food, and Rural Affairs (DEFRA). *UK Food Security Assessment: Detailed Analysis.* London: DEFRA, 2009; updated January 2010.

Dyson, T. "Why the World's Population Will Probably Be Less than 9 billion in 2300," in *World Population to 2300.* New York: United Nations, Department of Economic and Social Affairs Population Division, 2004.

El-Hage Scialabba, N., and C. Hattam, *Organic Agriculture, Environment and Food Security.* Rome: FAO, Environment and Natural Resources Service Sustainable Development Department, 2002.

Ericksen P, P, Thornton, A. Notenbaert, L, Crame, P. Jones, and M. Herrero. *Mapping Hotspots of Climate Change and Food Insecurity in the Global Tropics.* CGIAR Research Programme on Climate Change, Agriculture and Food Security (CCAFS) Report no. 5, 2011.

Euromonitor. *Who Eats What: Identifying International Food Consumption Trends*, 2nd ed. London: Euromonitor, 2011.

European Commission. *European Action Plan for Organic Food and Farming.* Brussels: Commission of the European Communities, 2004.

European Commission, Directorate-General for Agriculture and Rural Development. *China: Out of the Dragon's Den?* MAP Monitoring Agri-trade Policy, no. 01–08, May 2008.

European Commission, Directorate-General for Agriculture and Rural Development. *India's Role in World Agriculture.* MAP Monitoring Agri-trade Policy, no. 03–07, December 2007.

European Commission, Joint Research Centre Institute for Prospective Technological Studies. *Environmental Improvement Potentials of Meat and Dairy Products.* Brussels: European Commission, 2008.

European Commission, Joint Research Centre, Institute for Prospective Technological Studies. *Impacts of the EU Biofuel Target on Agricultural Markets and Land Use: A Comparative Modelling Assessment.* Brussels: European Commission, 2010.

European Environment Agency. *Water Resources across Europe—Confronting Water Scarcity and Drought.* EEA Report No. 2., March 17, 2009.

Evans, A. *The Feeding of the Nine Billion: Global Food Security for the 21st Century.* London: Chatham House, 2010.

Fischer, G., H. van Velthuizen, M. Shah, and F. Nachtergaele. *Global Agro-ecological Assessment for Agriculture in the 21st Century: Methodology and Results.* Luxembourg: IIASA, 2002.

Fonseca M. B. et al., *Impacts of the EU Biofuel Target on Agricultural Markets and Land Use: A Comparative Modelling Assessment.* Seville, Spain: European Commission Joint Research Centre Institute for Prospective Technological Studies, 2010.

Food and Agriculture Organization of the United Nations. *Food Outlook.* June 2010 issue.

Food and Agriculture Organization of the United Nations. *Agricultural Biotechnology—Meeting the Needs of the Poor?* Rome: FAO, 2004.

Food and Agriculture Organization of the United Nations. *Agricultural Trade, Trade Policies and the Global Food System.* Rome: FAO, 2008.

Food and Agriculture Organization of the United Nations. *Climate Change and Food Systems Resilience in Sub-Saharan Africa.* Rome, FAO, 2011.

Food and Agriculture Organization of the United Nations. *Feeding the World in 2050: World Summit on Food Security.* Rome, November 16–18, 2009.

Food and Agriculture Organization of the United Nations. *Food and Agriculture Statistics Global Outlook.* Rome: FAO Statistics Division, 2006.

Food and Agriculture Organization of the United Nations. *Food Price Index.* Rome: FAO, September 2011.

Food and Agriculture Organization of the United Nations. "Food Supply Situation and Crop Prospects in sub-Saharan Africa," no.2, August. Rome: FAO, Global Information and Early Warning System, 1999.

Food and Agriculture Organization of the United Nations. *Global Forum on Agriculture, Paris, 30 June 2009.* Rome: FAO, 2009.

Food and Agriculture Organization of the United Nations. *Greenhouse Gas Emissions from the Dairy Sector: A Life Cycle Assessment.* Rome: FAO, 2010.

Food and Agriculture Organization of the United Nations. *How to Feed the World in 2050: Critical Evaluation of Selected Projections.* Expert meeting. June 24–26, 2009.

Food and Agriculture Organization of the United Nations. *Livestock's Long Shadow—Environmental Issues and Options.* Rome: FAO, 2006.

Food and Agriculture Organization of the United Nations. *Price Volatility in Agricultural Markets: Evidence, Impact on Food Security, and Policy Responses.* ES Policy Brief no. 12. Rome: FAO, 2011.

Food and Agriculture Organization of the United Nations. *Report of the Special Rapporteur on the Right to Food.* United Nations A/65/281, General Assembly. August 11, 2010.

Food and Agriculture Organization of the United Nations. *The State of Food and Agriculture in Asia and the Pacific 2006.* Rome: FAO, 2006.

Food and Agriculture Organization of the United Nations. *The State of Food Insecurity in the World 2011: How Does International Price Volatility Affect Domestic Economies and Food Security?* Rome: FAO, 2011.

Food and Agriculture Organization of the United Nations. *World Agriculture: Towards 2030/2050. Interim report: Prospects for Food, Nutrition, Agriculture.* Rome: FAO, 2006.

Food and Agriculture Organization, Committee on World Food Security. *Price Volatility and Food Security: Report by the High Level Panel of Experts on Food Security and Nutrition.* Rome: FAO, July 2011.

Food and Agriculture Organization, Economic and Social Development Department, *Price Surges in Food Markets: How Should Organized Futures Markets Be Regulated?,* Policy Brief, no. 9, June 2010.

Food and Agricultural Research Policy Institute, Iowa State University. *2011 World Agricultural Outlook.* Ames, Iowa: FAPRI-ISU, 2011.

Food Chain Analysis Group, Department of Environment, Food, and Rural Affairs (DEFRA), *Food Security and the UK: An Evidence and Analysis Paper.* London: UK Government, DEFRA, 2006.

Frazão, E., B. Meade, and A. Regmi. *Converging Patterns in Global Food Consumption and Food Delivery Systems.* Washington, DC: USDA Economic Research Service, 2007.

Garnett, T. *Animal Feed, Livestock and Greenhouse Gas Emissions: What Are the Issues?* Food Climate Research Network, Centre for Environmental Strategy, University of Surrey. Paper presented to the Society of Animal Feed Technologists, Coventry, January 25, 2007.

Gehlhar M., and W. Coyle, *Global Food Consumption and Impacts on Trade Patterns.* Washington, DC: USDA Economic Research Service, 2008.

Gilmour, R. *A Poor Harvest—The Clash of Policies and Interests in the Grain Trade.* New York: Longman, 1982.

Global Food Markets Group. *The 2007/08 Agricultural Price Spikes: Causes and Policy Implications.* London: UK Government, DEFRA, 2010.

Goodland, R., and J. Anhang. *Livestock and Climate Change: What if the Key Actors in Climate Change Are Cows, Pigs, and Chickens?* Washington, DC: Worldwatch Institute, 2009.

Grievink, J-W., L. Josten, and C. Valk. *State of the Art in Food: The Changing Face of the Worldwide Food Industry.* Report for Cap Gemini Ernst & Young. London: Reed Elsevier, 2002.

Hansen, J. et al., "Earth's Energy Imbalance: Confirmation and Implications." *Science* 308, no. 5727 (2005): 1431–1435. doi:10.1126/science.1110252.

Heffer, P., and M. Prud'homme. *Fertilizer Outlook 2011–2015.* Paris: IFA, May 2011.

Heller, M., and G. Keoleian, *Life-Cycle Based Sustainability Indicators for Assessment of the U.S. Food System.* Ann Arbor: Center for Sustainable Systems, University of Michigan, 2003.

Henneberry, S. *Emerging Countries: Converging or Diverging Economies?* Milwaukee, WI: American Agricultural Economics Association, 2010.

Huffman, W. "Technology and Innovation in World Agriculture: Prospects for 2010–2019." Iowa State University Working Paper # 09007. April 2009.

Intergovernmental Panel on Climate Change (IPCC). *Fourth Assessment Report: Climate Change 2007: Contribution of Working Group 1.* Cambridge: Oxford University Press, 2007.

International Assessment of Agricultural Knowledge, Science, and Technology for Development (IAASTD), *Synthesis Report: A Synthesis of the Global and Sub-Global Reports.* Washington, DC: Island Press, 2009.

International Farm Comparison Network (IFCN). *Dairy Report 2011.* Prepared by Torsten Hemme and dairy researchers from 90 countries. Kiel, Germany: IFCN Dairy Research Center, 2011.

International Food Policy Research Institute (IFPRI). *Food Security, Farming, and Climate Change to 2050: Scenarios, Results, Policy Options.* Washington, DC: IFPRI, 2010.

International Fund for Agricultural Development (IFAD). *Soaring Food Prices and the Rural Poor: Feedback from the Field.* Rome: IFAD, 2007. Available at: www.ifad.org/operations/food/food.htm.

International Institute for Applied Systems Analysis (IIASA), *Probabilistic World Population Projections & Research Themes & Research Plan 2006–2010*, 2007 update. Laxenberg, Austria: IIASA, 2007.

International Monetary Fund. *Food and Fuel Prices—Recent Developments, Macroeconomic Impact, and Policy Responses.* Washington, DC: IMF, June 2008.

International Monetary Fund. *World Economic Outlook: Tensions from the Two-Speed Recovery.* Washington, DC: IMF, April 2011.

Institute for Agriculture and Trade Policy. *Commodities Market Speculation: The Risk to Food Security and Agriculture.* Minneapolis, MN: IATP Trade and Global Governance, 2008.

Institute of Grocery Distribution, *Market Index—Top 12 of 75 Markets.* Herfordshire: IGD, 2011.

Irwin, S.H., and D.R. Sanders. *The Impact of Index and Swap Funds on Commodity Futures Markets: Preliminary Results.* OECD Food, Agriculture and Fisheries Working Paper No. 27. Paris: OECD Publishing, 2010.

Jaggard, K. W., A. Qi, and E. S. Ober. "Possible Changes to Arable Crop Yields by 2050." *Philosophical Transactions of the Royal Society* 365B (2010): 2835–2851.

Joll, R., ed. *Human Development Report 1997*. New York: United Nations Development Programme, 1997.

Kearney, J. "Food Consumption Trends and Drivers." *Philosophical. Transactions of the Royal Society* 365B (2010): 2793–2807.

Koning N.B.J. et al., "Long-term Global Availability of Food: Continued Abundance or New Scarcity?," *NJAS: Wageningen Journal of Life Sciences* 55(3): 229–292.

Koyama, O. *Projecting the World Food Supply and Demand Using a Long-term Dynamic Simulator.* Ibaraki, Japan: Japan International Research Center for Agricultural Sciences, 2010.

Knox, J. W., T. M. Hess, A. Daccache, and M. Perez Ortola. *What Are the Projected Impacts of Climate Change on Food Crop Productivity in Africa and South Asia?: Systematic Review Final Report.* London: DIFD, 2011.

Kruse, J. *Income Growth in LDCs: Estimating Demand for Agricultural Commodities to 2050.* Milwaukee, WI: American Agricultural Economics Association, 2010.

Lu, S. "Understanding China's Retail Market." *China Business Review* (June 2010).

Lutz, W. et al., "The End of World Population Growth," *Nature* 412 (August 2, 2001).

Lutz, W., and K. C. Samir. "Dimensions of Global Population Projections: What Do We Know about Future Population Trends and Structures?" *Philosophical Transactions of the Royal Society* 365B (2010): 2779–2791.

Lutz, W., W. Sanderson, and S. Scherbov. *IIASA's 2007 Probabilistic World Population Projections.* IIASA World Population Program Online Data Base of Results, 2008. Available at: www.iiasa.ac.at/Research/POP/proj07/index.html?sb=5.

Malthus, T. R. *An Essay on the Principle of Population.* London: J. Johnson, 1798. Reprint, London: Macmillan, 1966.

Mwaniki, A. *Achieving Food Security in Africa: Challenges and Issues.* Ithaca, NY: Plant, Soil and Nutrition Laboratory, 2007.

Nachtergaele, F., R. Biancalani, S. Bunning, and H. George. *Land Degradation Assessment: The LADA Approach.* Rome: FAO Land and Water Division, 2010.

National Oceanic and Atmospheric Administration (NOAA) Geophysical Fluid Dynamics Laboratory (GFDL), "Patterns of Greenhouse Warming," *GFDL Climate Modeling Research Highlights* 1, no. 6 (January 2007).

Nelson, G. C. et al., *Climate Change: Impact on Agriculture and Costs of Adaptation.* Washington, DC: International Food Policy Research Institute, 2009.

Organisation for Economic Co-operation and Development (OECD). *Agricultural Policy Monitoring and Evaluation 2011: OECD Countries and Emerging Economies.* Paris: OECD Publishing, 2011.

Organisation for Economic Co-operation and Development (OECD). *The Economic Outlook and Policy Requirements for G20 Economies.* Paris: OECD, October 31, 2011.

Organisation for Economic Co-operation and Development (OECD). *OECD Environmental Outlook to 2050.* Paris: OECD Publishing, 2012.

Organisation for Economic Co-operation and Development–Food and Agricultural Organization of the United Nations (OECD–FAO). *Agricultural Outlook 2009–2018.* Paris: OECD, 2009.

Organisation for Economic Co-operation and Development–Food and Agricultural Organization of the United Nations (OECD-FAO). *Agricultural Outlook 2010–2019.* Paris: OECD, 2010.

Organisation for Economic Co-operation and Development–Food and Agricultural Organization of the United Nations (OECD-FAO). *Agricultural Outlook 2011–2020.* Paris: OECD, 2011.

Overseas Development Institute. *Making the EU's Common Agricultural Policy Coherent with Development Goals.*
    Briefing Paper 69. September 2011.

Paarlberg, R. *Food Politics—What Everyone Needs to Know.* New York: Oxford University Press, 2010.

Parry, M. L. "Impacts of Climate Change on Agriculture in Europe." IPCC Meteorological Office presentation to infor-
    mal meeting of EU Agriculture and Environment Ministers, London, September 11, 2005.

Parry, M. L., T. R. Carter, and N. T. Konijn, eds. *The Impact of Climatic Variations on Agriculture,* vols. 1 and 2.
    Boston: Kluwer Academic, 1988.

Pingali, P. "Malthus Is Still Wrong." Presentation to the 7th International Conference of the Asian Society of Agricul-
    tural Economists, Hanoi, Vietnam, October 13, 2011.

Pretty, J. et al., "The Top 100 Questions of Importance to the Future of Global Agriculture." *International Journal of
    Agricultural Sustainability* 8, no. 4 (2010): 219–236.

Rabobank. *Global Dairy Outlook: Enter the Giants.* Utrecht, The Netherlands: Rabobank, 2011.

Ratner, B. D. "Sustainability as a Dialogue of Values: Challenges to the Sociology of Development." *Sociological
    Inquiry* 74, no. 1 (2004): 50–69.

Regmi, A., and J. Dyck. *Effects of Urbanization on Global Food Demand: Changing Structure of Global Food Con-
    sumption and Trade.* WRS-01–1. Washington, DC: USDA Economic Research Service, 2007.

Roberts, T. L. "The Role of Fertilizer in Growing the World's Food." Paper given at COVAPHOS 111: International
    Conference on the Valorization of Phosphate and Phosphorus, Morocco, October 2004.

Sands, R. et al., *Impacts of Higher Energy Prices on Agriculture and Rural Economies.* Washington, DC: USDA
    Economic Research Services, 2011.

Saunders, C., A. Barber, and G. Taylor. *Food Miles—Comparative Energy/Emissions Performance of New Zealand's
    Agriculture Industry.* Research Report No. 285. Canterbury, NZ: Lincoln University, 2006.

Schipper, L. F., and I. Burton, *The Earthscan Reader on Adaptation to Climate Change.* London: Earthscan, 2008.

Schmidhuber, J., and F. N. Tubiello, "Crop and Pasture Response to Climate Change." *PNAS: Proceedings of the
    National Academy of Sciences* 104, no. 50 (2007): 19703–8. doi:10.1073/pnas.0701976104.

Sen, A. K. *Poverty and Famines.* New York: Oxford University Press, 1981.

Sexton, R. J. "Grocery Retailers' Dominant Role in Evolving World Food Markets." *Choices* (Journal of the Agricul-
    tural and Applied Economics Association) 25, no. 2 (2010).

Shapouri, S., S. Rosen, M. Peters, F. Baquedano, and S. Allen. *Food Security Assessment, 2010–20.* Outlook
    Report No. (GFA-21) 64. Washington, DC: USDA Economic Research Service, 2010.

Singh, R. B. *Towards a Food Secure India and South Asia: Making Hunger History.* Bangkok: APAARI, 2009.

Sjauw-Koen-Fa, A. *Sustainability and Security of the Global Food Supply Chain.* Utrecht, The Netherlands: Rabo-
    bank Group, 2010.

Smith, A. et al., *The Validity of Food Miles as an Indicator of Sustainable Development.* Final report produced for
    DEFRA. Oxon: AEA Technology, 2005.

Solomon, S., D. Qin, M. Manning, Z. Chen, M. Marquis, K. B. Averyt, M. Tignor, and H. L. Miller (eds.), *Contribu-
    tion of Working Group I to the Fourth Assessment Report of the Intergovernmental Panel on Climate Change.*
    Cambridge: Cambridge University Press, 2007.

Spielman, D. J., and R. Pandya-Lorch, eds., *Millions Fed: Proven Successes in Agricultural Development.* Washing-
    ton, DC: International Food Policy Research Institute, 2009.

Stevenson, J. R., N. B. Villoria, D. Byerlee, T. Kelley, and M. Maredia, "Green Revolution research saved an esti-
    mated 18 to 27 million hectares from being brought into agricultural production." *Proceedings of the National*

Academy of Sciences. West Lafayette, IN: Center for Global Trade Analysis, Agricultural Economics Department, Purdue University, 2012.

Sturgeon, T. J. "How Do We Define Value Chains and Production Networks?" MIT IPC Globalization Working Paper 00–010, 2000.

Tilman, D. et al. "Agricultural Sustainability and Intensive Production Practices." *Nature* 418 (August 8, 2002): 671–677.

UK Government. *Food 2030.* London: DEFRA, 2010.

UK Government, Cabinet Office, The Strategy Unit, "Executive Summary," in *Food Matters: Towards a Strategy for the 21st Century.* London: Cabinet Office, 2008.

UK Government, Cabinet Office, The Strategy Unit, *Food: An Analysis of the Issues. Report to Government.* London: Cabinet Office, January 2008; updated and re-issued August 2008.

UK Government Office for Science. *The Future of Food and Farming: Challenges and Choices for Global Sustainability.* London: UK Government Office for Science, 2011.

United Nations. *Demographic Yearbook: Data on Population of Capital Cities and Cities of 100,000 and More Inhabitants.* New York: United Nations, 2011

United Nations Programme on HIV/AIDS. *UNAIDS Report on the Global AIDS Epidemic.* New York: United Nations, 2010.

USDA Economic Research Service, *Cross-Country Analysis of Food Consumption Patterns: Changing Structure of Global Food Consumption and Trade.* WRS-01–1. Washington, DC: USDA Economic Research Service, 2010.

USDA Economic Research Service. "Global Food Markets" (last updated May 30, 2012). Available at: http://www.ers.usda.gov/topics/international-markets-trade/global-food-markets.aspx.

U.S. Energy Information Administration. *International Energy Outlook 2007.* Washington, DC: EIA, 2007.

U.S. Energy Information Administration. *International Energy Outlook 2011.* Washington, DC: EIA, 2011.

van der Mensbrugghe, D. *The Environmental Impact and Sustainability Applied General Equilibrium (ENVISAGE) Model.* Washington, DC: World Bank, 2008.

Verzandvoort, S., R. Rietra, and M. Hack Alterra. *Pressures on Prime Agricultural Land in Europe.* The Netherlands: Wageningen University, 2009.

von Braun, J. *The World Food Situation: New Driving Force and Required Actions.* Washington, DC: International Food Policy Research Institute, 2007.

von Braun, J., A. Gulati, and D. Orden. *Making Agricultural Trade Liberalization Work for the Poor.* Washington, DC: IFPRI, 2004.

Vorley, B., and UK Food Group. *Food, Inc.: Corporate Concentration from Farm to Consumer.* London: IIED, 2010.

Watanabe, M. H. Shiogama, T. Yokohata, T. Ogura, M. Yoshimori, J. Annan, J. Hargreaves, S. Emori, and M. Kimoto. *Model for Interdisciplinary Research on Climate (MIROC).* Tsukuba, Japan: MIROC Group for Climate Feedback and Sensitivity Studies, National Institute for Environmental Studies, 2012.

Woods, J. et al. "Energy and the Food System." *Philosophical Transactions of the Royal Society* 365B (2010): 2991–3006.

World Bank. *Disasters, Climate Change, and Economic Development in Sub-Saharan Africa: Lessons and Future Directions.* Washington, DC: World Bank, 2007.

World Bank. *Global Economic Prospects 2009: Commodities at the Crossroads.* Washington, DC: World Bank, 2008.

World Bank.: *World Development Report 2008: Agriculture for Development*. Washington, DC: World Bank, 2008.

World Bank, *World Development Report 2010: Development and Climate Change.* Washington, DC: World Bank, 2010.

World Commission on Environment and Development. *Our Common Future.* New York: Oxford University Press, 1987.

World Health Organization. *Global and Regional Food Consumption Patterns and Trends.* Geneva: WHO Press, 2009,

Yergin, D. *The Quest—Energy Security and the Remaking of the Modern World*, rev. ed. London: Penguin Books, 2012.

index